Financial Conditions
and
Macroeconomic
Performance

To

Hyman P. Minsky

Our mentor and critic

Hyman P. Minsky, distinguished scholar at the Jerome Levy Economics Institute of Bard College, and Professor Emeritus of Washington University-St. Louis, is a nationally known economist who, in the words of *Business Week* columnist Robert Kuttner, merits a Nobel Prize as one of the great institutionalists of the economics profession, a man "whose work begins with the complexity and turmoil of actual markets rather than with the presumed equilibrium of theoretical ones." Professor Minsky's best known works include *John Maynard Keynes* (1975), *Can 'It' Happen Again?* (1982), and *Stabilizing an Unstable Economy* (1986). Born in Chicago in 1919, he received his B.S. in mathematics from the University of Chicago and a Ph.D from Harvard.

Financial Conditions
and
Macroeconomic
Performance

Essays in Honor of Hyman P. Minsky

Steven Fazzari
and
Dimitri B. Papadimitriou
Editors

M.E. Sharpe Inc.
Armonk, New York
London, England

Available in the United Kingdom and Europe from M.E. Sharpe, Publishers, 3 Henrietta Street, London WC2E 8LU.

Library of Congress Cataloging-in-Publication Data

Financial conditions and macroeconomic performance: essays in honor of Hyman P. Minsky
edited by Steven M. Fazzari and Dimitri B. Papadimitriou
p.cm.
Based on papers presented at a conference honoring Minsky held at Washington University, St. Louis, Missouri.
Includes bibliographical references and index
ISBN 1–56324–016–5.—ISBN 1–56324–017–3 (pbk.)
1. Finance—Congresses.
2. Macroeconomics—Congresses.
3. Business cycles—Congresses.
4. Minsky, Hyman P.—Congresses.
I. Minsky, Hyman P.
II. Fazzari, Steven M.
III. Papadimitriou, Dimitri B.
HG63.F55 1992
339—dc20
92–20961
CIP

Printed in the United States of America

The paper used in this publication meets the minimum requirements of American National Standard for Information Sciences—Permanence of Paper for Printed Materials, ANSI Z39.48-1984

BB   10   9   8   7   6   5   4   3   2   1

CONTENTS

FOREWORD

HENRY B. KAUFMAN

Hyman Minsky has labored hard and well in the labyrinths of economics and finance where few have worked with clarity and coherence. While linking business with finance is essential to understanding how forecasts and events interact in our world, rational theories of this linkage have been sparse. Hyman Minsky, however, has provided a definitive analysis. The rest of us, of course, have free rein to question his logic and quibble with his assumptions. But these are largely secondary matters. The relevant point is that the overall thrust of his position is clear, and his conclusions are disturbing. Events of the post–World War II period have vividly supported his basic argument.

Hyman Minsky, through his analysis, saw early on the increasing fragility of our financial system. He began with the insight of Keynes concerning the volatility of investments, and then pointed out that the underlying uncertainty of the cash flow from investments has powerful repercussions on the balance sheet of business. In turn, the government intervenes in an attempt to reduce the risks in this process, essentially by taking expansionary policies that prevent a debt deflation. According to Hyman Minsky, such counteraction by government does not produce a long period of economic equilibrium, but, again, lays the groundwork for another investment boom driven by a wave of new debt. According to Minsky this sequence of booms, government intervention to prevent debt contraction, and new booms entails a progressive buildup of new debt, eventually leaving the economy much more fragile financially.

Having worked in the financial markets for my entire professional career, I became aware of the risk of a debt explosion in the 1960s and was attracted to Hyman Minsky's thinking. I saw this debt buildup through my work in the flow of funds. I attribute the subsequent rapid growth of debt to the removal of circuit breakers such as official interest rate ceilings, the rapid deregulation of markets and institutions, the many financial innovations that promoted debt, and the globalization of financial markets. In the wake of these sweeping changes, no effective official supervision was imposed over markets and institutions. Thus, regrettably, Hyman Minsky's view of increasing fragility has come true.

This volume is a fitting tribute to Hyman Minsky. It matters not whether we are monetarists, Keynesians, or disciples of any other economics persuasion. He deserves our accolades because of the persuasiveness of his analysis, and because he was a crusader. He foresaw the irregular weakening of our financial institutions that has brought the issue of financial fragility to dead center. It is now high time that we find the way out of this abyss.

PREFACE

In September 1965, Hyman P. Minsky was appointed professor of economics at Washington University in St. Louis, Missouri. He taught many generations of students, influenced the direction of the economics department, and contributed greatly to Washington's research reputation with his prodigious scholarly work. In June 1990, Minsky retired from his teaching duties to take up the position of distinguished scholar at the Jerome Levy Economics Institute of Bard College in New York.

To mark this occasion, several institutions collaborated to put on a conference in honor of Minsky's contribution to the economics discipline and to his institutional home of nearly thirty years. Major support for this event came from the Jerome Levy Economics Institute and from Mark Twain Bancshares of St. Louis, an institution with which Minsky has had a long association, most recently as a member of its board of directors. Additional support came from Washington University departments and student organizations. The conference commissioned essays that examined Minsky's contributions to economic theory and policy analysis written by scholars from all over the world who had a close association with Minsky, or who have been influenced greatly by his research. The conference was held in St. Louis on April 20 and 21, 1990 and included a keynote address to the Washington University community by Benjamin Friedman.

The conference essays are collected in this volume. Although they touch on many aspects of Minsky's work, they do not constitute an exhaustive survey of his contributions. The piece by Gary Dymski and Robert Pollin provides an overview of Minsky's research from the authors' perspective. The remainder of the essays cover topics chosen by their authors, developing aspects of their own research in ways that reveal the influence of Minsky's far-reaching contributions.

The conference and this volume of essays owe their existence to the dedicated work of many individuals. This project originated from discussions among Minsky's colleagues at Washington University. The conference was organized by Steven Fazzari, Edward Greenberg, and Laurence Meyer, whose initial idea sparked the conference. Financial support from the Levy Institute and Mark Twain Bancshares, our major donors, as well as various Washington University sources, made the conference possible. Trudi Spigel and her staff from the special programs office of Washington University provided invaluable advice and support in planning the logistical details of the conference. Karen Rensing, of the economics department, kept track of myriad clerical details and helped to organize the organizers. The participants in the conference, many of whom traveled to St. Louis for the occasion, contributed lively, sometimes heated, discussion that influenced the final forms of the papers collected here. Finally, we thank Hyman Minsky who has contributed so much, personally and professionally, to the discipline of economics, to Washington University and the Levy Economics Institute, and to us.

Steven Fazzari
Dimitri B. Papadimitriou
March, 1991

JEROME LEVY ECONOMICS INSTITUTE
OF BARD COLLEGE

Founded in 1986, the Jerome Levy Economics Institute of Bard College is an autonomous, independently endowed research organization. It is nonpartisan, open to the examination of diverse points of view, and dedicated to public service. The support of the Institute made this volume possible.

The Institute believes in the potential for economic study to improve the human condition. Its purpose is to generate viable, effective public policy responses to important economic problems. It is concerned with issues that profoundly affect the quality of life in the United States, in other highly industrialized nations, and in countries with developing economies.

The Institute's present research agenda includes such issues as financial instability, poverty and problems associated with the distribution of income, and economic growth. In all its endeavors, the Institute places heavy emphasis on the values of personal freedom and justice.

Financial Conditions
and
Macroeconomic
Performance

CHAPTER ONE

Introduction: Conversations with Hyman Minsky

STEVEN FAZZARI

I came to know Hyman Minsky toward the end of his time at Washington University when I joined the faculty as an assistant professor right out of graduate school in fall 1982. My conversations with Minsky since then have greatly influenced my research and professional development. When the authors of the papers collected in this volume were presenting their ideas at the conference honoring Minsky at Washington University, I was struck by how closely the major ideas in these papers related to the themes Minsky emphasized in conversation with his colleagues and students. Therefore, I try to show in this essay how the major themes in each contribution connect to the ideas Minsky emphasized, almost on a daily basis, to those around him. As a result, this chapter does not summarize the papers. The reader will have to go to the papers themselves to discover their individual messages. This introduction attempts to draw together the diverse ideas expressed in the individual chapters, relating them to the view of economic activity that Minsky conveys at a personal level. For an impression of how Minsky perceives the world he has experienced, see the following chapter, "Minsky on Himself," by Dimitri B. Papadimitriou.

Finance, the Economy, and Policy

Within the first minutes of any conversation with Hyman Minsky, one learns that economic theory is hopelessly sterile unless it recognizes the fundamental impact of finance. He would often talk about theories that abstracted from finance and money as "village fair" models, possibly applicable to tangential barter in a subsistence society, but wholly inadequate to the task of understanding the driving forces of modern capitalism. Not surprisingly, then, the central role of financial and monetary relations in the economy is emphasized in all the papers in this volume.

The author is associate professor of economics at Washington University, St. Louis. He thanks Edward Greenberg for excellent comments.

These effects arise at *all* levels of analysis. At the microeconomic level, for example, Kindleberger (chapter 5) explores the historical and logical foundations of financial intermediation in the functioning of the market system; particularly the importance of information in the intermediation process. Similarly, Fazzari (chapter 8) analyzes the microeconomic mechanism that links real investment with financial structure. At the macroeconomic level, the impact of finance on the aggregate performance of modern, "financially sophisticated" economies, to use Minsky's phrase, appears in most of these papers. Delli Gatti and Gallegati (chapter 9), for example, argue that the evolution of financial structure over the business cycle systematically pushes the system from a dynamically stable regime to instability. Similar themes are emphasized by Ferri (chapter 7). These are a few examples. Every paper in this volume reflects Minsky's vision of finance as central to an understanding of economic activity in our times.

Another strong impression that one gets from a conversation with Minsky is that theoretical economics and economic policy analysis are inextricably linked. As Friedman states in the keynote address for the conference (chapter 4), Minsky's ideas are relevant today, not just for economic theory, but also for the "actual prospects and risks facing our economy." The papers in this volume, particularly those by Dymski and Pollin, Ferri, Friedman, Kregel, and Wray, explore Minsky's particular view of financial capitalism and its implications for the conduct of fiscal and monetary policy, as well as for various proposals about institutional reform.

The Theory of Investment and Endogenous Money

Minsky sees himself as an expositor of "financial Keynesianism." At the core of his financial interpretation of Keynes' work is the theory of investment; fluctuations in macroeconomic activity primarily arise from fluctuations in investment.

In modern mainstream thinking, the key determinant of investment in plant and equipment is the (marginal) productivity of capital which is determined technologically. The income streams generated by the productivity of capital are appropriately discounted at a real interest rate common to all agents in the economy that, itself, can be explained ultimately by preferences and technology. Minsky does not deny a role for the productivity of capital in determining the expected cash flow generated by an investment project. In conversation, he accepts that the "Qs" (following Keynes' notation for the expected cash flows from investment) can be affected by the productivity of capital. The problem of meaningfully defining the physical quantity of capital as a single aggregate has little impact on his thinking. There are those, however, who believe his indifference to this issue weakens his overall impact. (See the end of the paper by Dymski and Pollin [chapter 3] for discussion.)

But to leave the determination of investment *entirely* to technology and the market interest rate, as is common in most neoclassical investment models, is to ignore the essential explanation for investment fluctuation: finance. Minsky talks about how the key decisions that drive investment, and therefore animate the business cycle in a modern capitalist economy, take place in the "board rooms" of major firms where the financing of major projects is granted or denied. Minsky calls this his "Wall Street" view (see Dymski and Pollin) to describe great pools of finance capital moving swiftly among places and accounts. More recently, he uses the term "money-manager capitalism" to describe the evolution of intermediation along these lines as discussed in Kindleberger's paper.

The conditions under which finance for investment is forthcoming drive variations of investment more than anything else. This view places Minsky out of the neoclassical mainstream. He emphatically denies the independence of *real* investment from *nominal* financial conditions. Minsky often says that the only "real" interest rate is the one that actually appears on financial contracts and affects cash flows: the nominal interest rate in conventional economic jargon. He denies the validity of the "Modigliani-Miller" theorem, not because of the subtleties of the tax law, but because of the structure of capitalism.

The paper by Fazzari (chapter 8) takes on the task of explaining why such a fundamental link between investment and finance must arise in a decentralized economy. The key insight, which Fazzari draws from recent developments in the mainstream literature and applies to Minsky's view, is that borrowers and lenders, by the very nature of their distinct roles, do not have the same information about the quality and likely success of an investment project, i.e., their information is "asymmetric." For this reason, what Minsky, following Keynes, calls "lenders' risk" arises. This risk will be magnified or attenuated by characteristics of the agents involved in financing an investment project (e.g., reputation and collateral), and the magnitude of lenders' risk can vary independently from the technological productivity of that project. Fazzari argues that asymmetric information is both inherent to capitalism and fundamental to understanding the investment-finance links that are central to Minsky's theory.

The paper by Dymski and Pollin and the paper by Wray also examine lenders' risk (as well as the corresponding concept of borrowers' risk). Wray, in particular, emphasizes the special relationship between borrowers and lenders and its importance in the process of investment finance. This relation is not impersonal like the market link between suppliers and demanders in the simplest microeconomic model. An exchange between borrowers and lenders does not depend solely on price. Kindleberger analyzes the special role of banks as financial intermediaries in an historical context. The complexity of this relationship between banker and entrepreneur is a cornerstone of Minsky's vision which has been discovered finally by mainstream economists (for a useful survey, see Gertler 1988). These developments in the mainstream are evidence of the pervasiveness of Minsky's vision.

The idea, emphasized especially by Fazzari, that these mainstream developments are consistent with Minsky's views, and indeed, may provide a new dimension to his insights, has spawned controversy which is reflected in several of the papers in this volume. Kregel argues that asymmetric information is not necessary to support financial instability at the macroeconomic level. If, for some reason, banks restrict credit, firms will be unable to finance investment. In the aggregate, reduced investment will force cash flow down, limit the ability of firms to service debt, and validate the bankers' original decision to tighten credit. In this sense, financial constraints on investment, regardless of their microeconomic basis, become a self-fulfilling prophecy. Dymski and Pollin argue that "fundamental uncertainty" about investment projects necessitates financial effects on investment whether or not the information available to borrowers and lenders is asymmetric. This argument is pursued further by Dymski (1991) in a paper inspired, in part, by the lively discussion of this point at the conference.

The microfoundations of financial effects on investment constitute only the starting point of Minsky's theory of investment. Any discussion of "financial constraints" with him quickly leads to the systemic instability induced by the investment-finance link. Investment creates financial relations that stretch both backward and forward in time. Minsky often emphasizes what Dymski and Pollin call the "financial trails" of investment. As Kregel points out (chapter 6), the decision to hold capital is also the decision to finance capital because past investment created a set of cash payment commitments. Firms' fulfillment of these commitments, or their failure, is a key element in determining the direction of the business cycle. In addition to these historically determined relations, Wray identifies another common thread that Minsky emphasizes about the systemic behavior of investment: investment today is only possible if investment in the future can be expected to generate the aggregate cash flows necessary to validate the liabilities that new investment creates.

These concerns have current relevance for the U.S. economy. As Friedman's lecture demonstrates, the proportion of corporate income that goes to service debt (that is, to validate historical commitments) has risen from about 16 percent in the financially robust 1950s and 1960s to approximately 60 percent in the 1980s. Friedman notes that although the U.S. economic structure may have changed in ways that can support such a dramatic increase in debt leverage, the danger of a collapse of investment finance looms on the horizon if an economic downturn results in widespread repudiation of these massive new debt obligations.

Because Minsky emphasizes the central role of finance for investment and the volatility it induces, he strongly rejects the idea that any meaningful measure of "money," the liability side of financial transactions, can be exogenous. This critique of conventional thought is not unique to Minsky's view. But his thinking drives in the direction of endogenous money. These ideas are discussed by Dymski and Pollin and developed in detail by Wray (chapter 10). He argues that to recognize the endogeneity of money resurrects the Keynesian concept of liquidity preference as a central cause of the volatility of macroeconomic activity. Yet, some of the endogenous money literature suggests that the Federal Reserve's attempt to impose quantity constraints on the banking system is irrelevant. As Wray makes clear, Minsky's view is more subtle. Financial innovation and liability management give banks great flexibility in determining the quantity of money. But quantity constraints imposed by the Federal Reserve can have important effects on the cost and availability of credit. Thus, Minsky's monetary theory is more complex than either the mainstream exogenous measure-of-money view, or the perspective that Federal Reserve quantity constraints are irrelevant for credit markets because only the discount rate matters.

Financial Instability

The theories of investment and endogenous money are the building blocks of Minsky's broader ideas about macroeconomics and are key to his central concern: the financial instability that drives fluctuations in the economy as a whole. This idea flows from the microfoundations of investment and financial markets discussed previously. As Dymski and Pollin emphasize, and any talk with Minsky confirms, the idea of macro instability induced by finance is part of Minsky's "preanalytic vision." He rejects the notion of a simple exchange economy in which money and finance are "veils" as a starting point.

Ferri's paper lays out the abstract character of economic activity that underlies Minsky's more particular contributions on financial instability. The formal structure of what Ferri calls Minsky's "general systems view" is inherently dynamic and nonlinear. This vision stretches back to his earliest published work, but in recent years he has adopted the perspective of the new mathematics of nonlinear dynamics, especially chaos theory. This general view of economic activity complements Minsky's more specific contributions on financial instability.

As Kregel makes clear, however, the *possibility* of instability as the result of nonlinear dynamics is not the essential issue. The key, rather, is the substance of the model's structure that generates nonlinearities and instability. Ferri argues that "money," broadly defined, is the central source of nonlinearity in the model that underlies Minsky's view. Nonlinearities arise when economic phenomena feed back on asset values. This analysis ties monetary theory, investment, and macrodynamics together to explain how financial instability emerges as an inherent feature of the capitalist business cycle.

The model presented by Delli Gatti and Gallegati (chapter 9) analyzes this phenomenon. In their structure the importance of internal funds for investment, and the endogenous generation of internal funds by the macro system, creates a nonlinear feedback loop that increases the Keynesian multiplier and can push the system's dynamics from a stable to an explosive regime. In this model, as Minsky often emphasizes, maintaining an adequate flow of internal funds to fulfill past commitments, "validating the liability structure" in Minsky's terminology, creates the basis for acceptable system performance.

But for Minsky, "stability is destabilizing" (see Dymski and Pollin); full employment is not a "natural equilibrium point but a transitory moment in a cycle." This result is implied by the Delli Gatti–Gallegati model. In most conventional analyses, to the extent that they address financial conditions at all, the financial structure becomes continually stronger as an upswing continues. For Minsky, however, the longer a boom continues, the more the liabilities of firms must be increased to finance investment, i.e., the greater the demands on current cash flows to finance debt payments. This increased "financial fragility" sows the seeds of the next downturn, placing financial instability in an inherently dynamic and cyclical context.

Wray argues that these financial dynamics will cause the ultimate demise of any constant money growth policy rule. If the Federal Reserve's policy is successful at constraining money growth in the face of a strong demand for credit created by boom conditions, the leverage and fragility of the system will rise. As this process continues, debt repudiation eventually follows, the Federal Reserve's lender-of-last-resort hand is forced, and the "monetarist" rule must be abandoned. Wray uses this idea to explain why the Federal Reserve's crisis containment function was called upon often in the 1980s: it was a result of their success in constraining the expansion of reserves that ultimately stretched the system's liquidity dangerously near the breaking point.

In day-to-day conversations, it is clear that Minsky has little patience with interpretations of his cyclical perspective that tie predictions of endogenous instability to "irrational" behavior on the part of investing firms or financing agents. The behavior at the micro level may be quite rational, even essential to survival. Banks must seek to expand finance and maintain market power to maintain their position in the competitive struggle. They may be quite aware of increasing systemic fragility, but this problem is financial externality over which individual agents have no control. The view that financial institutions need continually to seek market power shows, in Wray's opinion, Minsky's Schumpeterian roots, and thus, ties Minsky, as a Harvard graduate student, to his teacher (see chapter 2).

Minsky's perspective on financial instability clearly distinguishes his work from the mainstream neoclassical synthesis view of macro, which treats financial relations "summarily," as Dymski and Pollin put it. Most textbook Keynesian analyses relegate financial influences to money demand and the traditional LM curve. Recent work within the mainstream tradition, however, has proposed a more fundamental role for finance in the determination of macroeconomic activity (see the survey by Gertler, 1988). This work derives "credit rationing" and financial influences on investment from microeconomic fundamentals that include impediments to information transfer between borrowing and lending units.

There is a debate among the expositors of Minsky's ideas regarding the significance and relevance of this recent work in the development of what Minsky calls "financial Keynesianism." There is little doubt that these new developments have led, in some mainstream circles, to a broader set of financial influences on macroeconomic activity. As discussed previously, Fazzari's paper in this volume argues that these new mainstream insights are fundamental to understanding the reasons why finance matters for real activity at the microeconomic level and that the information problems that lie at the root of these financial effects are a basic characteristic of decentralized economic activity. The alternative interpretation, however, views mainstream ideas on information-based financial effects as but another in a long line of tangential "imperfections" on which neoclassical interpretations of Keynes (and Minsky) have rested. In this view, asymmetric information and the resulting financial effects are to the new generation what sticky nominal wages were to the previous generation.

Minsky takes a cautious, yet open, approach to these so-called "new Keynesian" developments. Their primarily static structure fails to capture the richness of his ideas on dynamic financial instability, and the structure of the formal models does not come close to encompassing the institutional detail of Minsky's "Wall Street" perspective. Yet Minsky seems to welcome the new insights, even if he does not embrace them fully. He is open to the view that greater understanding can be gained from the study of financial effects on macroeconomic activity with a variety of tools.

Policies to Contain Financial Instability

One cannot talk to Minsky about financial instability and economic theory without the conversation drifting to the conduct of economic policy. This practical side of his thinking is bound up with his macroeconomic theory, and it is reflected in the papers collected here. As Ferri points out, some of Minsky's earliest work emphasized how institutional structures could place limits on endogenous instability (i.e., "floors and ceilings"). These limits need not be tied to fixed behavioral parameters like autonomous investment or consumption. They could arise from apt policy intervention. In such a model, the incoherence of an endogenously unstable model may be "thwarted," to use Ferri's term.

The time series data generated by an explosive system that is constrained by institutional intervention may appear to have come from an inherently stable dynamic structure (see Blatt, 1978). But this result suggests an implicit danger for policy, emphasized by Ferri. If intervention is successful at constraining instability, researchers may be misled to conclude that the system is endogenously stable and that policy intervention is not required to maintain macro coherence. With the macro problems apparently suppressed, policy may strive for micro efficiency gains from financial deregulation. The latter may weaken the essential thwarting mechanisms, however, and set the stage for the system's explosive dynamics to cause a financial collapse.

In a similar vein, Dymski and Pollin discuss how the Federal Reserve's lender-of-last-resort intervention can put a floor on endogenous debt-deflation dynamics. But to the extent that historically successful intervention has prevented financial crisis, the disciplining mechanisms that discourage high leverage have weakened. With higher indebtedness, the frequency and magnitude of the Federal Reserve's intervention will increase, possibly to the point where crisis can no longer be contained. Such a scenario could well characterize the U.S. economy of the early 1990s.

In discussing policy as well as theory, Minsky often refers to the "two-price" system: the price of current output (including current investment goods) and the price of existing capital assets. Kregel's paper in this volume argues that Minsky's emphasis on this system elucidates Keynes' underlying price theory, and that this framework clarifies policy discussion. The twin pillars of Minsky's recommended policy structure are "big government" (a fiscal authority that engages in large spending and taxing programs) and a "big bank" (a lender of last resort).

The key role of big government operates through the "Kalecki mechanism," which Minsky has adopted as a cornerstone of his analysis of fiscal policy: economic downturns cause reduced profit flows. Reduced profits weaken the ability of firms to service existing debt commitments. Consequently, asset quality deteriorates and the price of capital assets declines relative to the price of current output. This, in turn, reduces investment and magnifies the downturn. Such a process has the potential to be unstable. But, according to Kalecki, government deficits support business profits. If the fiscal impact of the government is large enough to attenuate falling profits, the price of capital assets will be supported, and the downside potential of this channel can be contained. The Reagan fiscal policy of running large deficits as the U.S. economy recovered from the deep recession of the early 1980s could have been recommended on the basis of Kalecki/Minsky logic.

Big deficits, however, affect profits and the economy over a period of months or years. This policy cannot contain the speculative instability in asset markets that can arise in financial panics and that causes the price of capital assets to crash. The best medicine for panic conditions is intervention by the "big bank." As the discussions by Kregel and Wray make clear, the lender of last resort can support capital asset prices, maintain order in financial markets, and thwart debt deflation.

Such a coordinated policy stance may effectively constrain instability in particular instances. Dymski and Pollin, however, question the longer-term implications of successful macroeconomic policy. The success of big government and the big bank at preventing debt deflation renders inoperative the "natural" mechanism for shaking out financial fragility. In a Minskian mode, the result would seem to be greater leverage and greater fragility. Will policy success cause fragility to build to the point that even well-informed policy intervention cannot contain the system's dynamics? Will delaying the crash make it worse when it finally comes?

These concerns seem to find support in the U.S. financial excesses of the 1980s, and appear to be consistent with Minsky's overall approach. In conversation with Minsky one gets the impression that "It," by which he means an economic and financial collapse on the order of the Great Depression, does not have to happen again. He conveys a sense of faith in the power of policy, but he also conveys a sense of risk; that well-informed policymakers may not be in place at the critical time. Or they may not act quickly and decisively. And for these reasons, a dramatic collapse must still be feared.

Friedman's lecture also conveys a sense that the government, especially the Federal Reserve, can prevent disastrous financial crisis. But the negative effects of such policy on the economy emerge as inflation. High leverage means that the Federal Reserve cannot allow a serious recession, and the result is higher inflation. This point reflects a theme that Minsky often emphasizes: the need for the Federal Reserve to act as an effective lender of last resort may often be inconsistent with its other objectives, particularly the objective of maintaining low inflation.

Similar concerns about inflation as the cost of using monetary policy to contain financial instability appear in several other papers in this volume. Dymski and Pollin identify "an inflationary bias . . . built into the economy through this combination of systemic fragility and anti-deflationary intervention." Kregel links this point to the "two-price" system. Inflation of the "cost-push" variety works through the price level of current output. Monetary policy can eliminate this kind of inflation only by causing a recession and unemployment. In Kregel's words, this makes it "an extremely blunt tool" to use against wage-driven inflation. Monetary policy, however, has a more direct effect on the prices of capital assets through its impact on interest rates and the liquidity of the financial system. Therefore, it may be more effective in controlling what might be called speculative inflation in capital asset prices. But, as the dynamics of asset prices depend fundamentally on potentially volatile expectations, any attempt to curb inflation in financial markets runs the risk of setting off unstable reactions.

Emphasizing another major aspect of Minsky's vision, Ferri makes clear that the institutional structure of the system will not remain static. Policy mechanisms that contain instability will lead to institutional innovation that causes problems to emerge in new directions. A good example of this process is the creation of deposit insurance to deal with aspects of financial instability that contributed to the Great Depression. In the 1980s, deposit insurance, in the wake of deregulation, has contributed to new kinds of instability in the U.S. banking system. Minsky was fond of making his undergraduates see analogies between financial instability and the *The Wizard of Oz*. When Judy Garland, as Dorothy, lands her house in Oz and looks at the strange world around her, she tells her dog, "Toto, we're not in Kansas anymore." For Minsky, Dorothy's dilemma is similar to that of the Federal Reserve as it tries to contain financial instability in an ever-changing institutional setting.

Conclusion: Minsky's Intellectual Challenge

The sense one gets from conversation with Hyman Minsky is that modern capitalism, in what he calls "financially-sophisticated economies," is a complex and dynamic system. Its essential features cannot be captured in a static framework, nor can one abstract from finance and still have a model that describes modern reality. The endogenous dynamics of the system have the potential to break out into instability. Wise policy intervention is essential to containing the instability. Such intervention may lead to acceptable behavior for a time, but the risk remains that the system will overcome any particular structure of institutional containment mechanisms.

This is the Minsky vision. But as he retires from teaching, he sees the research program spawned by his vision as only beginning. He continues to develop it himself, and he encourages a new generation of economists to pursue the theoretical and econometric work that will probe the logic and application of his ideas. The papers in this volume are a sample of work that is in progress around the world to assimilate, critique, and develop Minsky's economics. Conversations with Hyman Minsky will pose a great intellectual challenge for some time to come.

References

Dymski, Gary. 1991. "Fundamental Uncertainty, Asymmetric Information, and Financial Structure: 'Post' versus 'New' Keynesian Microfoundations." Mimeo, University of Southern California, Los Angeles.

Blatt, J.M. 1978. "On the Econometric Approach to Business Cycle Analysis." *Oxford Economic Papers* 32:469–79.

Gertler, Mark. 1988. "Financial Structure and Aggregate Activity: An Overview." *Journal of Money, Credit, and Banking* 20:559–88.

CHAPTER TWO

Minsky on Himself

DIMITRI B. PAPADIMITRIOU

I first met Hyman Minsky in summer 1981 at the Trieste School organized by the Center for Advanced Economic Studies. I was familiar with his work, having used his classic book, *John Maynard Keynes*, in my seminar on post-Keynesian Economics. During the three weeks at the School he was always surrounded by many young scholars interested in his "financial fragility hypothesis" as the most relevant characteristic of today's advanced capitalism. With unfailing patience, warmth, friendliness, and good humor, he would listen, attentively and sympathetically, and then explain, generously and thoughtfully, the complexity and inherent instability of the financial structure of today's modern market economies. That summer marked the beginning of my friendship with Hy, and in 1990, after his retirement from Washington University in St. Louis, we became colleagues at the Jerome Levy Economics Institute where he is a distinguished scholar.

Hyman Minsky was born in Chicago in 1919. His father, Sam Minsky, emigrated from Russia after the failed revolution in 1905. Sam was active in the Socialist Party in Chicago and met Hy's mother, Dora Zakon, at a gala that the Jewish section of the party had organized to celebrate the one hundredth anniversary of the birth of Karl Marx. Hy is a product of the Lima, Ohio, Chicago and New York City public schools. He graduated from George Washington High School in New York City and went to the University of Chicago in 1937. This was the period when economics at Chicago was very intellectually open, exemplified by the radical Oscar Lange, the liberal Paul Douglas, the middle-of-the-road Jacob Viner, and the conservatives Frank Knight and Henry Simons (Minsky 1985).[1] Even though he received a B.S. degree in mathematics, Hy discovered, under the influence of Oscar Lange and Maynard Krueger, that his real calling was in economics. He attributes this interest in economics to the socioeconomic environment of his youth. He was active in the youth division of

The author is professor of economics, executive vice president of Bard College, and executive director of The Jerome Levy Economics Institute. He would like to thank Steven Fazzari for his excellent comments on a draft of this essay.

the American Socialist Party in Chicago. His first exposure to economics was through the integrated social science sequence course, distinctive to the Chicago undergraduate curriculum during the Hutchins era. He received further grounding in economics from the lectures of Lange, Knight, Douglas, Simons, and especially from conversations with Gerhard Meyer, who was always available to explain what was not clear, and with whom Hy became close friends. Other friendships, some of them long-lasting, as the one with the late Abba Lerner, were developed in Minsky's close knit environment of those Chicago years.

Chicago was not to be where Hyman Minsky would receive his master's and doctoral degrees. He began graduate studies at the University of Chicago in 1941, but Lange encouraged him to leave Chicago, at least for a while. So, in summer 1942, he joined the Leontief group at Harvard that was working on postwar planning and the embryonic input-output scheme. As he remembers, Lange was convinced of the importance of input-output as a planning tool for the socialist world. The group around Leontief included a number of economists and economists-to-be: Sam Westerfield, Caleb Smith, Penny Hartland, Alice Johns, and Fran Kramer. At Harvard in 1942–43, Hy met James Tobin, Robert Solow, Evsey Domar, and Andreas Papandreou. He remembers the walking tours that Evsey organized for the whole group. One trip in particular—climbing Mt. Washington in New Hampshire—started what Hy calls a long "romance" with the White Mountains. Every year when he returned to Harvard, and later while teaching at Brown University, before the start of the fall semester, he would spend a week or two hiking in these mountains.

Quite soon after Hy began his work on the Leontief project, Leontief asked him what his plans were for the following year. Hy's reply was that he planned to return to a fellowship at Chicago. When he mentioned the stipend, Leontief replied that Harvard could do better, and within a short while Hy received an offer of a fellowship in the Littauer School that was quite a bit better than the one from Chicago. Hy called Lange who was not in Chicago, but at an Army base in Virginia. Lange advised Hy to take the Harvard fellowship, especially as he did not expect to be at Chicago the following year. In Minsky's mind at the time, he would only stay at Harvard for a year or so. Then he intended to return to Chicago.

After this conversation, Hy saw Lange only when Lange lectured at Harvard during the fall of 1942, and later, several times in New York while Hy was in the Army and Lange was teaching at Columbia. After the war, when Lange was in New York as the Polish representative to the United Nations, Hy did not visit with him, although he recalls receiving invitations to visit whenever he was in New York. Hy interpreted the information that Lange was briefed presumably by the OSS before his famous mission to Moscow, as indicating that Lange may well have started his path in politics with the acquiescence of U.S. intelligence. Since Hy was visible in supporting the independence of the U.S. Berlin Social Democrats in the 1946 Einheit party struggle, he believed that it might be best if Lange did not meet with him. Hy is not sure whether he was overcautious.

Once summer 1942 ended, Hy enrolled in the Littauer School of Administration at Harvard, but after one semester he was inducted into the U.S. Army. From February 1943 to spring 1945, Hy was stationed in New York at the Brooklyn Army Base in the control and planning division. Sar Levitan, who by then was a Columbia Ph.D. (and is currently a member of the George Washington University faculty) was the officer in charge of the group preparing the general's monthly reports. The Brooklyn Army Base and the New York Port of Embarkation were really a very large enterprise, and Hy's time at the base was the equivalent to a staff job in a large business. In the spring of 1945, the expectation was that the war in Europe would be over soon. The Army organized ports from the personnel of the New York Port which were to handle the redeployment of forces from Europe back to the United States and to the Far East. Hy was volunteered for the headquarters of the 52nd Port of the Transportation Corps, and soon his port was off to Europe.

He recalls that within a week after being inducted, without any basic training, he was "shipped" to the Brooklyn Army Base in part because they needed individuals who had some knowledge of statistics. He was not fit to be a field soldier, being classified 1B due to his long history of hay fever, other autumn allergies, and asthma. Hy remembers the astonishment of his officers when they discovered that he had never fired a gun. Before he could go overseas, it was necessary for him to go to Fort Dix to "fire a gun." Hy's job at New York's Port of Embarkation was to work on a monthly report on the activities of the port and on various studies about its efficiency and operation. The assignment allowed him considerable time to "wander" in New York City. It was during this period that he attended Abraham Wald's lectures at Columbia University and renewed the old Chicago relationships with Lange, who was teaching at Columbia, and with Abba Lerner, who was to become a good friend, at the New School for Social Research. Hy had first met Lerner in Chicago at a reception in Paul Douglas's house following a lecture given by Angelika Balabanoff. He became particularly close to him when Hy joined the faculty of the University of California at Berkeley, where Lerner would visit from time to time. They remained close friends until Lerner's death in 1982.

During this period, Lerner was developing his *Economics of Control*. His work laid the groundwork for "the markets are always at equilibrium" idea. The processes of getting into and out of equilibrium, and of individual behavior in a world of uncertainty which made "equilibrium" an amorphous concept were, however, ignored.

Even though his army classification was 1B, in late 1945 Hy went overseas. He remembers being at sea when the submarine offensive in the Battle of Bulge took place. His first overseas station was in Newport, Monmouthshire, England. One responsibility Hy had was to make sure that the manifests were delivered for the stockpiled materials accumulated in Britain that were being shipped to France. He was once given an interesting assignment which proved to be personally quite important. His orders were to escort a shipment of nylons for the Women Army Corps to a depot outside Cambridge. The assignment gave Hy the opportunity to spend a weekend in Cambridge and meet a number of the well-known economists there including Richard Kahn and Piero Sraffa. He recalls attending a meeting of the Marshall Society chaired by Joan Robinson.

The war was winding down, and on September 23, 1945, the day of his 26th birthday, Hy was in Paris. His unit had broken up and he was transferred to the Office of the Chief of Transportation. He reported for duty each night at midnight at a very fancy office off the Champs-Elysees, and called the various ports of embarkation to get, from the duty officer, the number who had been loaded on ships to various destinations within the preceding twenty-four hours. In the morning, after distributing copies of this report to various officers, Hy was free to enjoy Paris.

This assignment unfortunately lasted only six weeks, and Hy was again transferred, this time to Frankfurt. As he puts it, "Frankfurt was bombed out and it wasn't Paris; and what do you do all day in Frankfurt?" While in Frankfurt, Hy ran into an officer in Military Government, Major Ed Reuss whom he had met at Maynard Krueger's house in Chicago. Reuss was a trade union leader who had ties to the Socialist Party. He asked Hy to visit with him at his office in Hoechst, which Hy did. Reuss said that David Saposs of the Manpower Division in Berlin needed reliable men, and asked Hy if he would be interested in joining Saposs. Minsky was, and soon—about Christmas time—he was in Berlin and assigned to the Reports and Planning Brigade of the Manpower Division under the direction of civilian David Saposs.

David Saposs was a labor economist with a doctorate from Wisconsin where he had been a student of the institutionalist John R. Commons. Saposs was a leading member of the Anti-Communist Left. Many of the people who worked with him at the Manpower Division were "politically reliable" from that point of view. Because of his background, Minsky was also politically reliable. Hy was discharged from the U.S. Army in early 1946, but stayed in Berlin as a civilian employee in the Manpower Division of the United States Military Government for six months before returning to Harvard in fall 1946.

The stint in the Army, especially his stay in Germany, played a pivotal role in framing the intellectual issues of economics that Hy would later pursue. In his own words, "[t]he experience in Germany and the interactions with Saposs impressed upon me the importance of the specific institutions and historical circumstances [for] what happens in the world. From that time on . . . I understood that theoretical abstractions are necessary to focus thinking—but abstract theory is the beginning of serious economic analysis, not the end product" (Minsky 1985, 212).

Saposs was involved with the labor union movement and before working for the NLRB, he had headed Brookwood Labor College, a socialist oriented training school for union officials. At this time, there was a considerable amount of politicking within the enlisted and civilian personnel of military government. The people in military government were, for the most part, committed ideologically to help build a new world order. Other people were there because of their anti-Nazi conscience. In retrospect, the internal composition of military government was a continuation of the American undergraduate campus debate of the 1930s between the Communist and the non-Communist left. In the Manpower Division, one prominent issue was the structure of the labor unions that would arise in Germany after the war. The American view was that there should not be a repetition of the pre-Hitler era of secular and sectarian unions, i.e., Catholic trade unions, Socialist trade unions, Communist trade unions. Furthermore, for the union leadership to be legitimate, it had to be cleared by military government officials in an effort to keep the union movement out of the hands of Nazi sympathizers. The political alliances within the American military government, especially in the Manpower Division, were complex, almost Byzantine. Various groupings within the labor movement were represented. There was the Communist Party background group that came out of the Hillman group within the Congress of Industrial Organization (CIO). The Reuther faction (largely Socialist) of the United Auto Workers (UAW) was well represented. Saposs had close ties both with the right wing Socialists in the States, who, by 1946 were mostly in the Democratic Party, and with the American Federation of Labor (AFL) leadership. Much of the effort in the Manpower Division was directed to blocking Communist influence in trade unions.

Although support of free and independent trade unions was the American policy, by winter and spring of 1946, trade union organization in the American Zone was lagging. The problem was, perhaps, due to the requirement that trade union leaders had to be certified by the American authorities and many of the field military government officers bought the line that Communists were the only true anti-Nazis. The American zone included conservative Bavaria and the socialist stronghold of Hess. Hy recalls a trip to the zone with Ed Reuss during which, along with Irving Brown, they met illegally with Social Democrats who had not been cleared for the trade union leadership by the military government. Irving Brown was the AFL representative in Western Europe. Financed by Jay Lovestone, the head of the AFL's foreign department, Brown was very important in aiding and abetting non-Communist trade union development.

David Saposs was concerned with the organizing of unions not proceeding at pace. He had to use his channels into the leadership of the AFL to alert them of the slowdown of union organizing activities in Germany. The slow pace of organizing also bothered the White House, and President Truman sent Joseph Keenan, the head of the American plumber's union, to Germany to get the wheels moving. The Keenan mission was to investigate why trade unions were not being organized. Saposs accompanied Keenan on his trip to the zone, and the report was that military government must recognize the legitimacy of Social Democrats.

In the winter of 1946, there was a movement to develop civilian governments in the zones and in Berlin. Four political parties were recognized: the Christian Democrats, the Liberal Democrats, the Social Democrats, and the Communists. It was clear that if there were free elections in Berlin and in the Soviet Zone, the Social Democrats would win. In the Soviet Zone, the Soviets forced a union of the Communists and the Social Democrats into a United Socialist Party, the "Einheit Party." (Officially East Germany was governed by the United Party until the Berlin Wall came tumbling down.) Some of the Social Democrats in the American Zone did not want unification with the Communists, and in opposing it, met with forceful pressure from the Soviet political officers. A support group of Social Democrats for the anti-unity party soon emerged, and the United States military government became funnels for help to them. Minsky and others helped the Social Democrats by providing moral and, at times, financial support in the form of tradeable goods that were received from U.S. union counterparts in Detroit. "I received many packages of cigarettes from Walter and Roy Reuther during those days," Hy remarks. He was active in supporting the Socialist Party's drive of independence from the Communists. The American military was finally convinced that there should not be a unification of the two parties unless a referendum of Social Democrats approved it. In February the referendum was held, and the anti-unity position won. All these efforts resulted in unions being recognized and growing at a rapid pace, with the Social Democrats as the dominant ideological force in nonsectarian trade unions. I asked Hy whether he ever felt that his activities in Germany contributed, in a way, to the beginning of the Cold War. He did not reply, and he did not have to; it was obvious that the thought had crossed his mind.

The decision to return to Harvard, Minsky said, was not based on financial considerations since Chicago had offered a better financial aid package. It was primarily for personal reasons, reinforced by the fact that his Chicago mentors—Lange, Simons, Viner and Douglas—would not be there, Viner having gone to Princeton, Lange back to Poland to work for the Polish Government, Douglas to run for political office, and Simons having recently died. Hy understood that the Chicago of the undergraduate years was not to be recaptured although many of his undergraduate friends were returning. At Harvard the atmosphere and teaching was not at all Chicagoan. The topics discussed in classes and seminars, as Hy remembers, were jumbled together. For instance, in Alvin Hansen's fiscal policy seminar, the rules of conventional and countercyclical fiscal policy applied in various ways and at various instances were hammered out according to the orthodox Keynesian program. Hansen, the leading disciple of Keynes in America, interpreted Keynes in rather a mechanistic fashion, virtually ignoring the significance of money and finance. Furthermore, uncertainty, which was fundamental in Keynes' understanding of the capitalist economy, was left out. The Hansen-Williams seminar which Minsky attended, both in his first semester at Harvard before the war and in the time after the war, influenced his later work. Hansen's position was that the behavior of a market economy could be controlled by aggregate interventions. Simons' view was that market structures matter in determining both efficiency and the efficacy of aggregate interventions. And Lange's view was that the allocation and the accumulation aspects of an economy can be separated in forming the structure of policy-oriented thinking. Combined, these theories characterize the basis for Hy's work.

Hansen was heavily influenced by the trauma of the Great Depression. He believed that achieving and sustaining a close approximation to full employment was much more important than any misallocative impact that interventions might entail. Furthermore, if market structures—monopoly in its various forms—blunted the effects of fiscal policy, the impact could be overridden by doing a bit more in the way of stimulation. It would be possible to do more with a given degree of fiscal stimulus, but if leakages in the form of price increases (due to the exercise of market power) were small, the impact of the leakages could be overcome.

We now know that fiscal policy can be entirely transformed into inflationary pressures with little or no beneficial effect upon output. During the period of 1933–39, the modest inflation was a relatively good thing, for it eased the debt burden that had been taken on in the 1920s and which became worse as deflation drastically lowered nominal cash flows. Inflation in 1933–39 was proinvestment, whereas in the 1970s and 1980s inflation disrupted the logic of investment by making it "rational" to be highly indebted. It also led to the belief that the nuances of investment were of secondary importance, for the rising of nominal values would bail out both the investor and financier alike.

In conversations with Minsky, he now believes that sustained high employment requires a labor movement that is willing and able to forgo wage increases in excess of productivity increases, and that such willingness and ability was present in the young trade unions of the 1940s and 1950s. Union leaders and members in the earlier periods remembered how weak trade unions had been, and realized that they were vulnerable to a loss of power if they ever lost political support. By the 1970s, union membership and leadership no longer remembered what it was like before the New Deal. Unions became a device that largely transformed aggregate stimuli into price increases. As time went by, the forbearance that made unions consistent with relative price stability in the 1940s and 1950s diminished.

Graduate study at Harvard, although enjoyable, was neither as intellectually intense as at Chicago, nor as exciting as the time in Berlin even though the end result in Berlin was not the building of a great new world out of the war that many had expected. "I really had no ambition when I came back," Hyman says. This disillusionment had several sources: family background, involvement in the Socialist movement, and the vulgar nature of the Soviet regime that violated all precepts of decency. In addition, there were those lists of names of individuals who had infiltrated as Communists into the government, the military, and various other agencies. This outcome was more or less a confirmation of the Right's approach in getting back at the supporters of Liberalism and Radicalism. When Hy returned from the Army, he and others—Tom Shellins, James Duesenberry, Evsey Domar, Richard Goodwin and Robert Solow from Massachusetts Institute of Technology (MIT)—would meet every so often to go over their papers and explore their ideas. Undergraduate Robert Solow and Hy had been quite close until the time Solow went into the Army. He remembers Solow and his wife-to-be, Bobbi, sitting for hours in his study. Harvard was not as intellectually intense an environment as Chicago, and the faculty tended to move ahead; push an idea forward, endorse, and impose it.

Schumpeter, of course, was an important figure there, and Minsky became acquainted with him early on together with John Williams who, aside from his faculty position at Harvard, was also the vice president of research at the Federal Reserve Bank of New York. Hy was the teaching assistant to Hansen and Williams in their joint money and banking course. It appears, however, from Hy's recollections that Harvard, for the three years he spent there, was not the center of his social life. Many acquaintances from Chicago had moved to Cambridge and were at MIT or in Boston. He vividly recalls meeting Julius Margolis at the stairs of Littauer as soon as he was back at Harvard from the Army. His close friends, with whom he shared an apartment, included Jerry Lettvin, Walter Pitts and Oliver Selfridge, all of whom were working with Norbert Weiner at MIT. Another person from those years that Hy remembers was Leon Lipson, whom he first had met in Berlin. Lipson, after receiving his degree from the Harvard Law School, went into private practice and then to Yale Law School, and at one point was the provost there. Hy soon got the reputation of being a smart guy at Harvard, and he is convinced that his grades were mostly based on this reputation rather than the work he did in class.

The University of Chicago continued to influence Hy since he maintained his contacts by spending time there during the Harvard intercessions when Chicago was still in session. During those return excursions, Hy would visit the Cowles Commission with his old friends, James Burtle and Carl Christ. It was at that time that Hy first met Kenneth Arrow and renewed his friendship with Leo Hurwicz whom he had first met when they both worked for Lange.

In 1949, Hy left Harvard to accept his first faculty appointment at Brown University. (The very first faculty position, however, was in the summer of 1947, when he was recruited by Bill Cooper to teach at Carnegie-Mellon—Carnegie Institute of Technology, as it was known then.) This was a good experience that led to making new friends such as David Fand and Padraic Frucht. Hy wanted to stay close to Harvard, yet far enough away to be independent. He made this decision despite the career opportunities that were coming up in the department, including Leontief's new economic research program. Hy sometimes wonders how his intellectual interests would have developed had he decided to stay at Harvard and join Leontief. While at Brown from 1949 to 1955, Hy wrote his doctoral thesis. Alvin Hansen expected him to work with him, but Hy started with Schumpeter with the topic that was going to explore the relations between market structure, banking, the determinants of aggregate demand, and business cycle performance. Because of Schumpeter's untimely death, the dissertation was finished in 1954 under the supervision of Professor Leontief. Hy feels indebted to him because, as he says, "Wassily was supportive despite the topic which was far from his interest; but he saw me through." During the Brown years Hy's academic visibility was in authoring book reviews and participating in the annual professional meetings. He was tenured there and promoted to the rank of associate professor.

In 1955, the same year he married Esther De Pardo, Hy was invited by Andreas Papandreou to the University of California at Berkeley. The visiting appointment in 1955–56 led to an offer to join the Department, which Hy accepted starting in 1957 after returning to Brown to fulfill the terms of his leave. He stayed at Berkeley, with the exception of one year off at the National Bureau of Economic Research (NBER), until 1965. At Berkeley, a number of articles were written and published including those that dealt with central banking, money markets, and multiplier-accelerator models. During the years at Berkeley, Hy developed a growing dissatisfaction with orthodox economic theory. The time at the NBER in 1960 was a terribly frustrating one for Hy because the data for what he wanted to do was not available. This was the year when he came to the conclusion that the flow of funds analysis, when it was transformed into how investments were, in fact, financed, missed the point. He began to argue that the flow of funds analysis should really emphasize cash flows where cash is committed by contracts, and today's cash is obtained by committing future cash. Minsky's cash flow perspective, developed during the year at the NBER, first surfaced publicly in "Comment on Friedman and Schwartz's Money and Business Cycles" (Minsky 1963).

Soon after Hy's second year at Berkeley, Aaron Gordon succeeded Andreas Papandreou in becoming chairman of the department. Henry Rosovsky became vice chairman, and Hy was named director of graduate studies. Together with the director of undergraduate studies, they constituted, in effect, an executive committee of the department. Thus, in addition to his academic duties, Minsky tried his hand at being an administrator. He was successful in that the Graduate Program was put on a sound basis. But soon he became dissatisfied with the change that was taking hold. The emphasis in teaching and research became increasingly abstract theory and econometrics to the neglect of institutions and history. He believed that the Berkeley doctoral program, which aimed at developing broadly educated economists, was superior to one that would have a narrower focus. The department offered an enormous breadth of courses, given by leading people, which made it distinctive. Aside from Tibor Scitovsky, and later Gerard Debreu, the senior faculty was not an assemblage of "stars." There was a high level of competence in Joseph Bain, Howard Ellis, and Aaron Gordon, all of whom were very good, but fell short of the "greats" in the discipline. The signs of change were there, however, and when they took hold they rendered Berkeley mediocre in almost everything except mathematical economics.

Still, the years at Berkeley were interesting in many respects. Hy remembers the time when Nicholas Kaldor, Aubrey Silverstein, Frank Hahn, and Donald Winch came to Berkeley at the same time, and Kaldor organized a private seminar that included Kenneth Arrow and Hollis Chenery from Stanford. The genesis of Minsky's *John Maynard Keynes* book owes a good deal to this seminar. The Keynes book was actually finished three years before it was published. The extra two-year publication lag was imposed because Columbia University Press wanted the book to come out simultaneously with two other monographs; one on Ricardo and the other on Marx. In the end, they had to publish it without the other two because of Hy's insistence and his threat of taking it to another publisher.

The capital asset pricing model, based on present value of future profits and central to the book, along with the view that the problem of capital asset pricing was critical, were extensively presented by Hy in lectures and seminars at a number of campuses and in his classroom at Berkeley. He was able to test these ideas on graduate students because of the flexibility he, Harvey Leibenstein, and Tibor Scitovsky had in teaching year-long courses on topics of their choosing. Hy's course had a heavy emphasis on industrial organization, money, and macroeconomics. The courses on monetary theory were split between Hy—who concentrated on the institutions and uses of money part—and Howard Ellis—who focused on the history of monetary theory. Hy was also responsible for the honors program, and among his students, he mentions the names of Victoria Chick, June Flanders, Nancy Gordon, Peter Gray, Robert Hall, Roger Miller, and Thomas Sargent.

Minsky had managed while at Berkeley to involve acquaintances from Harvard who were at the Bank of America in setting up an arrangement with the institution—the largest bank in the United States at the time—to fund seminars and lectures that would be given to the bank's staff as well as to Berkeley faculty and students. The arrangement had the added benefit of providing summer employment to students and entry into jobs at the bank, as well as supplementary funds to the department's budget. The interchange of ideas in these seminars helped fashion Hy's ideas about institutional innovation in banking. At that time, the Bank of America had invented the VISA card, or Bankamericard as it was then known. Hy's interest in the details of banking, the bank's internal operations, capital asset pricing, and cash flows, enabled him to work with the Mark Twain Banks when he moved to Washington University in St. Louis. His association with Mark Twain, as Hy admits, made Washington University more attractive than the invitations from other schools that came during his twenty-five-year tenure there.

The decision to accept the offer from Washington University in 1965 was the result of a disappointing 1964–65 year at Berkeley, a turbulent year where fundamental issues of freedom of speech and choice—especially for graduate students—were being tested by the University administration. Parietal rules, based on the *in loco parentis* assumption for undergraduates, were unacceptable to graduate students who took their objection to the streets. On the one hand people began to take sides, friendships were broken, and divisiveness developed. On the other hand some people tried to mend the splits. Henry Rosovsky, for example, became known as the great conciliator. What became clear, however, was that the administration failed to see the central issue. What emerged was a debate of administration versus student rights; Hy, to this day, feels that the administration should have been wiser.

The events at Berkeley crystallized a desire to look for a quieter place affording the opportunity to get some things done and then focus on the long term. As Hy puts it:

> I frankly went to Washington University with no intention of spending twenty-five years there. I thought I'd go there, get some things done and get out. But, I got involved with the banks and when the offer came through from the State University [New York], two or three years later, the bank made it worthwhile to stay. This happened a couple of times.

In 1969–70 Hy spent a sabbatical year in Cambridge further developing and presenting the ideas that were to appear in the Keynes book. He remembers that, on two or three occasions, he had long conversations with a young Ph.D who was teaching at the University of Bristol. These meetings would lead to a close and long-lasting friendship between Hy and Jan Kregel. After eight or ten years at Washington University and heavier involvement with the banks, it became difficult to think about leaving St. Louis.

Chronologically, a major point in Hy's academic career was the publication of his book, *John Maynard Keynes*, in 1975. This gave Hy the opportunity to become an important figure in the development of the post-Keynesian paradigm. In 1975 he did not necessarily view himself as a post-Keynesian. But there was overlap in his work on financial instability, and crisis with the work of Paul Davidson, Jan Kregel, and his former student Victoria Chick. He joined the editorial board of the *Journal of Post Keynesian Economics* that was launched by Paul Davidson and Sidney Weintraub in 1977. At about the same time, he also became involved with a number of organizations in Italy including the first faculty of the Trieste Summer School of Advanced Economic Studies, a relationship that has continued to the present and which necessitated that Hy begin his classes at Washington University two weeks later than scheduled each fall term until his retirement in 1990. Minsky has given many lectures throughout the United States and abroad including Britain, Holland, France, Italy, Hungary, and Australia.

In the course of our discussions, I asked Hy whether a connection can be made between the Henry Simons notion of the importance of the state of industrial organization, and the issue of macroeconomic financial instability. Simons,

Hy explained, in advocating the importance of the organization of production in a capitalist market economy, was implicitly stating that a financial structure was necessary for the system to be dynamic; and furthermore, debt deflations and consequent deep depressions were characteristics of any capitalist economy. Minsky's financial fragility hypothesis, inherent in an advanced capitalist system with a complex financial structure, owes a debt to the influence of Henry Simons. In linking the Simons view, Minsky, in his thirty-year-old article, "Central Banking and Money Market Changes," distinguishes two concepts of liquidity: one is the ability of the Federal Reserve to assure the values of particular assets because it will deal in them; the other is the concept of liquidity as cash flow. Cash flows and, in particular, assured cash flows of assets which appropriate these cash flows have markets. And assets, especially such as government liabilities, have assured markets. The pricing of various assets that emerges out of the cash flow structure is the "second price level."

The importance of Minsky's two price levels cannot be underestimated. It is basic to his interpretation of Keynes that, unlike the orthodox economist's belief in the neutrality of money, money is not neutral and, furthermore, mandates that two price levels must be recognized in an advanced capitalist economy. First, the price level of current output, and second, the price level of financial and real assets. These two price levels are determined from different relations and variables. The price level of current output is the device through which production and distribution take place and costs are recovered. It is dependent mainly on labor costs plus a markup. Alternatively, the price level of capital and financial assets incorporates uncertainty and is dependent on yields. Since yields represent streams of income through time, their current prices must reflect the current valuations of incomes that will be realized over time.

A case can be made that Minsky's analysis and interpretation of Keynes, although quite different from the standard neoclassical, may still be within the mainstream economic thought. He agrees that his is a special version of post-Keynesian economics, perhaps better named "Financial Keynesianism," and he remembers many instances of tension between the post-Keynesians and himself. One source of friction arose when Minsky would accept certain aspects of mainstream thought as contributing to his own views. In particular, he refers to his review of Leijonhufvud's book. Minsky (1968) emphasized the importance of the book. He stresses that he read the book very closely, and the line that he took in his review was that Leijonhufvud's distinction between Keynesian economics and the economics of Keynes was valid. While Leijonhufvud did write that the standard interpretation of Keynes was wrong, he provided no alternative, correct interpretation.

Hy insists that there is overlap in his work with that of Paul Davidson, some conceptual disagreements between them notwithstanding. He believes that *John Maynard Keynes* and Davidson's *Money and the Real World* got lost because, at the time of their publication, post-Keynesian economics was identified with the prevailing view of labor markets and wage controls necessary for the tax-based incomes policies developed by Sidney Weintraub.

Stabilizing an Unstable Economy was Minsky's most recent book, and I asked him to contrast, briefly, the ideas developed in this new book with those in *John Maynard Keynes*. The relationship between the two books, Hy contends, is that *Stabilizing an Unstable Economy* takes the same fundamental structure, but instead of treating it as a history of doctrine problem, treats it as a positive theory. In addition, the book is not an interpretation of Keynes alone. It follows Kalecki in linking profit flows to investment. Profits become both the lure of new investment and the result of realized investment. The history of the central bank and the way it functions when the banking sector is disrupted lies at the core of the book. The argument is developed to outline long-term policy recommendations for the effective and smooth functioning of the economic system.

Both *John Maynard Keynes* and the collection of articles in *Can "It" Happen Again* were preludes to *Stabilizing an Unstable Economy*. The most recent book deals with labor markets, trade unions, and market processes. In a way it is reminiscent of the Hansen-Simons dichotomy of macroeconomics and market structures. The book, in Minsky's mind, also takes a step toward integrating Schumpeter because the entrepreneurial aspect is emphasized and, as Minsky (1988) put it, in 1911 Schumpeter was closer to being a Keynesian than Keynes was.

One would surmise that Minsky's intellectual debts would be to Henry Simons and Schumpeter. "It is hard to say," Minsky responds. "Certainly Simons, Lange and Schumpeter were important, but generally I believe we are all products of our environment. The involvement with the Bank of America staff, and later with the Mark Twain Bancshares was also significant in the development of my ideas."

Hyman Philip Minsky is able to grasp and articulate a complicated argument. He is a warm, sympathetic, and supportive individual. I am proud to be one of his friends and closest colleagues.

Note

1. Minsky's undergraduate training in economics is chronicled in his very incisive and thoughtful article, see Minsky (1985).

References

Minsky, Hyman P. 1963. "Comment on Friedman and Schwartz's Money and Business Cycles," *Review of Economics and Statistics* 45 (supplement):101–111.
———. 1968. "Review of Axel Leijonhufvud's *Keynesian Economics and the Economics of Keynes*," *Journal of Finance* 23.

―――. 1985. "Beginnings," *Banca Nazionale del Lavoro Quarterly Review*, 154 (September):211–21.

―――. 1986. "Money and Crisis in Schumpeter and Keynes." In *The Economic Law of Motion of Modern Society: A Marx-Keynes-Schumpeter Centennial*, H.J. Wagener and J.W. Drukker, eds., pp. 112–22. Cambridge: Cambridge University Press.

CHAPTER THREE

Hyman Minsky as Hedgehog: The Power of the Wall Street Paradigm

GARY DYMSKI AND ROBERT POLLIN

Hedgehogs and Foxes

Sir Isaiah Berlin's justly famous essay on Tolstoy's theory of history begins with the following observation:

> There is a line among the fragments of the Greek poet Archilochus which says: "The fox knows many things, but the hedgehog knows one big thing." . . . [T]aken figuratively, the words . . . mark one of the deepest differences which divide writers and thinkers, and, it may be, human beings in general. For there exists a great chasm between those, on the one side, who relate everything to a single central vision, one system less or more coherent or articulate, in terms of which they understand, think and feel—a single, universal, organizing principle in terms of which alone all that they are and say has significance and, on the other side, those who pursue many ends, often unrelated and even contradictory, connected, if at all, only in some *de facto* way, for some psychological or physiological cause, related by no moral or aesthetic principle. . . . The first kind of intellectual and artistic personality belongs to the hedgehogs, the second to the foxes. (1953, 1–2)

Most research in economics is the work of foxes, extending, modifying, or testing conceptual, empirical, or policy questions. Such activity tends to obscure the small set of core ideas which underlay economists' models. These core ideas can be thought of as answering some basic questions about how the economy works: To what degree do capitalist economies promote equity and efficiency? What is the role for state intervention and public ownership? What economic

The authors are respectively assistant and associate professor of economics at the University of California, Riverside. They wish to acknowledge the constructive suggestions on a previous draft by John Caskey and James Crotty, and extend special thanks to Laurence Harris, Steven Fazzari, and Hyman Minsky for useful discussions and encouragement at various stages of this paper's development.

27

arrangements will best promote individual freedom, meaningful work, and material well-being? Taken as wholes, these core ideas constitute the preanalytic visions which, according to Schumpeter, "supply the raw material for our analytic effort" (1954, 41).

The most familiar preanalytic vision in contemporary economics is the Arrow-Debreu-McKenzie model (Weintraub 1979), which we refer to, hereafter, as the mainstream vision. The elements of this vision are: All economic agents are consistently rational; economic action is most naturally represented as the atomic movement of agents maximizing their own gain; and, since decentralized markets afford agents the most freedom of action, and agents know their own minds, market allocation is the best device for achieving economic coordination. The point of reference for the mainstream vision is the Walrasian general equilibrium.[1]

The ranks of economists who have developed their own preanalytic visions is small. On the one hand, there are only so many distinct and coherent answers to the core questions posed above. On the other, the mainstream vision has been developed by its practitioners to encompass a web of understanding so complete that different angles of vision seem uninformed.

Hyman Minsky's career stands apart. A hedgehog, he has remained formidably bound to his own "single universal organizing principle, in terms of which alone all that [he says] has significance." Minsky's vision, of course, is his "Wall Street paradigm." Through it, he has investigated a range of questions: A "financial" interpretation of Keynes; an attack on mainstream macroeconomics; a theory of investment and endogenous financial instability; an endogenous theory of money; an analysis of contemporary stabilization policies; and, most importantly, an original and fruitful analysis of the problems afflicting contemporary capitalist economies.

What is Minsky's Wall Street paradigm? It is useful to begin with some general observations. Minsky describes his approach as follows:

> In our economy the behavior of "Wall Street" is a determinant of the pace and direction of investment. A model of the economy from the perspective of "Wall Street" differs from the standard model of economic theory in that it first sees a network of financial interrelations and cash flows and then a production and distribution mechanism. A "Wall Street" paradigm is a better starting point for theorizing about our type of economy than the "barter" paradigm of conventional theory. (1977, 141)

Because cash flows and the network of financial interrelationships must be examined before considering issues of production and distribution, Minsky's Wall Street paradigm leads in many directions over the macroeconomics landscape. Yet it also leads to one central result which is fundamentally at odds with the mainstream view: Capitalist economies are inherently unstable, and disequilibrium and unemployment are their normal state of affairs. Minsky writes, "The capitalist market mechanism is flawed in the sense that it does not lead to stable price-full employment equilibrium, and that the basis of the flaw resides in the financial system" (1974, 267). This view could not be more at odds with the mainstream conclusions that money is a mere "veil" (as in the writings of Milton Friedman), that the corporate financial structure is "irrelevant" (the "Modigliani-Miller" theorem), or that federal deficit spending has no impact on the private economy (Barro's "Ricardian Equivalence").[2]

For Minsky then, the financial system is the root source of instability in capitalism; this is why Wall Street is the focus of his analytic vision. But the power of Minsky's vision can be grasped only when the pieces of his Wall Street paradigm have been assembled. Therefore, let us follow the thinking of this archetypical hedgehog through its various formulations.

Our discussion is organized as follows. We will begin with Minsky's interpretation of Keynes, the place from which Minsky's own analytical framework originates. In our next section we will contrast Minsky's approach to Keynes with that of mainstream macroeconomics. We first examine how the ideas of Keynes were appropriated into the Neoclassical synthesis, and then summarize Minsky's critique of this approach. Next, some of the main themes of the "new" neoclassical macroeconomics are described and we will show that Minsky's criticisms remain equally relevant to these recent developments. Next we will survey Minsky's basic analytical concepts: His theories of investment, endogenous financial instability, and endogenous money; and his analysis of interventionist policies. Then we will consider how well Minsky's approach can explain the macroeconomic experience of the postwar U.S. economy, both on its own terms and relative to more mainstream formulations. Finally, we consider some limitations of the Wall Street paradigm and offer concluding observations.

Minsky and Keynes

Any understanding of Hyman Minsky should begin with John Maynard Keynes because Minsky regards his own work, above all else, as an interpretation and extension of Keynes. Further, most positions in macroeconomics over the past fifty years amount to an acceptance or rejection, in varying degrees, of Keynes. Thus, the distinction between Minsky and his opponents can be understood by examining their perspectives on the great British economist.

In Minsky's interpretation of Keynes, capitalism is inherently unstable because of the volatility of private investment. Private investment drives the capitalist economy; its volatility is therefore the root cause of fluctuations in aggregate demand and employment. Investment is more volatile than other components of aggregate demand because it is based on investors' subjective evaluations of the future, and in particular on their expectations of future cash flows from profits. Investors cannot know in a precise deterministic or even probabilistic sense how profitable any given investment project will be.[3] To be sure, investors can take steps to reduce the risk of loss to which investment exposes them by diversifying their activities, selling project participations, and seeking insurance. But investment decisions must be made, nonetheless, under these conditions of fundamental uncertainty. As Minsky has pointed out, Keynes placed primary emphasis on this argument in his famous response to Jacob Viner, which stands as his only restatement of the essential message of the *General Theory*. The key passage in that paper is:

> By "uncertain knowledge," let me explain, I do not mean merely to distinguish what is known for certain from what is only probable. The game of roulette is not subject, in this sense, to uncertainty; nor is the prospect of a Victory bond being drawn. Or again, the expectation of life is only slightly uncertain. Even the weather is only moderately uncertain. The sense in which I am using the term is that in which the prospect of a European war is uncertain, or the price of copper and the rate of interest twenty years hence, or the obsolescence of a new invention, or the position of private wealth owners in the social system in 1970. About these matters there is no scientific basis on which to form any calculable probability whatever. We simply do not know. (1937, 213–14)

As Minsky reads Keynes, this fact of fundamental investment uncertainty is most clearly reflected in the financial aspects of capitalism: First, in the financial structures of firms; and, second, in the set of financial markets we associate with "Wall Street." Let us consider these two aspects in turn.

The financial structure of any individual firm consists of the relationship between the volume and characteristics of the various assets held, and the various liabilities which, together with net worth, support those assets.[4] It is usual for firms to mismatch the character of their assets and liabilities. Investment projects usually require firms to use shorter-term liabilities carrying certain cash commitments to finance long-lived assets with uncertain returns. Undertaking investment projects exposes firms to fundamental uncertainty, in the sense that they may yield cash flows substantially less than those anticipated. But the failure of any investment project implies more than mere disappointment, because the liabilities financing it give rise to cash commitments even if the assets they support become worthless. So investment expenditures leave financial trails and, hence, increase the exposure of both investing firms and their creditors to the risk of default and liquidation. The more a firm is leveraged—that is, the more debt obligations it carries relative to its equity base—the more likely that default on any project will require liquidation.

As Minsky reads Keynes, there are two ways in which Wall Street proper bears the burden of uncertainty. First, all firms can use financial markets to protect themselves against uncertain asset returns whether or not they undertake investment expenditures. This uncertainty takes the form of risks of two types for firms and individuals financing asset positions. The first is default risk; that is, the risk of a return on investment projects below the expected return. The second is market risk; the risk of loss from adverse price movements in financial markets. Default risk accrues to the residual claimants on the cash flows and net worth of firms undertaking investment expenditures. Any set of owners can dilute their share of default risk, and, hence, their burden of investment uncertainty, by selling additional equity claims or other subordinated debt claims. In this case claims sold in financial markets absorb some of the original owners' burden of investment uncertainty by spreading default risk over a larger number of financial market participants.

In addition, firms and individuals can trade financial instruments on secondary markets to assemble portfolios of financial assets with more desirable risk/return profiles. Minimizing losses from market risk, however, involves guessing the mood of the market, itself, which varies independently of the underlying productive conditions. Indeed, according to Keynes, market experts must be concerned "not with making superior long-term forecasts over [an investment's] whole life, but with foreseeing changes in the conventional basis of valuation a short time ahead of the general public" (1937, 154). Because of this extreme sensitivity to opinion, rumors and snap judgments hold considerable sway over the decisions of market participants. Thus, firms which turn to the financial markets to limit their exposure essentially exchange one form of uncertainty for another—they reduce default risk at the expense of increasing market risk. Moreover, the increased use of financial markets for this purpose may actually increase these markets' volatility and, hence, the extent of market risk.

Second, the financial markets carry forward the accumulated contractual obligations of all past investment decisions. All firms, especially nonfinancial firms, carry cash commitments based on the financial decisions they had made in previous time periods. These commitments were made based on expectations of future profit streams. Should these expectations be disappointed, firms become less capable of fulfilling their cash commitments. Default risk rises for these firms and, by association, for their creditors as well. Depending on the severity of this problem—the proportion of highly leveraged firms throughout the economy and the extent to which, in the aggregate, cash flows have fallen short—an interactive debt deflation can be set off through the defaults of a small number of highly leveraged firms. The financial market thus becomes the conduit through which disappointed expectations transmit instability to the economy as a whole.

In short, Minsky interprets Keynes as saying that fundamental investment uncertainty—as manifested in default and market risk—along with the economy's interlinked chain of financial commitments, makes firms' balance sheets fragile and engenders unstable financial markets. These conditions of financially fragile firms and unstable financial markets, moreover, dominate the relations of production and distribution in determining the pace of economic activity in capitalism. The argument for interventionist policies emerges through this inherent flaw in advanced capitalist economies with sophisticated financial markets. Government intervention is necessary, first of all, to reduce or eliminate the possibility of interactive debt deflations. This requires policies which prevent the spread of defaults from their point of impact to the remainder of the financial system. This intervention or promise of intervention—which is embodied in the central bank's lender-of-last-resort function, in deposit insurance, and in regulation of financial markets—reduces the volatility of financial markets.[5] In macroeconomic terms, this commitment by government is equivalent to setting a lower limit on profit flows.

But even if capitalism's downward instability can be reduced in this way, stable full-employment equilibria will not result. Reducing the risks of default and of debt deflations will, instead, encourage overoptimistic expectations and a debt-driven investment boom. Downward instability will thus be replaced by excessive leverage and persistent inflationary pressures. As Minsky writes:

> Because Keynes arrived at his views on how a capitalist economy operates by examining problems of decision-making under conditions of intractable uncertainty, in his system, stability, even if it is the result of policy, is destabilizing. Even if policy succeeds in eliminating the waste of great depressions, the fundamental financial attributes of capitalism mean that periodic difficulties in constraining and then sustaining demand will ensue. (1975, 12)

In Minsky's interpretation of Keynes, the capitalist investment process is inherently flawed because at its root is the uncertainty associated with profit-seeking activity which policy cannot eliminate. The manifestations of investment uncertainty—market and macro instability, and individual firms' failure due to interlinked defaults—can be changed, even ameliorated, through interventionist policies. But these policies cannot bring the economy to a stable full employment equilibrium. The alternative to downward instability is the upward instability produced by interventionist policies. According to Minsky, it is for this reason that Keynes advanced his oblique, yet famous, proposal that "a somewhat comprehensive socialization of investment will provide the only means of securing an approximation of full employment" (1936, 378).

Neoclassical Macroeconomics: The Descent to "Banality"

Minsky's angle of vision off of Keynes' shoulders has deviated sharply from that of almost all of his American colleagues. This section first shows how Minsky's vision differed dramatically from the "neoclassical synthesis," the mainstream vision which dominated U.S. macroeconomics from the 1950s to the mid-1970s. Since the mid-1970s, both a "new classical" school and a "new Keynesian" school have arisen in macroeconomics.[6] The latter, in particular, takes greater account of financial factors than the earlier neoclassical synthesis models. Because it remains faithful to the mainstream postulate that markets are globally stable, however, its treatment of financial issues remains restricted.

Minsky's Critique of the IS-LM Model

The overwhelming majority of U.S. Keynesians of Minsky's vintage fell into the "neoclassical synthesis," which combined an IS-LM system with a labor market framework along with some combination of the real balance effect and Phillips curve. According to Paul Samuelson (1955, 212), this neoclassical synthesis was "accepted in its broad outlines by all but about 5 percent of the extreme left and extreme right among writers."

This tradition, of course, was initiated by John Hicks's explicit effort to reconcile "Mr. Keynes and the classics," and, throughout, has attempted to merge what its practitioners perceived as most useful in both Keynes and the old classical system. As such, it represented a broad consensus that market mechanisms were efficient and stable. According to this approach, an economy not positioned at full employment can be brought there through several possible channels. Relying exclusively on the market mechanism, the existing unemployment will generate market-induced declines in wages which leads firms both to lower prices and hire more workers. The increases in employment and lower prices will then promote increases in aggregate demand. In addition, interventionist approaches can take two forms: monetary interventions to lower interest rates which would lead firms to borrow more for investment; and, fiscal interventions which would spur aggregate demand directly. Determining the appropriate path to full employment depends on how responsive one thinks the wage rate is to unemployment; how responsive investment is to interest rates; and how effective fiscal and monetary policies are at increasing aggregate demand. Within this agreed-upon framework, participants in macro debates chose between degrees of "monetarism" or "Keynesianism." Theoretical differences were discernible according to the means one preferred for achieving and sustaining full employment. Tellingly, financial relations were treated summarily; they appeared only in the form of a "money market" which was readily manipulable by central bank interventions.

In Keynesian variants of this framework, the key static impediments were rigidities which blocked out-of-equilibrium adjustment, including wage rigidities induced by labor unions or government policy, and price rigidities due to monopolistic market power or government policy. If not for these institutional rigidities, full employment could be readily attained through market adjustments. But because of these rigidities, the practical path to full employment was to employ monetary and fiscal policy, particularly, to stimulate effective demand. As long as government policy fine-tuned the economy, a classical economic system could be approximated indefinitely. As Olivier Blanchard has written, the neoclassical synthesis "did not expect full employment to occur under laissez faire; it believed however that, by proper use of monetary and fiscal policy, the classical truths would come back into relevance" (1987, 634).

While its principal models were static, the neoclassical synthesis did not completely ignore income variability. Endogenous variability in aggregate output was, interpreted as entirely a matter of well-behaved cyclical fluctuations. Following Samuelson (1939), a number of limit-cycle models based on the acceleration principle were proposed. These were based on two assumptions: first, that investment was a function of the lagged income level, implying that macro behavior could be reduced to a difference equation; and, second, that the time-trend of national income which resulted was globally stable.[7] The economy's motion through time was due to mild inventory cycles. Paralleling the summary treatment of financial relations, cyclical motion due to financial forces—not to speak of debt-deflations—was not considered important. In sum, endogenous instability in economic behavior was accounted for in models which demonstrated its relative unimportance.[8]

Minsky acknowledges that Keynes, by failing to fully "escape from habitual modes of thought" in the *General Theory*, left the door open for his neoclassical interpreters. However, this reigning U.S. postwar version of Keynesianism reduced "the Keynesian revolution to banality" (1986, 138). One of the major facets of Minsky's career was to criticize this approach in depth, even as he developed his own "fundamentalist" Keynesian analysis. How, according to Minsky, did the neoclassical synthesis miss what was essential in Keynes? There were three basic and interconnected errors.

(1) Persistent unemployment could never be explained as the result of mere market rigidities. Indeed, in Minsky's interpretation of Keynes, flexible wages and prices would only worsen conditions in a slump. Falling wages would lead to falling prices and expectations of further declines so that investment would be discouraged. At the same time, and perhaps most importantly, the real value of cash commitments would rise as wages and prices declined, increasing real debt burdens and, thus, raising the likelihood of widespread defaults.

(2) The role of financial commitments and financial markets narrows in the neoclassical synthesis to the LM equation. And even here, we assume that the central bank controls the supply of money. Endogenous financial influences thus reduce to the decision of asset holders about whether to carry money or bonds. There is no sense here of the predominant influence of financial relations and markets in determining the pace and direction of economic activity.

(3) The overarching error of this approach is its belief that "the proper use of fiscal and monetary policy" could make the economy behave as if it were a classical system. Of course, this error follows logically from the mistaken notion cited above that unemployment stems merely from rigidities, and not from fundamental uncertainty refracted through the financial markets. Endogenous instability is introduced only to be dismissively treated in limit-cycle models. For Minsky this last idea that a classical equilibrium system could be effectively

reproduced through policy above all expresses the "banality" of neoclassical Keynesianism—the loss of the critical and even the questioning stance toward capitalism that was so forceful in the work of Keynes himself.

How Different Is the New Macroeconomics?

The last two decades have witnessed a seachange in mainstream macroeconomic thinking. Turbulent macroeconomic events in the 1970s, together with three economic downturns, reduced the prestige of the neoclassical synthesis and helped to legitimize the "new classical economics." The new classicals asserted that capitalist macroeconomies should be modeled as consistent systems of equilibrium relations. From this position they launched a two-front attack on the neoclassical synthesis. First, they argued that the passive supply side of the neoclassical synthesis should be replaced by an autonomous aggregate supply function which flexibly, or even instantaneously, shifted with anticipated changes in macro conditions. Second, they argued that agent expectations (and, hence, behavior) should be modeled as forward-, not backward-looking. In particular, agents could predict government's policy choices, and adjust to anticipated government policy in advance of its execution. Therefore, government could have no effect on the economy except insofar as its policy rule changed in a completely unanticipated way.

What made this two-front attack so devastating was that it was launched in the name of more behaviorally complete and consistent models of macroequilibrium. In effect, its weapon of choice, simple (often representative-agent) aggregate equations with some behavioral basis, exposed the soft underbelly of the neoclassical synthesis; its lack of any "microfoundation." *The old IS-LM apparatus was dismissed as ad-hockery.*[9]

A younger generation of "new Keynesians" has now emerged in response to the new classicals. These new Keynesians begin by accepting the methodological critique of the new classicals, and hence by reaffirming their debt to Walras.[10] They then present models which derive "Keynesian" conclusions while exhibiting the basic mainstream postulates that markets are best modeled as equilibrating and agents as unswervingly rational. The basic premise of a new Keynesian counterattack is, then, to first identify a rigidity which prevents the economy from attaining a first-best Walrasian outcome, and then to identify how government intervention might improve things. A number of new Keynesian models have renewed the old idea of rigidities in labor markets due to asymmetric information (the "efficiency wage" approach, presented in Akerlof and Yellen, 1986), long-term contracts (Fischer 1978 and Taylor 1980), or the "menu costs" of changing wages or prices (Mankiw 1985; Ball, Mankiw, and Romer, 1988). There is also increasing appreciation of financial factors. Indeed, new Keynesians have identified two channels whereby financial-market imperfections affect macroeconomic outcomes. First, asymmetric information in credit markets can lead to persistent rationing equilibria. Second, some analysts have shown financial factors such as collateral, and not just monetary forces, playing a role in propagating macro shocks.[11]

However, this new Keynesian attention to financial relations does not mean they have appropriated Minsky. The New Keynesians accept the new classicals' premises of long-run equilibrium and of the need to microfound macroeconomic relations using the postulate of individual rationality. The financial factors which they have identified as affecting real outcomes, then, make no reference to Keynesian uncertainty. From their neo-Walrasian perspective, Minsky's broad view of financial/real imbalances is both methodologically indefensible and overly rich; his edifice taken as a whole represents an unnecessary detour in an analytical game whose highest art is defeating an enemy after granting all his premises but one.

Indeed, Minsky's critique of the "old" macroeconomics applies equally to the new. The new Keynesians are reinterpreting persistent unemployment as a result of market rigidities; without these rigidities, the optimal equilibria of the new classicals emerge via the invisible hand. The role of financial commitments and financial markets is broader than before, but still restricted. In a sense, financial relations simply offer the new Keynesians a new terrain for finding rigidities. There is no recognition of the deeper links between investment uncertainty, cash-flow commitments, and endogenous instability. Finally, not only has the new macroeconomics largely recreated the terms of debate of the old, it too lacks a critical stance toward capitalism and its institutions. The mainstream response to the turbulence of the 1970s and early 1980s has not been to challenge the relevance of Walrasian equilibrium, but to link its models ever more closely.[12]

Fundamentals of the Minsky Model

Minsky's work has never centered on exegetical debates with neoclassical Keynesians over the true interpretation of Keynes. Its major thrust, rather, has been developing a macroeconomic model corresponding to what he saw as Keynes' revolutionary message; that, "stability is destabilizing" under capitalism because of uncertainty and the centrality of financial relations. This model then constitutes the main features of Minsky's Wall Street paradigm. This work can be divided into four basic elements: his theory of investment; his model of endogenous instability; his theory of the endogenous money supply; and his analysis of the effects of fiscal and monetary policy. We consider these in turn.

Minsky's Theory of Investment

Minsky's model, as he puts it, is a financial theory of investment leading to an investment theory of instability. How does he reach this result? To a certain point, Minsky's theory of investment is closely reminiscent of Tobin's q theory.

Tobin (1969) conceptualizes an economy with two prices: the production price of currently produced capital and consumer goods; and the market price of existing capital assets. Then q is simply the ratio of the latter divided by the former. When q exceeds one, investment occurs, since any output put in place will be valued at a temporary premium in the capital market. The model can be solved for a deterministic equilibrium, within which agents are constrained only by budget, not financing, and expected returns in a stochastic sense are identical and known by all agents.

Tobin (1989, 105) believes Minsky's formulation of the theory of investment to be indistinguishable from his own. But Minsky's model diverges from Tobin's in its emphasis on the importance of finance.[13] To begin with, Minsky, like Tobin, does develop a model based on two price systems—one for current output, P_i, and, one for existing assets, P_k. The proximate determinants of the P_i schedule are conditions in the product and labor markets; in particular the mark-up of wages over costs for a given level of productivity. The price of existing capital assets, P_k, is set by the supply and demand for existing assets. But the supply of existing assets is fixed in the short run, and the proximate determinants of the demand for assets in place are their expected profit yield, and expected degree of liquidity. As such, P_k is governed by uncertainty over profit flows from the asset, and the ability to sell the asset at face value when desired. One could close the model here, with investment being determined by the ratio of the "objective" variable P_i and the "subjective" P_k; in this case, the model is, indeed, interchangeable with Tobin's. But for Minsky, the model up to this point is incomplete because it fails to consider how investment projects will be financed. As such, any effort to explain investment behavior by these factors alone will produce only "palpable nonsense" (1986, 188).

The next step for Minsky is to bring in financing considerations. Investment is financed either through drawing down existing assets from retained earnings, or through external finance. When it is externally financed, this brings new considerations into the investment project, those of borrowers' and lenders' risk. Minsky argues that borrowers' risk arises to the extent that purchasers of capital assets must debt-finance their investment projects and hence increase their exposure to default risk.[14] To compensate for their increased risk, borrowers lower the price, P_k, at which they are willing to purchase the asset. How much will P_k decline? According to Minsky, this cannot be measured objectively, but rather depends on borrower leveraging, on how external financing influences borrower assessment of project risk and return, and on the borrowing terms offered. The demand price for capital assets will fall when asset purchases are debt-financed, but by an analytically indeterminate amount. Lenders' risk arises because lenders will insist on being compensated for excessive risk and moral hazard (Keynes 1937, 144). Lenders' risk, therefore, exerts upward pressure on P_i, the supply price of investment goods. Bankers (or other lenders) extract compensation for their lenders' risk by imposing harsher terms on borrowers; i.e., higher loan rates, shorter terms to maturity, collateral, and restrictions on dividend payouts. The costs extracted for lenders' risk vary directly with the leveraging of the investing firm. While, as Minsky observes, lenders' risk "appear[s] on signed contracts" (1975, 10), the amount of lenders' risk that will be required on any investment project is, like borrowers' risk, analytically indeterminate. Minsky thus argues that investment will take place at a level that equates P_k and P_i, but only after P_k is influenced to an indeterminate degree by borrowers' risk, and P_i is altered by lenders' risk. For Minsky then, "the pace of investment will vary as borrowers' and lenders' risk vary" (1986, 193). Here is where we see the sharp departure from Tobin. Through the concepts of borrowers' and lenders' risk, Minsky incorporates both of the key ideas he takes from Keynes—fundamental uncertainty and the centrality of financial relations—and embeds them as primary determinants of investment behavior.

Endogenous Instability

The notions of borrowers' and lenders' risks in investment also lead directly to Minsky's concept of endogenous instability. After establishing lenders' and borrower' risks as important determinants of investment, one must next ask what lies behind these considerations. Here it is useful to distinguish what we may call the "statics" from the "dynamics" of Minsky's endogenous instability model. This section first develops its "static" elements by characterizing the financial fragility of firms, and then develops these elements into a dynamic conception of endogenous instability.

Hedge, Speculative, and Ponzi Finance

Minsky's theory of investment, as developed above, shows the consequences of the Keynesian uncertainty associated with any given investment project. The next step is to explore the implications of investment uncertainty for firms as entities subject to solvency constraints.

In principle, the activities of firms can be understood as bundles of investment projects. At any point in time a given firm will have any number of projects, all of them generating cash flows and creating liabilities. Net returns on these projects may exceed or disappoint expectations, and may even turn negative. The financial fragility of any economic firm is a positive function of the cash flows generated by each of its investment projects, weighted for that project's importance among the firm's overall asset holdings, and a negative function of the cash commitments associated with each of its liabilities.

Minsky suggests a way of characterizing the financial fragility of firms; as financial entities, they can be divided at any point in time into three categories—hedge, speculative, and Ponzi units. These terms are applicable to all firms. But as Minsky develops the concepts, they apply primarily to nonfinancial corporations.[15]

Hedge units are those with expected cash flows from operations exceeding expected cash commitments at all points into the future. Since cash flows are uncertain, all firms must allow for some variance around the expected levels of these flows. For the hedge unit, even the lower bound of the variance of expected cash flow exceeds cash commitments. As such, a hedge unit always carries positive present value. A hedge unit does face some degree of risk due to investment uncertainty. But its viability does not depend on financial market conditions, only on the normal functioning of the product and factor markets from which its cash flows derive. Speculative units are those for which, at some points in time, cash commitments exceed cash flows. Normally this will occur when repayment of principal is incorporated in cash commitments, a condition typically associated with short-term debt. As such, speculative units are forced to borrow the difference between cash commitments and cash flows when their short-term loans must be refinanced. As a result, speculative units, unlike hedge units, depend on the normal functioning of the money market—as well as on the product and labor markets—to remain solvent. Should short-term interest rates rise above expected rates in a period when the firm must borrow, its present value could turn negative and the firm become insolvent. As a result, the larger the weight of speculative financing in the economy, the greater the importance of containing upward pressure on interest rates.

Finally, for Ponzi units, cash commitments are normally greater than expected cash flows at most or all points in time. As such, these firms normally have to borrow to pay interest as well as principal on cash commitments. Ponzi units can be economically productive; they might include firms whose earnings are highly seasonal, or firms which depend heavily on take-out financing to undertake investment projects. But this category also includes firms whose assets yield little or no income, and whose owners expect large capital gains at some unknown date. Ponzi units are heavily dependent on the continuous sale of debt and are, therefore, even more exposed to the vagaries of money markets than speculative units. Ponzi units should also carry large supplies of liquid assets to get them through periods of money market difficulties. Whether they will or not depends on how "Ponzi" the unit really is. Certainly Charles Ponzi did not concern himself excessively with the size of his liquid reserves.

Identifying which category any firm falls into provides a measure of its individual financial fragility; classifying all firms in an economy according to these categories provides a means of assessing the level of economywide financial fragility at any point in time. Clearly, fragility is heightened when the proportion of speculative and Ponzi units is high. Both speculative and Ponzi units have an inelastic demand for borrowed funds, and rely on the money market to maintain solvency. These units' economic viability is thus threatened by rising interest rates. At the same time, their interest-inelastic demand exerts upward pressure on interest rates. The alternative path for such firms to raise funds is to draw down liquid reserves or sell other assets. But when assets are sold concurrently by many firms in a period of high interest rates, the price of the assets sold falls as well. In addition, speculative units selling their income-generating assets could transform themselves into Ponzi units.

In short, the higher the proportion of speculative and Ponzi financial units, the greater the fragility of the economy. Fragility in the Minskian sense has two components. First, the economy becomes less capable of absorbing shocks, so shocks are more likely to induce a financial crisis and incipient debt deflation. But in addition, the degree of borrowers' and lenders' risk also rises, and this should inhibit the growth of debt-financed investment activity.

The Thrust toward Fragility

What determines the proportions of hedge, speculative, and Ponzi units, and thus the degree of financial fragility? Here is where the dynamic component of Minsky's model emerges. Minsky argues that there is an inherent tendency for capitalist financial structures to move from states of robustness to fragility over time. This is due to the shift in expectations that occurs over the course of a business cycle, and the way this shift is transmitted through the financial system (so that, again, finance and uncertainty are the central elements of the argument).

At the trough of a business cycle, realized profits and profit expectations are low. At the same time, the financial structure is robust since the debt deflations which would have accompanied the previous downturn have brought a high proportion of Ponzi and speculative units to bankruptcy. As the economy moves up from the trough, profits begin to rise. But expectations are still low due to memories of the trough, and lenders' and borrowers' risk premia are correspondingly high; thus, financing patterns remain relatively cautious. As the upturn continues and realized profits exceed expectations, however, expectations shift upward. Animal spirits are now ignited, and firms become more willing to borrow in the pursuit of profit opportunities. In these circumstances, even more cautious firms feel pressure to either pursue all apparent profit opportunities or forfeit them to competitors.

As full employment is reached and sustained, "euphoric expectations" take hold. The growth rate of debt exceeds that of profits, since, for a given distribution of income between wages and profits, profit opportunities are constrained by the growth of productivity, while the extension of credit is not so constrained. The financial structure thus becomes increasingly fragile—i.e., vulnerable to an interactive debt deflation which induces a downturn. In addition, banks and other lending institutions generally accommodate—and even aggressively promote—the growing demand for credit. Their expectations may have shifted upward as well. But more importantly, they do not generally refuse loan requests by large-scale solvent customers.

This is the argument by which Minsky concludes that a period of full employment is not a natural equilibrium point for a capitalist economy. It is, rather, a transitory moment in a cycle; one which, in turn, leads to overheating and increasing financial fragility.

Endogenous Money

This model immediately raises two questions. First, corporations and their bankers may be afflicted with euphoric expectations, but what about central bankers? Why can't they simply rein in borrowing growth through the normal tools of monetary policy? The second question, posed by James Tobin, concerns the consistency of Minsky's treatment of expectations. Following the logic of the rational expectations hypothesis, Tobin asks: Shouldn't Minsky's cycles vanish as borrowers and lenders understand the deleterious consequences of euphoric expectations? Answering these questions requires that we consider the remaining components of the Minsky model—the theory of money supply endogeneity and the impact on system behavior of government policy.

According to Minsky, financial markets are essentially demand-driven due to nonfinancial corporations' inherent thrust toward speculative finance and the supportive posture of private banks. But what if private banks do not have adequate reserves to meet loan demand? This is the question Minsky addresses in his work on money supply endogeneity which originated with one of his first published papers (Minsky 1957).

The central bank, of course, sometimes accommodates rising credit demand through open market operations which increase the supply of nonborrowed reserves. It will sometimes choose not to accommodate, particularly when it feels compelled to restrain inflationary pressures.[16] When the central bank restricts reserve growth, banks with insufficient reserves who wish to meet credit demand have two options: borrowing either from the central bank's discount window or on the private money market. Because of the high *frown costs* associated with discount window borrowing, banks generally opt to raise funds from the money market. On the money market, financial institutions with excess reserves will lend to those with reserve shortages, either through repurchase agreements, the federal funds market, certificates of deposit, the Eurodollar market, or some similar avenue—that is, through the set of practices we now term "liability management."

It is easy to understand how a single institution could meet its reserve needs in this way. Whether rising credit demand in the aggregate can be accommodated through the private money market, however, is another question. Minsky argues that through increases in the velocity of circulation, rising credit demand can be met to a considerable degree within the private money market. Liability management, indeed, is the vehicle through which velocity rises. This practice involves a shift in banks' liability structure; out of demand deposit accounts, which carry low interest costs but high reserve requirements, and into certificates of deposit, Eurodollars, and federal funds, which carry higher interest costs but lower reserve requirements. As bank liabilities shift into the money market, the aggregate supply of loanable funds rises even when the Federal Reserve restricts the growth of nonborrowed reserves.

Initially, liability management will cause interest rates to rise as the interest rates on bank liabilities climb, and as banks maintain their interest spread and pass along these higher borrowing costs to nonfinancial borrowers. However, such upward pressure on interest rates is, itself, an unstable market condition. This is because this upward pressure can spur financial innovation.[17] When successful, financial innovation allows banks to procure a substantial volume of liabilities through a new institutional channel. By definition, banks can market their managed liabilities at a lower cost than was previously the case, so innovation produces a new institutional environment wherein rates on managed liabilities need not rise, even if the central bank continues to constrain nonborrowed reserve growth. Minsky's initial paper on the subject documented the early development of post–World War II liability management in the markets for repurchase agreements and federal funds, concluding that through such innovations, the money market could always stretch the limits of liquidity in a boom.

Minsky emphasizes as well that this endogenous reserve generation process will not necessarily create a fully adequate supply of loan funds. As he says ([1957] 1982, 171): "These institutional changes may not lead to a sufficient increase in financing ability to effect the same increase in financing as would have occurred if there had been no central bank constraint." When the money markets cannot sufficiently increase credit supply, a liquidity shortage emerges; intermediaries may be forced to call in loans and sell assets to meet their reserve needs, and the extension of new loans will diminish. These conditions will contribute to financial fragility, and may even detonate a financial crisis.

From this framework, we can see that central bank intervention can influence the character of the endogenous thrust toward instability, but cannot contain or reverse this process. Under a fully accommodative central bank, cash commitments rise at the pace set by the private market. This accommodative posture encourages interest-rate stability. At the same time, however, the increased loan riskiness associated with rising cash commitments relative to cash flows may cause interest rates to rise even in an accommodative environment. If central bank policy is restrictive, interest rates will rise more sharply and velocity will also accelerate, encouraging innovation. In short, financial market turbulence will gain momentum whether or not the Federal Reserve chooses a restrictive or accommodative policy. But the behavior of interest rates and velocity as well as the rate of institutional change will vary with the central bank's policy choices.[18]

Government Policy and Rational Expectations

The fact that the central bank cannot contain the thrust toward financial fragility would be less important if the market, itself, were able to contain the shift toward euphoric expectations. Why doesn't it, especially in light of recurrent experiences with financial panic? With the arguments of rational expectations proponents in mind, James Tobin has legitimately raised this question in a review of Minsky's work. Minsky never provides an answer to this question as posed. We can readily extrapolate an answer, however, based on the analytical framework of his Wall Street paradigm.

In fact, there are two levels at which one should address this question within Minsky's framework. The first entails incorporating particular institutional features of advanced capitalism, especially the impact of large-scale government intervention in the post–World War II economy. The second involves an alternative specification of rationality.

Minsky's theory of money supply endogeneity leads clearly to the conclusion that monetary growth policies are not effective at controlling financial market forces, and are particularly inefficient in controlling the thrust toward speculative finance. At the same time, Minsky also argues that two other policy instruments (federal government deficit spending and lender-of-last-resort interventions by the Federal Reserve) are extremely effective, if not at achieving full employment, at least in limiting the downside variability of incomes and liquidity during economic downturns; particularly in periods of incipient financial crisis. Drawing from Kalecki's well-known accounting identity that, in a closed economy, profits equal investment plus the government deficit, Minsky argues that the effect of deficit spending during a downturn is to establish a floor for profits. At the same time, lender-of-last-resort interventions are able to counteract the liquidity shortages of distressed financial firms. Because of the powerful effects of these policies, Minsky believes firmly that another large-scale debt deflation and depression, such as occurred in the 1930s, will not happen again.

But Minsky is also clear that solving the problem of debt deflations by no means implies that interventionist policies can promote full employment equilibrium. Rather, Minsky argues that interventionist policies serve to validate the existing fragile financial structure; and problems emerging out of the existing structure are allowed to continue, and even deepen. It is in this context that Minsky would explain why, for contemporary capitalist economies, the clarion call of rationality does not seriously inhibit the movement toward financial fragility. According to Minsky, market participants do, in fact, behave rationally when they continually pursue risky financial practices even as the level of financial fragility rises. This is because deficit spending and lender-of-last-resort interventions, and the potential costs associated with risky financial practices, are, to a considerable extent, socialized—government rather than firms absorbs these costs. Indeed, the socialization of financial market risk promotes fragility since, as Minsky says, "once borrowers and lenders recognize that the downside instability of profits has decreased, there will be an increase in the willingness and ability of business and bankers to debt finance. If the cash flows to validate debt are virtually guaranteed by the profit implications of big government, then debt-financing of positions in capital assets is encouraged" (Minsky 1986).

Does Minsky's analysis lead to the conclusion, reminiscent of new classical economics, that financial fragility can ultimately be blamed on government rather than on market forces? History cautions against such a conclusion, since financial crises have been, as Professor Charles Kindleberger put it, "hardy perennials" in the history of capitalism, and particularly in the epochs preceding World War II when government intervention was not as powerful as it is today.[19] Why then, even under small government capitalism, did we observe a persistent Minskian pattern toward increasing fragility and crisis? Why didn't rational expectations stem the tide in the periods before government intervention weakened the market's power to punish excessive risk-taking?

Tobin surmises that Minsky "would give an empirical answer: The participants in every new era of prosperity extrapolate it, finding many reasons not to temper their optimism by the lessons of history" (1989, 106). This answer is consistent with Minsky's approach but, we would argue, appropriates Minsky's line of reasoning only partially. Deeper factors, involving both a fallacy of composition and what James Crotty calls an "asymmetric reward structure," are also at work. Let us consider these in turn.

Fallacy of Composition

If a single firm perceives advantages in taking on more debt, this will not lead the system, as a whole, to a state of fragility as long as the majority of firms still remain hedge finance units. We should assume, especially in earlier historical epochs when economic information was not extensive or widely dispersed, that single firms did not know the financial status of other firms; or even if they did, were not able to gauge when the borrowing of other firms as well as their own borrowing would transform a robust financial structure into a fragile one. Under these circumstances, a rise in aggregate fragility would not inhibit the behavior of a rationally calculating single firm.

In fact, even the "lessons of history" from previous financial crises would not provide a clear message to speculative or Ponzi firms. According to Minsky, financial crises ensue only after the economy experiences a shock. To be sure, shocks, themselves, are not the causes of crises. A robust financial structure will be resilient and withstand the shock. Nevertheless, it is the shock which detonates the crisis. As such, financial market participants would be able to blame the crisis on the shock, not on the risky practices they and others had pursued. For them, the lesson of history may be that their financial posture was reasonable, but that a onetime shock, for which they bore no responsibility, brought the system, and themselves, to a crisis.

In such circumstances, one may simply say that market participants possess imperfect information. *If* they understood the full Minsky model, they would, for example, be able to establish the link between their own behavior and the repercussions of the shock, and not fall prey to the fallacy of composition. But it would be difficult to assume market participants should understand such aggregate economic relationships, especially in historical periods when information on such aggregates, to say nothing of theorizing about them, was limited; and when a purely individual calculus would tend to encourage euphoric expectations and risk-taking.

Asymmetric Reward Structure

Even if market participants did have full knowledge of the Minsky model, and were aware that financial crises will occur at some point, that still would not enable them to predict *when* the financial crisis will occur. In the meantime, aggressive firm managers and bank loan officers will be rewarded for pursuing profitable opportunities and gaining competitive advantages. Cautious managers, operating from the understanding that boom conditions will end at some uncertain point, will be penalized when their more aggressive competitors surpass their short-run performance.

When boom conditions do end, aggressive managers will already have been promoted, while cautious managers will have been demoted, if not dismissed. Moreover, during the slump, all aggressive managers will fail together, so no single individual will be singled out for blame. This is in contrast to the boom, where the miscalculating cautious will have been isolated. *This, then, is the crux of the asymmetric reward structure—aggressive behavior is rewarded more and punished less than cautious behavior, even though the "lessons of history" should promote a well-honed sense of caution.*[20]

Minsky and the Real World

So we see that Minsky's Wall Street paradigm—the "one big thing" that this hedgehog knows—does provide an internally coherent and innovative analytic framework. But in itself, this is a limited achievement. The only important measure of his work is how well it helps us to make sense of the real world. This, in fact, is the standard against which Minsky, himself, has always evaluated both his own contributions and those of his professional colleagues.

The Contemporary U.S. Economy

To evaluate Minsky's usefulness for understanding the real world, we must look to the post–World War II U.S. economy as our primary testing grounds. Virtually all of Minsky's empirical writings are concerned with the contemporary United States and even his theoretical models presuppose the U.S. institutional framework.[21]

According to Minsky, the U.S. economy emerged out of the Depression and World War II with a highly robust financial structure. The Depression had bankrupted the weakest financial units. During the war, moreover, war-related federal government borrowing grew rapidly, while private sector borrowing was restricted. Thus, in the early postwar years, nonfinancial firms were predominantly hedge units, and financial asset holders carried federal government debt with virtually no risk of default. Because of these circumstances, in Minsky's view, economic growth was vigorous for 20 years after the war, business cycles were mild, and financial crises appeared to be relics of the pre-Keynesian past.

However, this phase of robustness gradually deteriorated because, according to Minsky, the successes of the early postwar period bred a disregard for the possibility of failure. In 1966, the United States experienced its first post-war financial crisis, the "credit crunch" associated with the squeeze on profits, higher interest rates, and the Federal Reserve's decision not to raise the Regulation Q ceiling interest rate. For Minsky, this event signaled a new postwar phase in which the financial structure could be characterized as having migrated well into the region of fragility.

The Deepening Trend toward Fragility

Minsky is correct that beginning in the mid-1960s, we observed a rising trend in the nonfinancial economy's ratio of borrowing to income; a rough measure of cash commitments to cash flows. We have seen in this period the process of financial innovation gather relentless momentum, circumventing, and then rendering ineffectual, the system of financial regulation created during the Depression. The monetary decontrol legislation of 1980 and 1982 merely formalized the by-then effective collapse of the financial regulatory structure. It is also true that since the 1966 credit crunch, financial crises have recurred regularly—in 1970 (Penn Central), 1974 (Franklin National), 1980 (silver market), 1982 (Mexico), 1984 (Continental Illinois), 1987 (stock market), and 1989 (junk bonds, stock market).[22] For the most part, these crises have also gained in severity over time. Finally, in accordance with the predictions of Minsky's framework, accompanying these indicators of rising fragility are: growing federal deficits in the 1970s and especially in the 1980s; and the increasingly frequent use of lender-of-last-resort interventions and emergency bailouts by the Federal Reserve and affiliated agencies.

It is crucial to recognize that when one incorporates the effects of interventionist policies into Minsky's framework, we are no longer describing simply a cyclical pattern of rising fragility, debt deflation, and the gradual return to robustness. This is because debt deflations are now thwarted by successful interventionist policies. As a result, the movement toward fragility is not reversed. This movement, rather, becomes a persistent trend, transforming the most basic structural parameters of the U.S. economy.

This idea of a persistent trend toward increasing fragility is crucial for Minsky's analysis of the contemporary period. It is the foundation from which other developments in the U.S. economy become explicable. The experience with inflation is one example. The large infusions of liquidity associated with interventionist policies are inflationary, according to Minksy, as they inject purchasing power into the economy at a rate far greater than they promote new production. This is not to say that interventionist policies within the fragile financial structure are the only thing that influences the behavior of the price level. Rather, an inflationary bias has been built into the economy through this combination of systemic fragility and antideflationary interventions; a condition which, in Robert Heilbroner and Peter Bernstein's apt description, "affects the economy like a subacute infection—not really serious but always there, ready to flare up into a really debilitating condition" (1989, 134).

In addition, investment behavior has been altered by the persistent fragility trend. Because a financially fragile economy is susceptible to rapid and unforeseeable reversals in business conditions, the time horizons of investors have shortened. Investors have thus become increasingly resistant to the idea of undertaking long-term projects like building new physical plant. This is why, in Minsky's framework, the types of investments that are sought increasingly are short-term commitments in the financial sphere and in speculation. Thus, according to Minsky, the trend toward fragility feeds upon itself and becomes ever more entrenched in the contemporary U.S. economy. At the same time, the shortening of time horizons and corresponding decline in real investment suggest that productivity growth will also decline as the trend toward fragility persists.

Finally, in Minsky's analysis, there are no readily apparent resolutions for this persistent trend, short of the old-time medicine of debt deflation. However, the costs of debt deflation are worsening as the migration toward fragility proceeds. To paraphrase a remark by Albert Wojnilower, one is more likely to survive a single engine airplane's crash from 2,000 feet than a 747's plunge from the heavens. This is not to say that the fragility trend is linear. Cycles do occur around it. But the timing and severity of each cycle is highly contingent, depending on how far into the fragile region the economy has moved, and on the extent and character of the government's anti-interventionist efforts.

Minsky and the Mainstream Foxes

How persuasive is Minsky's story? One way to measure this is by how well it fares against a veritable forest of foxes, who, knowing "many things," can produce detailed analyses of particular circumstances to explain each episode of financial crisis, or even broad patterns of financial change. A composite fox might argue as follows: Continental Illinois failed in 1984 because of the fall of oil prices and a still stifling regulatory environment. The stock market crashed in 1987 because of overzealous program trading and the misguided confrontational rhetoric of both the German Bundesbank and the U.S. Treasury. The S&Ls collapsed due to the transition from a regulated to a deregulated financial market—whether one focuses on the regulations or their elimination as the specific culprit is relatively unimportant. The demise of the junk bond market was due to the insider trading scandals or its converse, the harassment of traders through RICO laws—again, the specifics of how one interprets this episode are relatively unimportant. Even the longer-term pattern of rising indebtedness and fragility can be explained in this fashion, for example, as due to an unprecedented series of severe macro shocks in the 1970s and irresponsible fiscal policy in the 1980s.[23]

In short, the mainstream alternatives to Minsky's hedgehog approach entail identifying shocks and government policy failures as the causes of financial crisis episodes. Such explanations are fully consistent with neoclassical economists' overarching vision that the macroeconomy constitutes an equilibrium system. Working from that vision, we would explain economic dislocations as resulting not from normal systemic behavior, but in any specific instance, from distortions of the inherently equilibrating market forces. It is, therefore, these distortions which must be analyzed and not the system's behavior itself.

Of course, shocks, human error, and other distortions all play a role in any given situation. Minsky would never deny that. It, therefore, becomes difficult on a case-by-case basis to weigh the relative merits of Minsky's hedgehogism versus the neoclassical foxes, especially in a brief amount of space. Given this problem, one reasonable test of relative merits may be to compare the current positions of Minsky and the mainstream on fiscal and monetary policy. This offers the advantage of considering not onetime episodes, but rather longer-term patterns where specific details count for less.

With respect to monetary policy, we may begin with a categorical, but we hope not terribly controversial, judgment that mainstream approaches have fared poorly in explaining recent behavior. We feel confident in issuing such a sweeping judgment because this is precisely the conclusion reached by Professor Benjamin Friedman in a remarkably candid recent article (1988b). Friedman begins his discussion by acknowledging that while monetary conditions from mid-1982 to 1987 were generally favorable, mainstream monetary theories could provide no guidance in explaining observed behavior. He writes:

> Economists hoping to say something useful about monetary policy have had a tougher time. The quantitative relationships connecting income and price movements to the growth of familiar monetary aggregates, including especially the M1 measure of the money stock that had been the chief focus of monetary policy during 1979–82, utterly fell apart during this period. ... Economists who preferred to think about monetary policy in different terms had no more success in fitting the major developments of this period into some alternative conceptual framework. Relationships connecting income and prices to the monetary base, or to measures of credit, fell apart just as visibly as did those centered on M1. (1988b, 51–52)

As a result, Friedman concludes that "it is difficult to escape the conclusion that there is now a conceptual vacuum at the center of the U.S. monetary policymaking process." Why did this vacuum emerge? Friedman's basic answer, though expressed in less direct terms, is that substantial institutional changes in financial markets were responsible. These changes include innovations in domestic financial markets which have blurred the distinction between transactions and savings balances, and the increasing importance of international economic factors in influencing U.S. monetary policy. Since institutional change has never been a basic component of mainstream monetary analysis, the models broke down when such changes gathered momentum.

But a similar conceptual vacuum does not apply to Minsky's endogenous money approach, which is based on the idea that modern financial markets are always capable of substantial innovation when profit opportunities are sufficiently enticing. As such, what Friedman acknowledges as anomalies within mainstream theory are readily explicable within Minsky's endogeneity model. The various assets comprising "the money supply" are distinguished, as are all assets, by their relative degrees of liquidity, risk, and yield. Minsky's theory would expect the blurring of distinctions between different financial assets to occur regularly in modern financial markets, since aggressive financiers will attempt to maximize both the liquidity and yield of all financial instruments. Moreover, Minsky's approach explains more than just the anomalies of the mid-1980s. Major monetary puzzles of the 1970s as well, such as the collapse of the Goldfeld money demand function and the frequent definitional changes in the monetary aggregates, can also be explained as resulting from endogenous market processes overturning relationships that mainstream theorists had believed were stable.[24]

Concerning fiscal policy, and in particular discussions of contemporary federal deficits, we again confront important anomalies when mainstream analysis is our guide through the bramblebush. Consider the predominant "crowding out" perspective on federal deficits, which reaches the important conclusion that large-scale federal deficits have been responsible for the high real interest rates and low real investment growth rates of the past decade.[25] The basic premise underlying this conclusion is that the U.S. was effectively at full employment over most of the 1980s. As such, federal deficit spending was incapable of raising real incomes, and therefore could not increase aggregate savings. This means that federal deficits simply absorbed savings that otherwise would have been available to the private sector. The relative scarcity of savings would then imply upward pressure on interest rates for private sector borrowers. Facing higher rates, private business has become discouraged from borrowing and investing. From the crowding out viewpoint, then, the federal deficit has been largely responsible for both the high real interest rates and low investment growth rates of the 1980s.

What is wrong with this perspective? It is of course true that investment growth has been low and interest rates high over the 1980s. It is not the case, however, that private corporations have been, in any reasonable sense, crowded out of financial markets by the federal government. In fact, as recognized by Benjamin Friedman, a major proponent of the crowding-out hypothesis, "corporations have borrowed record amounts" since 1983. The problem was not that the corporations were short of credit, but rather, as Professor Friedman also recognizes, "they used an unusually large part of these funds for purposes other than productive new investments" (1988a, 264–65). In other words, what needs to be explained is not crowding out at all, but rather, why corporations, carrying more than ample investible funds, are using a significant proportion of these funds for mergers, acquisitions, and similar unproductive activities. Thus, the crowding-out theory cannot account for the major initial phenomenon it purports to explain—the borrowing behavior of private corporations.[26]

What about Minsky? His approach, of course, anticipates that deficits should grow over time as fragility deepens. As such, the impact of deficits in a fragile environment is double-edged; they help prevent debt deflations, and thereby the collapse of real investment, but only by encouraging further ventures into speculative and Ponzi finance. Within this framework, Minsky would naturally anticipate high levels of federal deficits and private corporate borrowing to emerge concurrently, the pattern we actually observe from 1983 onward. At the same time, we can see in Minsky's framework why the growth of borrowing should be associated with a relative decline in productive investment and more speculation—patterns that we also observe in the 1980s. This is because, as we move to a more fragile state, lenders' and borrowers' risk increases and time horizons shorten. Thus, from Minsky's viewpoint, large-scale federal deficits should be accompanied in the private sector by high levels of borrowing, but also by a decline in productive investment. In short, what seems anomalous from a crowding-out view emerge as normal phenomena within Minsky's conception.

The Limits of Minsky's Vision

We have argued that Minsky's Wall Street paradigm illuminates important features of contemporary U.S. capitalism which mainstream approaches cannot explain. But for all its power of illumination, the Wall Street paradigm also leaves large murky areas and anomalies of its own. It is important that these also be recognized.

Here we need touch only lightly on a most obvious failing; as an arch hedgehog, Minsky has never seriously attempted to "know many things." In other words, he has never sought to build a body of rigorous evidence to support his basic positions—an effort which may have led him to question, modify, or even strengthen his perspective. Nor has he attempted to test whether the patterns he describes may be explained equally well, or even more effectively, by any alternative framework as, for example, Benjamin Friedman does in the article on monetary policy cited above. To recognize this is not to suggest that Minsky is unscientific, but simply, again, that he is unequivocally a hedgehog. Almost by definition, the task of empirical verification is one best left to foxes.

Our real criticism of Minsky is not that he is too little a fox but, after all, insufficiently the hedgehog—a visionary whose vision is too narrow. The fact is that the Wall Street paradigm provides an overly constricted view of the essential characteristics of a modern capitalist economy. As we have discussed, the Wall Street paradigm, "first sees a network of financial institutions and cash flows, and then a production and distribution mechanism." Working from this premise, Minsky relegates to a second order of concern, and, indeed, never addresses seriously questions located within the "production and distribution mechanisms" that are not only intrinsically vital, but that also bear directly upon the problems of finance, instability, and crisis that are central to his vision.

This lacuna is evident even in his most basic formulations. For example, in Minsky's view, investment is determined by the intersection of two functions: the demand function P_k, which reflects anticipated yields from capital assets and borrowers' risk; and the supply function P_i, which reflects the costs of labor and purchased inputs, as well as financing costs and the associated level of lenders' risk. Minsky's analysis actually focuses on only selected elements of this framework; specifically, the P_k function and the role of lenders' and borrowers' risk. The P_i function, involving conditions in the labor and product markets—that is, wage rates, productivity rates, and markups of prices over prime costs—never warrants his serious attention. Such issues are relegated to Minsky's "black box." [27]

And what emerges when one opens the "black box"? To begin with, Minsky's approach implies that distributional questions, as reflected in the determination of wage rates and markups, do not have major macroeconomic implications. But this is incorrect, even within the confines of Minsky's model. Among other things, distributional questions will affect realized profit flows and the expected level of profitability. As such, distributional shifts will influence the P_k as well as the P_i curve, and thus play a substantial role in determining the rate of investment. Such ideas played a major role in the early business cycle models of Marx, Veblen, and Mitchell—all of whom then explicitly linked their cycle models to analyses of financial instability.

In fact, as became clear in later work developed in the Keynes/Kalecki tradition, the direction in which distributional change will affect profit expectations and investment is indeterminate, since it depends on the relative weight of two distinct and possibly countervailing effects. The first effect is that capitalists will benefit immediately from a rising profit share out of national income. But in addition, after a lag, capitalists also benefit on the demand side from a high aggregate wage bill, even to some extent if the relative share of national income favors wages over profits. But the presence of such complex influences only makes the problem of distribution within macroeconomics less tractable, not less important. Certainly, Wall Street denizens whose informational concerns extend beyond ARIMA models should want to somehow make sense of the macro implications of distributional questions. [28]

Minsky's "black box" approach to production and distribution also implies that productivity questions are relatively unimportant for macroeconomics. This, again, is incorrect even within a Minskian framework. A decline in productivity growth means declining income growth. This will imply a sharpening of distributional conflict, thereby increasing the variability of the distributional effects described above. Moreover, a major terrain of distributional conflict will be the federal budget, as various sectors will seek to protect themselves against declining pretax incomes by lowering their tax burdens and/or increasing their support from government. Thus, variation in productivity can affect profits, wages, investment, taxation, and the budget deficit. Empirically, as noted earlier with respect to the U.S., the advanced capitalist economies have all experienced a decline in productivity growth from the late 1960s to the present. This is also exactly the period, according to Minsky, in which the migration toward an increasingly fragile financial structure occurs. Minsky's writings offer only passing (if suggestive) references to this conjuncture of declining productivity growth and increasing fragility, even though the connection would appear to be fundamentally important.[29]

At one level, one appreciates why Minsky has adopted his particular intellectual stance. He wants to insist—indeed, to shout from the rafters—that we cannot understand the nature of contemporary capitalist economies without assigning primary importance to financial relationships. According to Minsky, when one abstracts from finance, one is no longer talking about real-world capitalism. That is why he strongly repudiates the contemporary "surplus" school of thought stemming from Sraffa, even though both Minsky and the Sraffians are members, in good standing, of the same non-neoclassical tradition. Minsky says Sraffian analysis is just as "irrelevant to the understanding of modern capitalist economies" as neoclassical theory, since both ignore finance in their models (1988, 1). But an aggrieved Sraffian could easily respond to Minsky, that a model which ignores the relationships of production and distribution is equally incomplete. And it would be no excuse to suggest, as Minsky seems to do when he juxtaposes his Wall Street approach with the neoclassical "barter paradigm," that the analysis of production and distribution is inevitably misguided because neoclassical thinking predominates. Kalecki, Kaldor, and Robinson, as well as Sraffa, were all great post-Keynesians who devoted much of their intellectual energies to the understanding of production and distribution under capitalism. There is no reason why Minsky should have put the lifetime contributions of these figures to one side.

Not surprisingly, the implications of Minsky's truncated vision extend beyond his model, into the realm of policy ideas, and the very *Weltanschauung* flowing from his work. Keynes observed in the *General Theory* that "the outstanding faults of the economic society in which we live are its failure to provide for full employment and its arbitrary and inequitable distribution of wealth and income" (1936, 372). Minsky writes more tepidly that "the major flaw of our type of economy is that it is unstable" (1986, 9). To be sure, Minsky takes pains to state his commitment to a more equitable form of capitalism, even, as he puts it, at the expense of some efficiency. But such ideas are mere asides in his overall framework. The major thrust of his work could lead one to conclude that the fundamental distributional questions—of unemployment, inequality, and ultimately of economic power in capitalist societies—could largely resolve themselves if capitalist finance can be stabilized.

Minsky, in other words, never confronts the obvious point that economic democracy does not prevail under capitalism—that wealth and power go hand in hand. The macro policy implications of this simple point were dissected brilliantly by Kalecki in the years immediately after he and Keynes explained the principle of effective demand. According to Kalecki, the intellectual means were then at hand to achieve full employment through interventionist government policy. But this did not mean that the capitalist economies would implement full employment. This is because unemployment serves a function under capitalism; it maintains the power of the capitalists, especially the power of the sack. Kalecki also anticipated that military spending would be a preferred means of generating countercyclical budget deficits, since alternative forms of government spending, for public investment or subsidizing mass consumption, would also threaten the market power and class prerogatives of capitalists (Kalecki 1971, ch. 12).

Minsky often stresses the need for unflinching criticism of capitalism, even if just to make the system work more effectively. But he, himself, pulls punches by ignoring these basic Kaleckian insights. As a result, the policy ideas Minsky advances in *Stabilizing an Unstable Economy*, while humane and often insightful, are essentially apolitical (and thus, uncharacteristically mild) because they do not address the implications of unequal wealth and power in capitalist societies.[30] One can see in this discussion how Minsky is attempting to specify Keynes' vague proposal for a "somewhat comprehensive socialization of investment." But one would not be surprised had these ideas been penned by a liberal neoclassical Keynesian, a James Tobin, for example; one whom, in the terrain of theoretical combat, Minsky would regard as more foe than friend. Tobin himself implies as much in his 1989 review.

This is all to say that Minsky has made important contributions to modern economics, but, as with all major figures, in a flawed and incomplete form. He has advanced new ideas and taken risks, and one should never expect original thinking to emerge finely honed and neatly packaged. As Joan Robinson once observed, only plodding minds go step by step, being careful to avoid slips. Original thinkers stride along, leaving a paper chase of mistakes behind them. Minsky's bold vision of post-Keynesian monetary macroeconomics has almost single-handedly forced those who would listen to recognize the centrality of finance, for the development of Keynesianism and, more broadly, for the building of relevant macroeconomic models. As such, he has deepened our understanding of the most basic elements of contemporary economic life: unemployment, inflation, stagflation, business cycles, fiscal policy, the role of central banks, and of course, the problems of financial instability and crises. And because Minsky has pushed his vision so forcefully, one can also readily follow his paper chase of mistakes. Minsky once said of Joan Robinson that "she was often wrong in especially incisive ways" (1986, xiv). The same applies to Minsky. He has left much for others to do, both building from his insights and transcending his errors.

We live in curious economic times in which the slogans of free market economics are being celebrated in unprecedented fashion. For obvious reasons, such thinking has emerged most dramatically in Eastern Europe, the Soviet Union, and China. In these regions, for example, competitive banking and financial markets are now broadly perceived as essential instruments for insuring the efficient and productive allocation of investment funds. The destabilizing potential of capitalist finance is ignored.[31] But as the reconstruction of these economies advances, their infatuation with Milton Friedman will fade. The works of Hyman Minsky will then stand as a challenging guide to a more humane economic future.

Notes

1. Since everyone loves the underdog, undoubtedly all schools of thought would like to reserve the term "mainstream" for the competition. The term is deployed here as a means of describing the basic principles which link pure theorists, policymakers, and all economists in between whose work is based on this vision.

2. The theoretical foundation for these positions is acknowledged straightforwardly by Frank Hahn (1983, 1) in his account of the role of monetary phenomena in an Arrow-Debreu model: "The most serious challenge that the existence of money poses for the theorist is this: the best developed model of the economy cannot find room for it." The notion that money is a mere "veil" for Milton Friedman may appear confusing, if not downright contradictory, given that his work—the foundation of modern "monetarism"— focuses so sharply on the role of monetary variables in affecting macroeconomic activity. The key to understanding this apparent paradox is that Friedman and other monetarists see monetary fluctuations as determined by government intervention, which are exogenous to market forces. Within this framework—and more generally, within the Walrasian system of general equilibrium—monetary variables exert no influence on real economic activity. General equilibrium is determined exclusively through the interaction of real economic forces, the endogenous variables in the system. This apparent paradox within monetarism is captured well in John Gurley's bit of doggerel: "Money is a veil/but when the veil flutters/the economy sputters."

3. The root cause of this uncertainty can be interpreted in either of two ways: (1) the complexity of the economic interactions determining the return on any given project, which are too large to be known with any precision in advance; or (2) the existence of an irreducible element of indeterminacy in a "real time" activity—that is, any activity in which the two steps of initiation and realization are separated in time. See Davidson (1978) for an analysis of "real time" and how it affects economic behavior.

4. Throughout this paper, the term "firm" refers to both firms and wealthowners considered as distinct operating entities. The "characteristics" of assets and liabilities consist of their defining elements: the length of time they must be held to yield a return, the certainty of that return, their term to maturity, and their liquidity (marketability).

5. The point of government intervention should not be to insure individual firms

against loss from default, which means socializing the risks individuals bear when pursuing profits. Instead, the goal should be to insure against the *adverse systemic consequences* which would result in an overreaction by the financial system to any one firm's default. In practice, it is difficult to insure against systemic risk without offering to bail out all market participants, as illustrated by the current debacle of savings and loan defaults in a regime of deposit insurance.

6. A key event in establishing the neoclassical synthesis was the publication, in 1949, of Hansen's *Monetary Theory and Fiscal Policy*. The "Lucas supply curve" was first set forth in Lucas and Rapping's 1969 paper, "Real Wages, Employment, and Inflation," published in the same year that former President Nixon declared us, "all Keynesians now." The influence of the new classical macroeconomics was solidified in the early and mid-1970s, especially with the publication of papers by Barro (1974) and Sargent and Wallace (1975) which dramatically demonstrated its policy implications.

7. Other permutations of this basic idea were also suggested. This literature is discussed at length in Gapinski (1982, chs. 4 and 6).

8. For example, Goodwin first proposed his path-breaking model of nonlinear dynamics in 1950. The implications of this model for chaotic and persistently disequilibrium dynamics were not explored in any depth by other theorists until the late 1970s.

9. It is useful to contrast Minsky's critique of the neoclassical synthesis with that of the new classical economists'. Both critiques deny the old neoclassical position that government intervention can stabilize the economy. Minsky locates the destabilizing pressure in financial relations and fundamental uncertainty—that is, in the "market"—and argues that government intervention can reduce the magnitude of macrofluctuations. The new classicals, by contrast, argue that government itself is the destabilizing force; markets, left alone, would equilibrate.

10. The acceptance of Walras by modern mainstream economists has shifted their analytical entry point. Previously, the entry point was the institutional particulars of the real-world problem being studied. Now, theorists must specify exactly how and why their models deviate from the pure competitive equilibrium. Indeed, the trend now is toward explaining institutions themselves in terms of agent rationality, information efficiency, and market forces: that is, not as ex-ante constraints but as optimal ex-post achievements. This has driven economists in every field, including the new Keynesians, back to very simple models in which phenomena are investigated at a very primitive level to determine basic causal links. This return to the building blocks of analysis, however, has largely meant a withdrawal from engagement with the fundamental policy questions which the more ambitious—if less "rigorous"—Keynesian models of an earlier generation could readily incorporate. This trend is particularly pronounced in monetary economics.

11. This growing literature is reviewed in Gertler (1988).

12. Blanchard and Fischer (1989, xi) preface their text on contemporary mainstream macromodeling: "On the surface, macroeconomics appears to be a field divided among schools, Keynesians, monetarists, new classical, new Keynesian, and no doubt others. Their disagreements . . . leave outsiders bewildered and skeptical. This is not our assessment of the field . . . macroeconomics shares many basic models and views." Nevertheless, such ecumenicism among contemporary mainstream macroeconomists does not extend to Minsky's contributions—Blanchard and Fischer fail to cite Minsky even once in their 650-page text.

13. Tobin's model is driven by an explicit assumption that financial markets equilibrate, and by an implicit assumption that product (and hence labor) markets do as well. If this latter implicit assumption were not granted, then Clower's (1969) observation that excess demand in one market implies excess supply in another would have to be granted, and the model respecified.

14. Minsky (1975, 109) explains that debt financing "lowers the margin of security" on the project; in effect, external financing precommits some of the project's cash flow as a cost and reduces the share left for the firm.

15. Some economists have objected to Minsky's use of the terms "speculative" and "Ponzi" finance to describe ordinary financial practices. Raymond Goldsmith has even denounced these usages as "demagoguery" on Minsky's part (Kindleberger and Laffargue 1982, 43). But surely economists have committed more flagrant linguistic misdeeds without having had images of breastbeating Il Duces invoked. Would Goldsmith similarly accuse Milton Friedman of demagoguery for having promulgated the utterly misleading concept of a "natural rate of unemployment?"

16. Greider (1987) emphasizes the connection between inflation and restrictive monetary policy in his account of Federal Reserve behavior in the late 1970s and early 1980s.

17. Dymski (1988) develops a model of liability-managing banking firms which shows how these firms are linked through the money market, and how the interest rate in that market depends on relative supply and demand pressures. Dymski (1989) extends Minsky's model of financial innovation by banks by arguing that innovation can develop both because of unexploited profit-making opportunity and also because rising interest rates in existing bank borrowing markets squeezes bank lending margins.

18. Minsky's position on money-supply endogeneity represents only one approach to this widely discussed question in the post-Keynesian tradition. See Moore (1988) for a more fully developed alternative approach, and Pollin (1991) for a survey and empirical evaluation of the alternative views. Harris (1990) provides a wide-ranging discussion of the state of post-Keynesian monetary theory, which he, perhaps, more aptly terms "structuralist monetary theory."

19. Kindleberger's 1977 book is a serious effort at applying a Minsky-inspired model to understanding the historical experience of financial crises in Western Europe and North America from the 1750s to the 1970s. It is notable in Kindleberger's "stylized outline" of the historical experience that the number of "manias, panic, and crashes," does, indeed, diminish in the 1950s and 1960s, consistent with the Minsky position that government interventions have inhibited debt deflations and downward instability. But Minsky's position and Kindleberger's evidence appear inconsistent with the recent striking finding of Romer (1986) that, "the stabilization of the post-war economy is a figment of the data." Romer's argument—that prewar, small government capitalism was no more unstable than the postwar big government economy—presents a clear challenge to adherents of post-Keynesian analysis. From a Minskian perspective, a relevant distinction here would have to be between downward and upward instability. Romer's work has drawn numerous responses from new Keynesian economists (for example, DeLong and Summers [1988]). Also see Felix (1984) for related work on this question.

20. As Crotty writes, "to fail with the crowd will do no harm to your career, while to fail all alone is disastrous. And you fail by being conservative in a boom that lasts for any reasonable period." Crotty's observations, of course, are closely allied to Keynes' famous discussion on "The State of Long Term Expectations" in chapter twelve of *The General Theory*. There, Keynes (1936, 158) states, "Worldly wisdom teaches that it is better for reputation to fail conventionally than to succeed unconventionally." We are grateful to Professor Crotty for explaining his concept of asymmetric reward structures in a lengthy private correspondence from which the above quotation is taken. We also note that Steven Fazzari suggested essentially the same argument in his comments on a previous draft of this paper.

21. The fact that Minsky refers almost exclusively to the contemporary U.S. economy raises the question of how generalizable his model is to other countries or time periods. Kindleberger (1977), of course, makes the strong case for the usefulness of Minsky's

framework for understanding the broad sweep of financial history. Beyond this, the contemporary Third World debt crisis is an obvious candidate for applying at least some of Minsky's lessons. Two efforts that attempt this are Darity and Horn (1988) and Pollin and Alarcon (1988).

22. One might add to this list the "silent run" on savings and loans in 1989 and 1990. Wolfson (1986) documents these events through the 1984 Continental Illinois episode, and also attempts to place them in a broader theoretical context. The clustering of episodes of financial crisis since 1984 already makes Wolfson's work seem somewhat dated, a fact which only affirms that financial instability has become a regular feature of our present economic landscape.

23. Another mainstream approach to rising indebtedness and financial instability is to define it as a nonproblem. For example, in considering the significance of rising corporate indebtedness, Lawrence Summers (1988, 131) declared it to be as important to economic policy as are "disputes with Norway over fishing rights are to foreign policy."

24. The difficulties posed for mainstream monetary theorists by a quarter-century of structural change are especially well illustrated by the infamous "search for the missing money" in the mid-1970s (Goldfeld 1976). Faced with a breakdown in the empirical fit of the Goldfeld money demand equation, mainstream monetary economists responded by attempting to identify the "break point" that, once found, would, presumably, again leave a behaviorally accurate equation. The vagaries of this search were such that some of the proposed break points were time periods in which no institutional or policy change of any importance had occurred. See Simpson (1980) for a discussion which links the issue of redefining monetary aggregates to that of financial innovation and, more specifically, to the problem of "missing money."

25. Crowding out, of course, is not the only significant mainstream position concerning contemporary fiscal deficits, the main alternatives being the Ricardian equivalence perspective initiated by Barro and Robert Eisner's "real deficit" framework. The spring 1989 symposium of the *Journal of Economic Perspectives* provides a good overview of these alternative approaches. Pollin (1992) presents a more critical overview as well as an attempt to explain contemporary deficits within a macroeconomic framework inspired by Marx, Keynes, and Kalecki.

26. Of course, controversy surrounding the crowding-out argument extends beyond this point; in particular, to the question of whether the stimulus to aggregate demand generated by deficit spending represents a net increase, or simply a transfer of purchasing power, from the private sector to the government. But even prior to addressing this controversy, we find it significant that private firms have simply not been inhibited from borrowing during the period of high deficits—i.e., whatever else has occurred because of deficit spending, private borrowers have not been "crowded out."

27. A similar criticism is developed in more depth in Pollin (1986) and Crotty (1986; 1990).

28. Wolfson (1986) provides a good introduction to the early cycle models of Marx, Veblen, and Mitchell (as well as that of Minsky), and discusses the way each linked business cycles and financial instability. Wolfson also explores the various factors generating financial crises in the post–World War II U.S. economy. He finds that the single greatest influence inducing financial crises is a decline in the interest coverage ratio, and that, in turn, the largest single factor generating a declining interest coverage ratio is a decline in corporate profitability. But to gauge the empirical significance of distributional influences, one must still consider the extent to which distributional shifts affect profitability. This has been a question of considerable empirical concern in recent years, especially among those exploring Marx's arguments about how variation in the "reserve army of labor" can squeeze profitability. Some relevant studies include Boddy and Crotty

(1975), Weisskopf (1979), Henley (1987; 1989), and Sherman (1990). In general, these studies find that the cyclical rise in labor's share of national income—corresponding to an increase in wage rates greater than the rate of productivity growth—does exert downward pressure on profitability, contributing to cyclical downturns. The relative importance of this factor among others is disputable; its influence appears to have been greater in the 1950s and 1960s than more recently. The difficulty in empirically determining the overall effect of a rising wage share is at least partially due to the countervailing influences of wages on profitability as a factor in demand as well as in costs. Marglin and Bhaduri (1990) develop a model delineating the complex paths through which profits are affected on both the cost and demand side by wage/rate variation.

29. Mainstream overviews of the decline in productivity growth are presented in a Fall 1988 symposium of the *Journal of Economic Perspectives*. An explicitly post-Keynesian perspective on declining productivity growth, based on Verdoorn's law, was suggested by Kaldor (1966) and critically discussed by Rowthorn (1975). Neo-Marxian analyses are developed in Bowles, Gordon, and Weisskopf (1983) and Glyn (1990).

30. Chapters twelve and thirteen of this 1986 book contain Minsky's most complete exposition of his ideas on policy.

31. Writing on the Chinese financial reforms, Dymski and Veitch (1990) argue that liberalizing banking and finance without altering the deep institutional structure of the socialist economy—and especially socialized ownership of assets and centralized control over the allocation of scarce resources—has led to excessive risk-taking, credit over-expansion, and price inflation. A related view of the introduction of financial markets into socialist economies is Singh (1989).

References

Akerlof, George, and Janet Yellen, eds. 1986. *Efficiency Wage Models of the Labor Market.* Cambridge: Cambridge University Press.

Ball, Laurence, N. Gregory Mankiw, and David Romer. 1988. "The New Keynesian Economics and the Output-Inflation Tradeoff," *Brookings Papers on Economic Activity*, No. 1, pp. 1–65.

Barro, Robert. 1974. "Are Government Bonds Net Wealth?" *Journal of Political Economy* 82 (November).

Berlin, Isaiah. 1953. *The Hedgehog and the Fox.* New York: Simon and Schuster.

Boddy, Radford and James Crotty. 1975. "Class Conflict and Macropolicy." *Review of Radical Political Economics* 7 (Spring): 1–27.

Bowles, Samuel, David Gordon, and Thomas Weisskopf. 1983. "Hearts and Minds: A Social Model of U.S. Productivity Growth," *Brookings Papers on Economic Activity*, No. 2, pp. 381–441.

Blanchard, Olivier. 1987. "Neoclassical Synthesis." *The New Palgrave*, pp. 634–36.

Blanchard, Olivier, and Stanley Fischer. 1989. *Lectures on Macroeconomics.* Cambridge: MIT Press.

Clower, Robert. 1967. "A Reconsideration of the Microfoundations of Monetary Theory." *Western Economic Journal* 6 (December): 1–8.

Crotty, James. 1986. "Marx, Keynes, and Minsky on the Instability of the Capitalist Growth Process and the Nature of Government Economic Policy." In *Marx, Schumpeter, and Keynes: A Centenary Celebration of Dissent*, pp. 297–326. Suzanne Helburn and David Bramhall eds., Armonk, NY: M.E. Sharpe, Inc.

———. 1990. "Owner-Manager Conflict and Financial Theories of Investment: A Critical Evaluation of Keynes, Minsky, and Tobin." *Journal of Post Keynesian Economics* 12: 519–542.

Darity, William, and Bobbie L. Horn. 1988. *The Loan Pushers: The Role of Commercial Banks in the International Debt Crisis*. Cambridge: Ballinger Publishing.

Davidson, Paul. 1978. *Money and the Real World*, second edition. New York: Macmillan.

Dymski, Gary A. 1988. "A Keynesian Theory of Bank Behavior." *Journal of Post Keynesian Economics* 10 (Summer): 499–526.

———. 1988. "Uncertainty, Illiquidity, and Bank Innovation," MRG working paper no. 88–13 (November). Los Angeles, University of Southern California.

Dymski, Gary and John M. Veitch. 1990. "Yin and Yang in Chinese Financial Reform: Decentralized Risk-Taking Versus Centralized Risk-Bearing," MRG working paper no.90–1 (March). Los Angeles, University of Southern California.

Felix, David. 1984. "The Impotence of Macroeconomic Policy Activism: A Critical Appraisal of the New Classical Macroeconomics." *Journal of Economic Issues* 18 (September): 825–59.

Fischer, Stanley. 1978. "Long Term Contracts, Rational Expectations, and the Optimal Money Supply Rule." *Journal of Political Economy* 85.

Friedman, Benjamin. 1988a. *Day of Reckoning: The Consequences of American Economic Policy under Reagan and After*. New York: Random House.

———. 1988b. "Lessons of Monetary Policy from the 1980s." *Journal of Economic Perspectives*,2 (Summer): 51–72.

Gapinski, James. 1982. *Macroeconomic Theory: Statics and Policy*. New York: McGraw-Hill.

Gertler, Mark. 1988. "Financial Structure and Aggregate Activity: An Overview." *Journal of Money, Credit, and Banking* 20: 559–88.

Glyn, Andrew. 1990. "Productivity and the Crisis of Fordism." *International Review of Applied Economics* pp. 28–44.

Goldfeld, Stephen. 1976. "The Search for the Missing Money." *Brookings Papers on Economic Activity*.

Goodwin, Richard. 1950. "A Non-Linear Theory of the Cycle." *Review of Economics and Statistics*.

Greider, William. 1987. *Secrets of the Temple*. New York: Simon and Schuster.

Hansen, Alvin. 1949. *Monetary Theory and Fiscal Policy*. New York: McGraw-Hill.

Hahn, Frank. 1983. *Money and Inflation*. Cambridge: Cambridge University Press.

Harris, Laurence. 1990. "Structuralist Monetary Theory." *Cambridge Journal of Economics*.

Heilbroner, Robert and Peter Bernstein. 1989. *The Debt and the Deficit: False Alarms/Real Possibilities*. New York: Norton.

Henley, Andrew. 1987. "Labour's Share and Profitability Crisis in the United.States." *Cambridge Journal of Economics* (December): 315–30.

———. 1989. "Aggregate Profitability and Income Distribution in the UK Corporate Sector, 1963–85." Manuscript. Kent, England: Keynes College, University of Kent.

Kaldor, Nicholas. 1966. *Causes of the Slow Rate of Economic Growth of the United Kingdom: An Inaugural Lecture*. Cambridge: Cambridge University Press.

Kalecki, Michal. 1971. *Selected Essays on the Dynamics of the Capitalist Economy*. Cambridge: Cambridge University Press.

Keynes, John Maynard. 1936. *The General Theory of Employment, Interest, and Money*. London: Macmillan.

———. 1937. "The General Theory of Employment." *Quarterly Journal of Economics* 51 (February): 209–23.

Kindleberger, Charles P. 1977. *Manias, Panics, and Crashes*. New York: Basic Books.

Kindleberger, Charles P. and Jean P. Laffargue, eds. 1982. *Financial Crisis: Theory, History and Policy*. Cambridge: Cambridge University Press.

Lucas, Robert, and Leonard Rapping. 1969. "Real Wages, Employment and Inflation." *Journal of Political Economy* 77 (September/October): 721–54.

Mankiw, Gregory. 1985. "Small Menu Costs and Large Business Cycles: A Macroeconomic Model of Monopoly." *Quarterly Journal of Economics* 100 (May): 529–37.

Marglin, Stephen, and Amit Bhaduri. 1990. "Profit Squeeze and Keynesian Theory." In *The Golden Age of Capitalism: Lessons for the 1990s,* Stephan Marglin and Juliet Schor, eds. London: Oxford University Press.

Minsky, Hyman. 1974. "The Modeling of Financial Instability: An Introduction." *Modeling and Simulation* 5: Proceedings of the Fifth Annual Pittsburgh Conference, Instrument Society of America, pp. 267–73.

———. 1975. *John Maynard Keynes.* New York: Columbia University Press.

———. 1977. "A Theory of Systematic Fragility." In *Financial Crises: Institutions and Markets in a Fragile Environment,* Edward J. Altman and Arnold W. Sametz, eds. New York: John Wiley and Sons, pp. 138–52.

———. 1982. "Central Banking and Money Market Changes." In *Can "It" Happen Again?: Essays on Instability and Finance.* Armonk, New York: M.E. Sharpe, pp. 162–78.

———. 1986. *Stabilizing an Unstable Economy.* New Haven: Yale University Press.

———. 1988. "Sraffa and Keynes: Effective Demand in the Long Run." Working paper no. 126 (November). St. Louis: Washington University.

Moore, Basil. 1988. *Horizontalists and Verticalists: The Macroeconomics of Credit Money.* Cambridge: Cambridge University Press.

Pollin, Robert. 1986. "Alternative Perspectives on the Rise of Corporate Debt Dependency: The U.S. Postwar Experience." *Review of Radical Political Economics* 18 (Spring and Summer): 205–35.

———. 1991. "Two Theories of Money Supply Endogeneity: Some Empirical Evidence." *Journal of Post Keynesian Economics* 13 (Spring): 366–98.

———. 1992. "Budget Deficits and the U.S. Economy: Considerations in a Heilbronerian Mode." In *Social Forces and Economic Questions: Essays in Worldly Philosophy,* Ronald Blackwell, Jaspal Chata, and Edward Nell, eds. New York: Macmillan.

Pollin, Robert and Diana Alarcon. 1988. "Debt Crisis, Accumulation Crisis and Economic Restructuring in Latin America." *International Review of Applied Economics* 2 (June): 127–54.

Romer, Christina. 1986. "Is the Stabilization of the Postwar Economy a Figment of the Data?" *American Economic Review* 76 (June): 314–33.

Rowthorn, R.E. 1975. "What Remains of Kaldor's Law?" *Economic Journal* 85.

Samuelson, Paul A. 1939. "Interactions Between the Multiplier Analysis and the Principle of Acceleration." *Review of Economics and Statistics* 21 (May): 75–78.

Samuelson, Paul A. 1955. *Economics,* third edition. New York: McGraw-Hill.

Sargent, Thomas, and Neil Wallace. 1975. "Rational Expectations, the Optimal Monetary Instrument, and the Optimal Money Supply Rule." *Journal of Political Economy* 83 (April).

Schumpeter, Joseph A. 1954. *A History of Economic Analysis. New York: Oxford Press.*

Sherman, Howard J. 1990. *The Business Cycle: Crisis and Growth Under Capitalism.* Princeton, N. J.: Princeton University Press.

Simpson, Thomas D. "The Redefined Monetary Aggregates." *Federal Reserve Bulletin* (February): 97–114.

Singh, Ajit. 1989. "The Institution of a Stock Market in a Socialist Economy: Notes on the Chinese Economic Reform." Manuscript, Cambridge: University of Cambridge.

Summers, Lawrence. 1988. ''Comment on Bernanke and Campbell,'' *Brookings Papers on Economic Activity,* No. 1, pp. 130–36.

Taylor, John. 1979. "Staggered Wage Setting in a Macro Model." *American Economic Review* 69 (May): 108–13.

Tobin, James. 1969. A General Equilibrium Approach to Monetary Theory." *Journal of Money, Credit, and Banking* 1 (February): 15–29.

———. 1989. Review of *Stabilizing an Unstable Economy*. *Journal of Economic Literature* 27 (March): 105–108.

Weintraub, E. Roy. 1979. *Microfoundations*. Cambridge: Cambridge University Press.

Wolfson, Martin. 1986. *Financial Crises*. Armonk, New York: M.E. Sharpe.

CHAPTER FOUR

Risks in Our High-Debt Economy: Depression or Inflation?

BENJAMIN M. FRIEDMAN

Writing at the beginning of the 1980s, Hyman Minsky pointed out that "The most significant economic event of the era since World War II is something that has *not* happened: there has not been a deep and long-lasting depression" (Minsky 1982, xi). Anyone familiar with Minsky's work would know that by this statement he also meant that there had not been a world-scale, or in the United States not even a national-scale, financial crisis—or more specifically, to use Minsky's classic description from nearly 30 years ago, "large-scale defaults by both financial and nonfinancial units, as well as sharply falling incomes and prices" (Minsky 1963, 101).

Minsky's dauntingly impressive body of work, spanning most of the postwar period, has added importantly to our understanding of financial crises and their implications for nonfinancial economic activity. It also has added to our knowledge of the fundamental nature of the financing of a private enterprise economy which, at times, can go awry, even in the tangibly dramatic ways that financial crises and depressions through the centuries have demonstrated. Indeed, in many respects Minsky's contributions have not merely added to our understanding. They have created whole new opportunities for understanding, as Minsky has opened original conceptual avenues for thinking about these complex and important market phenomena. I, therefore, feel very honored to speak at a conference honoring Hy and his splendid intellectual achievements.

Surely it is a powerful testament to the continuing force of those achievements that Minsky's work is as relevant today as it ever was, not only for economic theory but also for its application to the actual prospects and risks now facing our economy. In the early 1990s, it remains true that "It" (to use Minsky's preferred designation) has not happened again. Nevertheless, the

The author is William Joseph Maier Professor of Political Economy at Harvard University. This paper was presented as the keynote lecture of the conference honoring Hyman P. Minsky, April 20, 1990. It draws, in part, on earlier work, especially Friedman (1990, 1991).

events of the 1980s in the United States—including the greatly increased use of debt throughout society, and especially the proliferation of debt-financed mergers and acquisitions, and leveraged buyouts in the corporate business sector—have again raised fears of a financial crisis, with threatening implications for output, incomes, jobs, and capital formation.

Given the historical underpinnings of so much of Minsky's own analysis, it is useful to begin by recalling that the events of 1929–33 did not constitute the sole, or even necessarily the most prominent, episode of financial crisis in the history of free enterprise economies as we know them. To be sure, Black Thursday on Wall Street in 1929, and even more so the failure of Credit-Anstalt in 1931 and the worldwide banking collapse of the next two years, were hardly minor hiccups. But other major episodes that are familiar to more than just economists include the bursting of the Tulip Mania in the seventeenth century, the South Sea Bubble and the East India Company crisis in the eighteenth century, the failure of Baring Brothers in the nineteenth century, and, closer to home, the series of banking panics that were so familiar to our own economy before the founding of the Federal Reserve System. By now all this is standard lore, typically recalled with substantial color and, oddly enough, even with a hint of nostalgia at times.

Perhaps more importantly, financial crises have typically played a major role in fluctuations of nonfinancial economic activity. In the United States a financial crisis has occurred just prior to, or at the inception of, each of the half-dozen or so most severe recorded declines in economic activity. Before World War II, financial crises also occurred in conjunction with most other U.S. business fluctuations.

At the same time, it is far from obvious that the effects of financial crisis, damaging as they seem at the time, are uniformly harmful. Joseph Schumpeter, to whom Minsky has often pointed as a major influence on his own thinking, thought that financial crises, and the depressions that they bring, also play a cathartic role, clearing out the economy's underbrush, the better to foster dynamic new developments thereafter. Given that "It" has not happened for half a century, there may, therefore, be grounds to question whether at least some parts of our own economy have not begun to ossify.

In light of this historical perspective, what are the events of the last ten years that have so rekindled concerns about the likelihood of financial crisis after such a long hiatus? To begin, the use of debt by just about all sectors of the U.S. economy virtually exploded in the 1980s. Before then, the outstanding debt of all obligors in the United States that are not themselves financial intermediaries was remarkably steady. Not just for years, but for decades, the debt ratio held at about $1.35–1.40 of debt for every $1 of the annual national income. By 1990, however, the U.S. economy's debt ratio was above $1.80.

The U.S. Government accounted for roughly one-third of this rise in the economy's total indebtedness. The reason, of course, is the chronic imbalance between the federal government's expenditures and revenues that has become the hallmark of U.S. fiscal policy since 1981. The Reagan deficits produced the only sustained peacetime rise in the ratio of federal debt to gross national product in the entire two-hundred-year history of the United States. Even so, nobody has seriously suggested that the U.S. Government will, therefore, default on its obligations. The unprecedented increase in government borrowing is a serious problem for the United States, to be sure. This borrowing absorbs our saving, reduces our investment, retards our productivity growth, and impairs our ability to compete in world markets—but not because the resulting higher level of federal debt outstanding increases the risk of financial crisis. That risk, if indeed there is one, presumably arises from the debt of the private sector which accounted for the other two-thirds of the 1980s increase in the economy's total indebtedness.

Within the private sector, increased borrowing by both individuals and businesses has contributed about equally to this phenomenon. Until recently, discussion of these issues focused more on borrowing by individuals. I believe, however, that borrowing by businesses presents the greater risk to the economy. The reason is the dramatic difference in the use to which individuals and businesses have put the proceeds of their respective borrowing. Individuals have borrowed in record amounts since 1980, but they have also accumulated record amounts of assets; including not merely stock market assets and real estate, the prices of which can rise and fall, but a whole range of liquid assets such as deposits and stable-price debt instruments. By contrast, businesses, for the most part, have borrowed not to put in place any new assets at all, but simply to pay down equity.

By now surely everyone is aware of the incredible wave of mergers, acquisitions, leveraged buyouts and stock repurchases that swept over so much of corporate America in the latter half of the 1980s. This phenomenon has attracted more attention than any other financial development since the Great Depression. One reason for all this attention is that so many of the transactions have extinguished from the publicly held business sector companies that used to be household names: RCA, Gulf Oil, Kraft, Levi Strauss, Macy's, Revlon, Singer Sewing Machine, Bell & Howell, Twentieth-Century Fox, and plenty of others. Another reason is that some of these transactions have been genuinely huge. The $25 billion that an LBO group paid in 1989 for just one company, RJR Nabisco, amounted to one-half of one percent of the entire country's annual product. No doubt yet another reason for the attention given to these events is just the inherent fascination always associated with the making of huge fortunes by specific individuals, rather than by faceless corporate entities.

For our purposes, however, the common thread in each of these transactions is that a company has borrowed in order to pay down either its own equity or the equity of a company that it is acquiring. In short, the corporate sector as a whole has borrowed primarily for the purpose of substituting debt for equity. During 1984–89 the net pay-down of equity (that is, equity securities retired over and above the gross proceeds of new equities issued) by U.S. corporations engaged in nonfinancial lines of business was almost $600 billion.

One implication of this development, of course, is that corporate balance sheets have suffered. I believe, however, that the erosion of corporate balance sheets is less important than the parallel deterioration of business cash flows. On average, in the 1950s and 1960s, it took sixteen cents out of every dollar that corporations earned (measured before interest and taxes) to pay their interest bills. In the 1970s, as nominal interest rates rose and corporate earnings faltered through a series of recessions, the average corporation's interest bill consumed thirty-one cents of every dollar of its earnings. Since 1980, despite a seven-year economic expansion with strong growth of earnings, and despite falling nominal interest rates—both of which should have allowed corporate America to reduce its debt-service burdens—U.S. companies have borrowed so much that it now takes nearly sixty cents out of every dollar of earnings just to pay the interest bill.

It is always possible that these aggregate statistics are misleading; perhaps those corporations that borrowed the most were simply those with the greatest unused debt capacity. Recent research based on individual company data has shown that this is not so, however.[1] Company by company, just as in the aggregate, U.S. business corporations are becoming ever more highly indebted.

Some observers have suggested that these higher debt service loads will not constitute a problem. Michael Jensen (1984, 1986, 1988, and 1989), for example, has advanced three hypotheses that lead to that conclusion. First, Jensen has argued that the change in organizational structure accompanying many of these transactions, in particular leveraged buyouts, will lead to operating efficiencies that, in turn, will deliver faster growth of corporate earnings with which to service the higher debts. Secondly, he has suggested that a more highly leveraged capital structure will reduce lenders' incentive to liquidate a going concern in the event of bankruptcy should the anticipated earnings not materialize. And third, he has suggested that recent developments in corporate financing, for example, strip financing, interest rate caps, and interest rate swaps, reduce corporations' exposure to risk anyway. Another line of thinking in this same vein is that of Steven Roach (1989), who has argued that leveraged buyouts primarily take place in less cyclical industries in which cash flows are more reliable than for the average company. Yet a further argument along the same lines points to the fact that even after all of the borrowing done during the 1980s, the typical American corporation remains less highly leveraged than the typical firm abroad.

These are all serious arguments, and addressing them is not straightforward. For example, nobody knows whether U.S. corporations can safely live with the leverage that is typical of their German or Japanese counterparts. One reason for doubt is simply the difference in market structures. U.S. firms' debt securities tend to be widely held in an open market setting. By contrast, the German banks that are the primary lenders to German corporations are also major equity holders in these companies, and they typically play a major role on their boards of directors. Similarly, Japanese corporations tend to belong to large associations of corporations (*keiretsu*, the postwar equivalents to the prewar *zaibatsu*), which typically include not only operating companies, but also banks. A further reason why higher leverage may be possible abroad is that foreign economies are characterized by different presumptions than in the United States about the responsibility of government to intervene on companies' behalf should the need arise; and, conversely, the right that this intervention provides government to steer companies' affairs.

On the more specific effects of high-leverage transactions here in the United States, there is worrisome evidence that leveraged buyouts, in particular, may actually stunt rather than bolster companies' earnings growth. For example, Bronwyn Hall (1988) has shown that after leveraged buyouts, firms' expenditures for research and development typically fall. A recently completed Harvard thesis (Rudd 1990) has shown that the same is true for firms' capital expenditures.

Evidence from another Harvard thesis (Fox 1990) has shown signs of pervasive deterioration in the "credit quality" of firms undergoing leveraged buyouts between the mid-1980s and the later part of the decade. For example, firms that were LBO targets in the early 1980s typically had greater cash flows (relative to either assets or sales) than comparable firms that did not experience LBOs. More recently, however, LBO-target firms have experienced both an absolute decline in their cash flow ratios and a decline relative to other comparable firms. Similarly, in the early 1980s, firms that were LBO targets typically had higher liquidity ratios than comparable firms, but, again, this is no longer true. Firms that were LBO targets in the early 1980s also tended to do less capital spending (relative to sales or assets) than other comparable firms, thereby confirming the suggestion by Jensen and others that they had an excess of "free cash flow" with which to service their higher debts. More recently, however, LBO targets have done more capital spending than other comparable firms.

In the final analysis, the proof of these bonds is in their payoffs, and on this score, the track record has not been encouraging. It was hardly surprising that the 1981–82 recession raised the business bankruptcy rate in the United States to levels not seen since the 1930s. By most measures the 1981–82 recession was the worst business downturn the U.S. economy had experienced since the Great Depression. What was surprising, however, is that the bankruptcy rate not only did not decline after the recession ended, but continued to rise for four additional years. Only in 1987 did the pace at which firms went bankrupt level off, and even then it remained at a level well beyond any previous experience since World War II.

Moreover, in addition to the mere number of firms going bankrupt, the dollar volume of liabilities on which firms have defaulted (scaled, for example, in relation to national income) also rose to new highs in the 1981–82 recession, and also failed to decline after the recession's end. This observation is particularly important, because many people have claimed that the profusion of bankruptcies in the 1980s was largely a result of a surge in new business startups (since it is well known that new businesses tend to go bankrupt at a greater rate than established concerns). If that were the explanation, however, the bankruptcy rate would have risen but not the dollar volume of defaulted liabilities, because new startups typically do not have large amounts of liabilities. In fact, the ratio of defaulted liabilities to national income has been at postwar record highs as well.

Examining the more specific evidence on defaults on securities issued in the course of leveraged buyouts is especially instructive. A standard finding is that the default rate for the entire universe of "junk" bonds outstanding is about 8 percent. Recent research has pointed out, however, that because the junk bond market has grown so rapidly during recent years, the universe of such bonds outstanding at any given point of time always consists, disproportionately, of bonds issued just within the last two to three years. To gauge the genuine default prospect of these securities, it is necessary to distinguish the debt by how long it has been outstanding. Research by Asquith, Mullins, and Wolff (1989) has shown that the default rate for junk bonds in the United States rises from 3 to 8 percent after the bonds have been outstanding for only three years to 25 to 33 percent after ten years.

Most significantly, all this has happened in the unusually favorable context of the longest uninterrupted business expansion in U.S. peacetime history. The crucial question is what is likely to happen next time the economy experiences a major recession, comparable to the downturns of 1957–58, 1973–75, or 1981–82; in other words, a recession involving sharply declining earnings for the typical firm, as well as declining market values of those assets that firms with inadequate earnings might otherwise liquidate to supplement their ability to service their debts. One of Hyman Minsky's most famous (and most frequently misunderstood) notions is that sometimes firms must "sell position in order to make position." In an economy in which the market value of a firm's assets is declining, selling position in order to make position does not work. I believe that under current circumstances, a major recession (like 1981–82) would present a not insignificant risk of debt default on a scale large enough to create the kind of rupture in the financial system that, as Minsky's work has so persuasively shown, can have very serious consequences for the continuity of nonfinancial economic activity.

Even so, I do not conclude that a financial crisis, much less a consequent depression, is a likely outcome of the excess of business borrowing undertaken during the 1980s. The reason is that economic policymakers, in particular our monetary policymakers at the Federal Reserve System, have learned Minsky's lesson. The experience of the United States since World War II makes clear that a serious recession is likely to occur only if the Federal Reserve either deliberately brings it about or, at the least, tolerates the decline once it has begun for independent reasons. Given the financial risk consequent on a major recession under today's highly indebted conditions, I believe that the continuing rise in corporate indebtedness in the United States will soon—if it has not already begun to do so—significantly constrain the willingness of the Federal Reserve to initiate or even to tolerate a business recession of any major depth and duration.

In effect, rising corporate indebtedness has locked the Federal Reserve System into a no-deep-recession monetary policy. But if that is true, the experience of the United States since World War II also strongly suggests that a no-deep-recession-at-any-cost monetary policy will also, over a substantial period of time, be an inflationary monetary policy. Although it is theoretically possible to achieve both price stability and steady real growth without the occasional punctuation provided by significant economic downturns, nothing in our economy's history indicates that doing so is practically feasible. Instead, experience suggests that if rising business indebtedness increases the risks associated with economic downturns, and hence makes policymakers less likely to accept them, it, therefore, imparts an inflationary bias. In light of the uncertainties about monetary policy that now exist for independent reasons (for example, the collapse of the money-income and money-price relationships), this bias is likely to meet even less resistance than would have been the case not so many years ago.

In simple shorthand, then, the borrowing that U.S. corporations and other businesses have done since the end of the 1981–82 recession has shifted the short- and intermediate-run trade-offs confronting monetary policy, importantly including not just the single set of most likely outcomes under any specific set of circumstances, but also the attendant risks. Given those shifts in the relevant trade-offs, it is implausible to expect the Federal Reserve to respond to events as it would have had these changes not occurred. But if the reason why today's enlarged debt burdens will not lead to debt deflation, or even worse, is that they have effectively locked the Federal Reserve into a no-serious-recession monetary policy, the record of inflation and business cycles since World War II gives little reason for confidence that the ultimate consequence of increased business indebtedness will not be a return to high inflation.

Hyman Minsky persuasively argued years ago that meeting its responsibilities as lender of last resort is often—perhaps even typically—inconsistent with the central bank's ability to meet its other responsibilities; most evidently, the responsibility to maintain price stability. What we face in the current situation is the prospective exercise of the Federal Reserve's lender-of-last-resort responsibility; that is, not just acting before, rather than after, a systemic debt default becomes acute, but acting in such a way as to prevent the emergence of underlying economic conditions likely to foster a systemic debt default problem in the first place.

But Minsky's conclusion about the conflict between the central bank's lender-of-last-resort responsibility and its other responsibilities surely applies in this prospective context as well. If the rise in business indebtedness has rendered the U.S. economy too fragile (in the financial sense) to withstand any but short and shallow recessions—at least in the eyes of our central bankers—the most likely consequence of that fragility will be to render U.S. monetary policy increasingly impotent either to reduce inflation from the current level, or to resist a renewed acceleration of prices should it occur.

Note

1. See Bernanke and Campbell (1988) and Bernanke, Campbell, and Whited (1990).

References

Asquith, Paul, David W. Mullins Jr., and Eric D. Wolff. 1989. "Original Issue High Yield Bonds: Aging Analyses of Defaults, Exchanges, and Calls." *Journal of Finance* 43 (September):923–52.

Bernanke, Ben S., and John Y. Campbell. 1988. "Is There a Corporate Debt Problem?" *Brookings Papers on Economic Activity*, No. 1, pp. 83–125.

Bernanke, Ben S., John Y. Campbell and Toni M. Whited. 1990. "U.S. Corporate Leverage: Developments in 1987 and 1988." *Brookings Papers on Economic Activity*, No. 1, pp. 255–86.

Friedman, Benjamin M. 1990. "Implications of Increasing Corporate Indebtedness for Monetary Policy." Group of Thirty, *Occasional Papers*, No. 29.

———. 1991. "Views on the Likelihood of Financial Crisis." In *Reducing the Risk of Financial Crisis*, Martin Feldstein, ed. Chicago: University of Chicago Press.

Fox, Christopher J. 1990. "Changes in the Insolvency Risk of LBO Transactions: Evidence from the 1980s." Unpublished thesis. Harvard University.

Hall, Bronwyn. 1988. "The Effect of Takeover Activity on Corporate Research and Development." In *Corporate Takeovers: Causes and Consequences*, Alan Auerbach, ed. Chicago: University of Chicago Press.

Jensen, Michael C. 1984. "Takeovers: Folklore and Science." *Harvard Business Review* 62 (November/December): 109–121

———. 1986. "Agency Costs of Free Cash Flow, Corporate Finance and Takeovers." *American Economic Review* 76 (May): 323–29.

———. 1988. "Takeovers: Their Causes and Consequences." *Journal of Economic Perspectives* 2 (Winter): 21–48.

———. 1989. "The Effects of LBOs and Corporate Debt on the Economy." *Tax Policy Aspects of Mergers and Acquisitions*. Part I, U.S. Congress, House of Representatives, Committee on Ways and Means. 101st Congress, 1st Session.

Minsky, Hyman P. 1963. "Can 'It' Happen Again?" In *Banking and Monetary Studies*, Deane Carson, ed. Homewood, Ill.: R.D. Irwin, 101–111.

———. 1982. *Can "It" Happen Again? Essays on Instability and Finance*. Armonk, New York: M.E. Sharpe.

Roach, Stephen S. 1989. "Living with Corporate Debt." *Journal of Applied Corporate Finance* 2 (Spring): 19–30.

Rudd, Jeremy B. 1990. "The Effects of Corporate Debt on Corporate Investment." Unpublished thesis. Harvard University.

CHAPTER FIVE

Intermediation, Disintermediation, and Direct Trading

CHARLES P. KINDLEBERGER

I owe a large intellectual debt to Hyman Minsky who got me to think about instability in financial markets. It may be appropriate in a paper with this title to indicate that I got to Minsky's writings through the intermediation of Martin Mayer, author of *The Bankers* and many other popular works on the economy of our time. I mentioned my interest in financial crises, and Mayer asked whether I knew of Minsky's work. Like many an intermediary, he had, as far as I was concerned, a monopoly of information. After this information had been diffused, I have profited greatly over the years by dealing with Hy in "direct trading."

The concept of intermediation I propose to discuss is primarily economic and financial. Allow me, however, to display my interdisciplinary knowledge by noting that the idea is of greater applicability. Talcott Parsons somewhere wrote that governesses or nannies intermediate between parents and children, especially, I admit, in England. And that in the military, noncommissioned officers intermediate between commissioned officers and privates. To use a different social science, President Theodore Roosevelt intermediated between Japan and Czarist Russia in Portsmouth in 1905, as President Jimmy Carter did between Egypt and Israel at Camp David, and is attempting to do again, as I write, between Ethiopia and its former province, Eritrea, now independent.

Sometimes middlemen are not in the middle, so to speak. Michel Crozier's (1964) *The Bureaucratic Phenomenon* notes that face-to-face communication in governmental hierarchy in France is fraught with tension so that an official at level E will communicate with his superior at D by going above him and dealing through C. More nearly akin to economic and financial considerations is the public relations officer with a monopoly of information who stands between high governmental or business officials and the public.

On a macrosociological level, the existence of a large middle class contributes to political stability as it narrows the gap for bright and aggressive members of

The author is Ford International Professor of Economics, Emeritus at the Massachusetts Institute of Technology.

the lower class to cross as they rise. The middle class also cushions the decline of the elite, including younger sons in a system of primogeniture, and reduces the risk of polarization of society.

To extend the sociological aspects of the subject one iota, observe that when children grow up they no longer need the intermediation of a nanny, if they ever did, and communicate with their parents, in direct trading, often with ruthless bluntness.

But let me narrow the focus to economics and finance. More than a quarter of a century ago, John Gurley and Edward Shaw (1960) produced a path-breaking book, *Money in Theory of Finance*, which developed the theory of intermediation as the key to monetary and other financial institutions. As they viewed the process, financial structures in an economy developed in evolutionary fashion; from self-financing, to direct financing, to indirect financing through financial intermediaries. Some, but not overwhelming, attention was paid to disintermediation as a pathological process. They did not, however, envisage a further step, relevant today, of a return to direct financial contacts between borrower and lender when the advantage of the banking intermediary has been lost. I have in mind, especially, direct purchases of certificates of deposit and securities issued by large industrial corporations, bought by large pension funds and insurance companies. But first I want to extend the economic theory of intermediation to markets in general, and offer an analogy between goods markets and financial markets, using a bit of the economic history with which I have been keeping myself pleasantly occupied for some years. I will not test your patience by going back millennia in history, but start with such a stapling center as Amsterdam.

Amsterdam happened to be well-located, close to the junction between the Atlantic (and the Mediterranean) and the Baltic and North Seas, handy to Britain, and connected by the Rhine and the Meuse to a vast hinterland. After the fall of Antwerp to Spanish attackers in 1585, Amsterdam became an entrepot center. Its merchants were divided among the First, Second and Third Hand—from which we get these expressions. The First Hand, engaged in "distant trade," brought goods from abroad to the city and took them away again. The Second Hand broke bulk, stored goods, performed other intermediating functions, and repackaged the goods. Repackaging, for example, was necessary if grain from Danzig in Poland was not to explode under the hot Mediterranean sun as a consequence of spontaneous combustion, as it was being delivered say to Leghorn. Wines from Bordeaux were brought to Amsterdam in casks and sometimes bottled there, as free ports do today. The Third Hand sold at retail the small proportion of the total trade that remained in the United Provinces of Holland.

The First Hand had a monopoly of information and of capital; information as to what goods were available where, and what were wanted where. It intermediated by place and risk, and with the help of the Second Hand, by scale. The Second Hand also intermediated by social status, as it traded with the imperious leaders of the Dutch Republic—the First Hand—which clung tightly to power.

Adam Smith wrote the Bible for economists, *The Wealth of Nations*, and it is perhaps impious on my part to take exception to two of his remarks about merchants. In the first, he claimed that a little grocer in a seaport town had all the attributes of a great merchant except capital (1776, 112). This is far from the case as one contemplates the need to learn languages, and to acquire much wider knowledge of accounting, exchange rates, the qualities of goods, their prices, and the markets where they can be bought cheapest and sold at the highest prices. In the second, he stated that the merchant should normally be located at one end of a trade route or the other, in the instant case at Königsberg in East Prussia or Lisbon in Portugal, rather than midway between. But he stayed in Amsterdam and brought his goods there because he was uneasy at being separated from his capital and wanted it under his view, despite the double charges for loading and unloading along with some duties and customs (p. 422). This explanation ignores the functions of intermediating by size and risk, and it assumes that the merchants were, at least in some degree, irrational. By calling attention to the extra charges of handling merchandise in an entrepot center, however, Dr. Smith made clear the origins of direct trading when the monopoly of information of the great merchants had been dissipated by diffusion, and these costs could be saved.

But intermediation in trade does not persist. When the information monopoly that gave rise to it dissipates, direct trading is substituted for intermediation in goods. Exeter undertook to trade its serges directly to Spain, and Hull its woolen piece goods to Hamburg. London was for long the great exporter of raw materials from the Empire, but in due course, Scandinavia would trade directly with Australia, for example, and British reexports shrank to a small percentage of total exports from figures that previously approached 30 percent. Some intermediation in goods continues, to be sure, where simple processing was called for by the economics of transportation, especially down-scaling the final delivery of goods shipped in bulk from the original source. Where it was possible to save handling and the middleman's profit, however, direct trade took over as knowledge of needs and availabilities was widely diffused.

Let me indulge in a bit of Ciceronian rhetoric and say I would enjoy going on discussing intermediation in trade and its replacement by direct trading if space permitted—the Hanseatic merchants, hated by the inland towns on the ground that the merchants set prices at which the towns had to trade and had the power to ruin a country (Moser 1944, 197); Sweden trying to bypass Lübeck in the seventeenth century by selling its copper directly to Amsterdam (Glamann 1971, 456); German and Italian merchants deserting the Lyons fairs at the end of the sixteenth century to exchange goods through the Alpine passes, escaping the heavy taxation of the French monarchy (Boyer-Xambeu, Deleplace, and Gillard 1986, 155); nineteenth-century British merchants who slowed down technical change in cotton yarns and machine tools, telling producers "they don't want them like that" while simultaneously telling customers "they don't make them like that" even though the elimination of the middleman would allow producer and buyer to discuss together and agree on the nature of improved quality and whether it was worth the cost (Kindleberger 1964, 148–49); and, the elimination of jobber and wholesaler by American corporations as they rose in scale from local to regional to national and took the marketing function into the firm for direct buying and selling (Chandler 1962).

Middlemen have long been excoriated and defended. Oscar Wilde said that a publisher is simply a useful middleman between author and reader with no right to express an opinion on the value of what he publishes, while Disraeli wrote "It is well known what a middlemen is: he is one who bamboozles one party and plunders the other" (Cole 1989). A newspaper columnist on economics has felt the need to defend middlemen (Warsh 1989). I neither defend nor attack, but observe that intermediaries exist at an early stage of trade, and are usually replaced in due course by direct trade to save transport costs and one layer of profit. The market in the middle may have an artificial monopoly which it guards jealously, as did the Merchant Staplers of Britain selling wool on the continent (Braudel 1986, 448–49), or Danzig with the "privilege of being the only professional middlemen between Polish and West European merchants" (Federowicz 1976, 362). But competition nibbles away at most monopolies in goods, and monopolizing intermediators, as a rule, give way to direct trade.

Our interest, however, is in finance, not trade. Financial centers last longer than trade centers, I hypothesize, because the costs of transport in money—more generally transactions costs—are trivial compared with those in goods. Many trade centers, notably Amsterdam, London, and New York, shifted over from trade to financial intermediation when their informational monopolies in goods eroded and their appetite for risk diminished with rising wealth. But let me proceed more slowly by discussing the various bases for intermediating between borrower and lender.

One ancient basis had to do with social status. Nobles would be contaminated if they dealt directly with commoners, but had less hesitation in doing so through the intermediation of scriveners, notaries, goldsmiths, bankers; in France, *officers* and *financiers* who were holders of particular offices bought from the king. A rapid expansion of intermediary lending can be seen in comparative statics in the rise of the number of scriveners from "several" in the first decade of the seventeenth century to "at least 30 by 1630" (Parker 1974, 537).

One particular form of social intermediation was intimately bound up in risk—lending to the sovereign. The king could not be sued to collect unpaid debts owed by him, so that there was a need for special protection. This included lending on the crown jewels, the grant of a monopoly in the form of a tax, or the collateral of productive assets such as the silver mines of the Tyrol or the mercury mines of Almaden in Spain, both acquired by the Fuggers when their loans were defaulted on. The Spanish *asientos* (a form of loan to the King) were usually accompanied by a permit, which had value, to export silver. Or a member of the king's household, like Sir Stephen Fox in the court of Charles II, would borrow from the public to lend to the king, because the king was unlikely to welsh on a debt to an intimate (Clay 1978). Lionel Cranfield was a courtier of James I who lent to the monarch and borrowed to do so, including once from the merchant and early economic writer Thomas Mun, author of the great book, *England's Treasure by Forraign Trade*. One is surprised to find R.H. Tawney surprised to find that in 1641, financiers called upon to lend to the crown borrowed from others to be able to do so (1958, 107). And of course in France, many of those who paid the court large sums for offices to farm taxes or to take over various monopolies, like that in tobacco, borrowed from the public to obtain the needed capital (Dent 1973).

This antiquarian information has some relevance to the world of today because of the issue of syndicated bank debt by sovereign Third World countries. (This problem was discovered by most of the world in August 1982 when the Mexican debt crisis was revealed, but was apparent to academic observers more than half a decade earlier [see Goodman, ed., 1977]). There is something of a puzzle here that despite an impressive record of default by sovereign debtors, the investing public, including bankers who are presumably sophisticated in such matters, has often taken a childishly optimistic view of foreign government debt. I need not go back to the miserable record of Edward III of England whose defaults were said to have ruined the Bardi, Peruzzi, and Aicobaldi banks of Florence and Lucca (but see Hunt 1990) or to those of Philip II of Spain which undid the Fuggers, Welzers, and the bankers of Genoa. To a world that believes in any degree of rational expectations it is bizarre that French investors were trusting of Czarist Russia in the years from 1888 to 1913. A false analogy presumably was developed between lending to one's own sovereign, who could pay his debts by printing money, and lending to a foreign sovereign who lacks capacity to produce foreign exchange.

After intermediation by social status and to overcome sovereign immunity, I come to intermediation by place. In his classic, *Lombard Street*, Walter Bagehot discusses how the bankers of rich agricultural counties like Somersetshire and Hampshire discounted the bills of the industrial counties of Yorkshire and Lancashire ([1873] 1978, 53), illustrating the process with the testimony of a London bill broker before an 1810 Commission of Inquiry (ibid., 191–93). He claimed, moreover, that the practice still prevailed 60 years later, though in his introduction to Bagehot's *Collected Works*, R.S. Sayers denies it (ibid., 35, 193).

Intermediation by place took other forms. In England, areas with excess savings initially bought bills on places with deficits, through London brokers, but gradually they established a branch in London, or bought out an existing bank there. Banks needing money did the same to obtain funds. London banks in due course established national networks to bring savings efficiently from where they were abundant to where they were needed. For a time, provincial banks with a branch or subsidiary in London could pay depositors at the head office a fixed low rate of interest, whereas the London rate varied with bank rate. In time, the provincial depositors learned to move their funds to London when bank rate went to 4 percent or above. When enough depositors learned this, such a bank as Lloyds of Birmingham learned that it had to maintain a single deposit rate for the entire system (Sayers 1957, 165, 270).

In France, as Jean Bouvier's masterly account of the growth of the *Crédit lyonnais* tells us, Henri Germain started the bank in Lyons, which was heavy with capital accumulated in the silk business, went to Paris in due course to place the monies, and then built a network throughout France. The *Crédit lyonnais* favored those communities with excess savings, at the expense of those that were eager for loans, in order to accumulate funds to use in foreign lending. Deep students of my work on financial centers may remember the riddle: What do the Midland Bank, the Dresdener Bank, the Bank of Montreal, Bank of Nova Scotia, First Boston Corporation, and the *Crédit lyonnais* have in common? The answer is that the head office of each is located in a different city (or area) than that noted in the institution's name (1978, 67).

Place intermediation, through commercial banks in the United States, has been held back by rules against branch banking, rules now in process of being eased. Savings banks and savings and loan associations, both of which originally provided finance for home building, furnish a good example of the process. In the last decades of the nineteenth century, mortgage markets were regionally segmented by size of city and region, with a spread that ranged from 5.60 percent in cities within 25 miles of New England population centers with more than 100,000 people, to 9.76 percent for banks in the West within 25 miles of towns of 8,000 to 25,000 (Snowden 1988, 278). Such segmentation continued into the early twentieth century for savings institutions. There were some national players like insurance companies that were embarrassed when they felt it necessary to foreclose on farm mortgages in the 1930s, but these were not large enough to close the gap. With a wave of building in the West after World War II, especially in California, a number of thrifts in that state advertised in New York papers for deposits by mail at rates one percentage point or more above rates in the East. Further integration of the market for mortgage money came through Veterans Administration lending and the creation of the Federal National Mortgage Association and the Government National Mortgage Association, known familiarly as "Fannie Mae" and "Ginnie Mae," respectively. When savings bank disintermediation began in the late 1970s and early 1980s, savings banks replaced lost local deposits by borrowing on the national market for CDs. Most recently the packaging of mortgage lending has been undertaken by private as well as government institutions, and some of these packages of diversified mortgages (and automobile loans, installment and credit-card paper, and in Britain, export credits) are sold internationally. The intermediation through risk involved in this diversification is discussed below. It is not clear to me whether the private "securitization" of mortgage loans is diversified as to place, like those of Fannie and Ginnie Mae, or are localized.

The securitization of mortgages involves intermediation by size as well as place, and in this instance there is no progression for the small borrower that leads on to direct trading. I do have an illustration of direct trading replacing intermediation in information, if not in mortgage money on houses. In 1974 in discussing the finance of off-shore drilling for oil and gas, I asked a banker in Aberdeen whether he would seek information on the subject from his London correspondent who would get it from New York. The answer was that Aberdeen would deal directly with Houston.

Intermediation by size is wider and more commonplace than the foregoing illustration of securitization of mortgages, auto loans, installment paper, and the like. Typically people of small means deposit their savings with intermediaries who lend it in larger volume. This is the essence of the classic function of banks in the "mobilization of loan capital," to use an expression of Ehrenberg ([1895] 1928, 328–29). A strong element of intermediation by risk is involved, because the small saver is typically uninformed about the credit standing of the ultimate borrower and relies on the banking intermediary to lend only to creditworthy individuals and firms. The ignorance of the small depositor, as opposed to the reputed financial sophistication of the large, is of course the basis for limits on governmental deposit insurance in the United States, limits that have been increased with inflation and real wealth from $5,000, originally to $10,000, then $40,000, and now $100,000. There are, moreover, occasions, such as the financial crisis involving the Continental Illinois Bank, when the Federal Deposit Insurance Corporation has guaranteed foreign deposits of more than $100,000 in order to stop a run on a bank, making clear that the purpose of deposit insurance is more to stop runs—the extreme form of disintermediation—than it is to protect small savers. One could perhaps argue that wealthy foreigners may legitimately be more ignorant of the condition of American banks than U.S. residents, but the reasoning is not persuasive. As a classic example of intermediation by size, some years ago it was common knowledge that the Eurodollar market would not take deposits of less than $25,000, nor make loans below $1 million.

Intermediation by size occurs outside of banks in odd-lot houses that break bulk for small investors trading in securities in amounts of less than one hundred shares. At the other end of the scale, trading in lots of thousands of shares is mostly undertaken directly off the floor of the intermediating Stock Exchange, to get the benefit of lower or zero commissions.

Direct dealing between borrower and lender for large loans, cutting out the intermediation of banks, is one of the major innovations in finance in recent years, according to the Cross report (BIS 1986). Pension funds and insurance companies, dealing in large sums of money, are able to judge credit risks through treasurer departments peopled with finance analysts, and to lend with assured safety on certificates of deposit issued by nonfinancial companies or on securities placed directly with them. The banks have begun to miss out on a large portion of industrial loans for the larger companies, and this development is responsible for their intense lobbying for the repeal of the Glass-Steagall Act of 1933 that separated institutions into banks on the one hand, and investment houses on the other, forbidding banks to underwrite the issue of securities. Some of the smaller banks with a deep clientele of middle-size industrial companies with small financial staffs and a need for financial advice that banks traditionally provided, continue to do well. I vividly recall, however, hearing from the chief executive officer of a $400 million-a-year sales company—a big number at the time—that he refused to maintain a compensating balance at his bank, and when the bank president protested and justified such a balance on the ground of providing the company with a variety of services, he interrupted to say that the banks should charge the company for any service it asked for. He not only would not carry a compensating balance, but would, in fact, ride the float and make the treasurer's office in his company a profit center.

The loss of the loan business of large companies has led the banks to seek other sorts of business; some as more nearly "merchant banks," giving financial advice to various kinds of business for fees. Other banks began dealing in financial instruments such as swaps, repos, futures, and the like; still others providing accounting and transfer services to such institutions as mutual funds. In many instances, the loss of the ordinary run of large business loans has led banks to take more risky roads into construction loans, bridge loans for takeover firms, and junk bonds. It is not clear to me whether the surge in Third World debt in the 1970s was related to the shrinkage of ordinary loan outlets or not. In any case, the rise of direct trading between trade and industry on the one hand, and nonbank financial firms on the other has diverted a great many banks from their wonted paths into risky endeavors in which they now find themselves uncomfortable or worse.

The $100,000 limit on deposit insurance led to another form of intermediation by size that was less than salubrious for the economy as a whole; namely, the growth of deposit brokers who took large sums of deposit money and divided them into amounts of less than $100,000 to distribute among weak thrift institutions that had to pay more than standard deposit rates to attract funds. The practice keeps third-rate institutions alive longer than they would otherwise remain. A high deposit rate is normally a sign that the saving bank is in trouble, but the practice of breaking bulk of large sums to provide the weak bank with extra protection is dysfunctional for the system as a whole. It both encourages risk-taking and paralyzes the conservative and well-managed thrifts through disintermediation.

Bank competition for deposits led the way, from demand deposits that earned no interest, to Negotiable Orders of Withdrawal (NOW) accounts that did, thus depriving the banks of seignorage. Before the innovation, demand depositors could have been regarded as exploited by banks, which got something for nothing, or very little. Alternatively, demand deposits could be viewed as providing needed liquidity, such liquidity being a service rendered by the bank in time intermediation. Whichever view one takes of non-interest-bearing demand deposits, their demise and the need to "buy" deposits has reduced the earnings of banks on intermediation by size. Foreign banks in Paris which had to buy all their deposits were at a strong disadvantage vis-a-vis domestic banks which attracted the deposits of Frenchmen on which no interest was paid (Koszul 1972). The shift to NOW accounts in the United States has meant that domestic banks had to buy their deposits, as do foreign banks, increasing the degree of international competition.

Banks intermediate not only by place and size of wealth-holding, but also by time and risk. For time, it is evident that savers and borrowers have different time preferences. Savers want liquidity, borrowers to have their debts stretched out in time. Banks intermediate by lending long and borrowing short. They can provide liquidity to savers because not all savers will want their money simultaneously—a diversification effect. J.K. Price in discussing British overseas trade historically notes that wholesalers in Britain provided easy credit to exporters who, in turn, gave long credits to their foreign customers. The lengths of credit were equivalent, and most merchants had balance sheets dominated by accounts receivable and debts owed, with little in the way of fixed capital (1989, 278). This reflects a fairly primitive stage in financial development to such an extent that it merits attention.

There was an era in which savings institutions narrowed the gap in time between assets and deposits by requiring notice on deposit withdrawals. Commercial banks made sharp distinctions between demand and time deposits. Fixed terms remain in effect, today, on certificates of deposit, but most savings and time deposits are available on demand. And demand deposits—NOW accounts—earn interest along with time deposits. The threat of disintermediation runs from bank deposits, both commercial and thrift, to money funds, which have the advantage over banks in that there are no legal reserve requirements. Most, too, allow a certain amount of check-writing, or easy indirect access to the money on demand. The sharp rise in interest rates at the beginning of the 1980s led to outflows of money from banks to money funds from which it was loaned back to banks again, in certificates of deposits, at higher interest rates. This was not so much disintermediation, perhaps, as reintermediation.

An ironic point is worth mentioning. The small saver in a poor neighborhood generally left his money in savings banks at five or five-and-a-half percent interest, without realizing that money funds were available to pay higher returns. The sophistication that produced disintermediation from banks to money funds in prosperous cities and towns was absent in poor neighborhoods. Thus their savings banks, and similar institutions such as credit unions, continued to earn good returns in the 1980s, when the institutions that had been well-located in terms of wealth suffered from disintermediation. With higher interest rates they lost deposits and had to borrow in the open market so as not to have to sell their fixed-rate assets—mortgages and bonds—at the lower prices produced by increases in interest rates.

Intermediation by time is still required, but is taking place increasingly through futures markets as opposed to direct dealing. Banks and nonfinancial firms can find that pattern of liquidity that suits them in terms of cash flows in and out through forward contracts that adjust the time profile of anticipated receipts and payments. There remain solvency risks in such contracts, but their use is to fine-tune liquidity. Some years ago I observed that a number of companies would adjust their time preferences as to liquidity through their own intermediation, borrowing long in the Eurobond market when they planned a project, and depositing the funds in the Eurodollar market, so as to have the funds on hand when they were needed. This could be regarded as a form of direct trading within the firm, with the cost of purchasing liquidity represented by the difference between the long- and short-term rates of interest.

Another form of direct trading is the practice of Japanese groups that combine banks and insurance companies with manufacturing and chemical companies so as to be certain to have a source of financing always available. This is a form of vertical integration that applies also in some industries, controlling sources of supply and outlets in order to avoid the risk of interruption from breakdown of the market for inputs or outputs. Where inputs are bulky and difficult to store, as in coal or oil, control through ownership was thought necessary since interruption could not be forestalled by the maintenance of sizable inventories. Some of this vertical integration varied with the business cycle, to be sure; oil companies being readier to own tankers in tight markets and to rely on the market when tanker rates were slack. The move to just-in-time scheduling of materials and components made possible by computers reduces, further, the need to store inputs, just as futures contracts make it less necessary to store cash.

Intermediation by risk is connected with that by time and size. The small saver lends to one intermediary who both accumulates savings for large loans, and diversifies by lending to more than one borrower. The diversification should reduce default risk, although if the intermediary is badly or dishonestly managed, perhaps excessively speculative in its investments, the depositor's presumed gain through reduced default-risk from diversification is lost.

In addition to default risk, there is interest-rate risk. With a true time deposit, the depositor has a chance of gain when competitive interest rates decline, an opportunity-cost loss if they rise. The major interest-rate risk in intermediation, however, is that of the bank, as it lends long and borrows short. If its assets are in fixed-rate loans, securities, or mortgages for extended time periods, and interest rates rise, it may both lose depositors and suffer reductions in the value of its assets, even though the latter loss may be disguised by continuing to carry the assets on the books at cost. In recent years, banks and other lenders have sought to escape interest-rate risk by changing the rates paid for deposits on the one hand, and those charged on loans and mortgages on the other. But of course variable rates do not reduce risk overall. They shift it from the bank to the depositor and the borrower .

In one view the role of the intermediary in reducing risk for the lender (or depositor) is less connected with information than with reputation (Terlizzese 1989). The good reputation of a bank or other intermediary rests in the belief of the depositor that the intermediary understands the nature of risks and how to manage them. That view has had to undergo modification when the carefree lending and buying of junk bonds following the 1982 deregulation of the thrifts was exposed to light. But of course information and reputation are closely connected.

International intermediation by reputation has come to attention recently with some striking examples. Christopher Platt has examined the books of the Baring Brothers bank in London in the 1840s and been struck by the fact that gross and net lending by Britain to France differed sharply since much of the French bonds issued in London were bought by Frenchmen. There were elements of size involved, to be sure, as the London bond market was larger than that in Paris, and hence more liquid. But French investors felt safer lending to their own government and new railroads through the City, rather than directly, on the basis that the city's reputation for financial acumen was greater. Later, London issued bonds for the Argentine government bought by Argentinians as well as by British and other investors. There was an element of exchange risk here, as there may have been in European issues of dollar bonds in New York after World War II bought by Europeans. Such risk was minimal in the London-French case of the 1840s given the long-established gold standard. Platt notes that the standard estimates for the British capital outflow before 1914 must be reduced considerably to make allowance for these purchases by the borrowing countries. While this is doubtless true for France and Argentina, there is not, so far as I am aware, evidence that similar differences between net and gross existed for dominion borrowers such as Australia, Canada, and New Zealand.

Somewhat further away from this lending from national creditors to a national debtor through the intermediation of an outside country is that seen by Bacha and Diaz-Alejandro (1982), in their well-known article "International Financial Intermediation: A Long and Tropical View." Here, firms and governments in Third World countries borrowed from U.S. banks at a time when wealth-holders in those countries undertook to protect their capital by escaping foreign-exchange control and piling up deposits in U.S. banks, often the same ones. There was no intention on the part of, say Argentine or Mexican, capitalists to lend to their governments through foreign banks; it was nonetheless a form of international intermediation by size and exchange risk.

Still another form of international intermediation by reputation involving the Third World occurred after the OPEC price rise of 1973. One oil expert thought it would have been desirable for the OPEC countries to sell oil to non-oil Third World countries on credit terms (Levy 1982, 245, 266). The producing countries evidently thought otherwise, presumably on the ground that the credit standings of the importers were weaker than those of world-class banks. In consequence they sold only for dollars, with cash on the barrelhead, so to speak. This produced "recycling" as it was then called, but which, in our terms, is international intermediation by reputation, the OPEC countries lending to the Eurodollar market, and the Eurodollar banks lending to the Third World, both oil producers such as Mexico and Venezuela, and the importers.

I have pointed out that the displacement (to use Minsky's term), or exogenous shock, that gave rise to the lending in the first place antedated the November 1973 price rise by a couple of years. In 1970 and 1971, the United States tried to lower interest rates in the interest of President Nixon's reelection campaign at a time when the Bundesbank was tightening interest rates to curb inflation. Money poured out of the United States into the Eurodollar market. As interest rates fell, the world banks sought out new borrowers and found them in the Third World.

Intermediation then, by social status, place, time, and various sorts of risk, whether because of monopolized information or reputation, is continuously threatened by disintermediation, which may be intermediation through a different medium and by direct trading. I hazard the guess that intermediation by social status is a thing of the past, although the point about blue-collar neighborhoods being less subject to disintermediation than white-collar areas suggests a vestigial remnant of the effect. Intermediation by place would seem to be stretched to the limit in a world of ubiquitous computers connected by modems, facsimile machines, and copiers. That by time, and to a certain extent by risk, will compete with new financial instruments such as swaps, options, and the like. The troubles of the junk-bond market would appear to dampen the enthusiasm of some groups for intermediation by default risk, for example in the funds collected by leveraged buy-out (LBO) firms to use as bridge loans or equity investment in takeovers.

While intermediation by size changes its form as pension funds and insurance companies achieve a scale where they trade directly with large borrowers issuing notes and securities, that for smaller amounts will doubtless continue. The banking function of providing financial services to smaller companies that choose not to build their own treasurer's department to cover all their financial needs will last. In theory, there should be an advantage in having an outside opinion to guard against intellectual autointoxication, but the herdlike behavior of financial markets in the 1980s raises the question whether outside opinion-givers are independent of the waves of financial fashion.

It is likely that the size of companies moving to direct trading will shrink with time, but intermediation as a basic economic function is almost certainly here to stay. At the last minute, however, strong evidence of the loss of business to direct trading at major U.S. banks came with the second quarter of 1990 profit returns, and the efforts of Citicorp and Chase Manhattan to reduce their staffs.

> The need for cost-cutting is especially evident for banks like Chase and Citicorp, which have been hurt by a decline in wholesale lending and other financing for large corporations. While the banks still maintain expensive net-

works of foreign offices, corporate treasurers have learned how to borrow money more cheaply in the securities markets or from foreign banks. (*New York Times* 1990, 29)

An awareness of economic history might have forestalled the buildup now being trimmed down.

References

Bacha, Edmar Lisboa and Carlos F. Diaz-Alejandro. 1982. *International Financial Intermediation: A Long and Tropical View*. Essays in International Finance, No. 147. Princeton, N.J.: Princeton University International Finance Section.

Bagehot, Walter. 1873 (1978). *Lombard Street*. In N. St. John-Stevas, ed., *The Collected Works of Walter Bagehot*, volume 9. London: *The Economist*, pp. 45–233.

Bank for International Settlements. 1986. *Recent Innovations in International Banking*. The Cross Report, prepared by a study group established by the central banks of the Group of Ten countries. Basle: B.I.S.

Bouvier, Jean. 1961. *Le Credit Lyonnais de 1863 a 1882: Les Annees de Formation D'une Banque de Depots*, 2 volumes, Paris: SEVPEN.

Boyer-Xambeu, Marie-Therèse, Chislain Deleplace, and Lucien Gillard. 1986. *Monnaie Privée at Pouvoir des Princes*. Presses de la foundation nationales des sciences politques.

Braudel, Fernand. 1986. *Civilization & Capitalism, 15th–18th Century*. Vol. 2. *The Wheels of Commerce*, (translated from the French by Sian Reynolds), New York: Harper & Row.

Chandler, Alfred D. 1962. *Strategy and Structure: Chapters in the History of Industrial Enterprise*. Cambridge, Mass.: Harvard University Press.

Clay, Christopher. 1978. *Public Finance and Private Wealth: The Career of Sir Stephen Fox, 1627–1716*. Oxford: Clarendon Press.

Cole, William Rossa. 1989. "Author and Editor Against the Publisher." *New York Times Book Review* (September 3): 1.

Crozier, Michel. 1964. *The Bureaucratic Phenomenon*, Chicago: University of Chicago Press.

Dent, Julian. 1973. *Crisis in Finance: Crown, Financiers and Society in Seventeenth France*. New York: St. Martin's Press.

Federowicz, Jan K. 1988. "Anglo-Polish Commercial Relations in the First Hall of the Seventeenth Century." *Journal of European Economic History* 5: 359–78.

Glamann, Kristof. 1971. "European Trade, 1500–1750." In *The Fontana Economic History of Europe: Volume 2, The Sixteenth and Seventeenth Centuries*, Carlo M. Cipolle, ed. Glasgow: Collins/Fontana, pp. 427–526.

Goodman, Stephen, ed. 1978. *Financing and Risk in Developing Countries*. New York: Praeger.

Gurley, John G. and Edward S. Shaw. 1950. *Money in a Theory of Finance*. Washington, DC: Brookings Institution.

Hunt, Edward S. 1990. "A New Look at the Dealings of the Bardi and Peruzzi with Edward III." *Journal of Economic History* 50: 149–62.

Kindleberger, Charles P. 1964. *Economic Growth in France and Britain, 1851–1950*. Cambridge, Mass.: Harvard University Press.

———. 1978. *Economic Response: Comparative Studies In Trade, Finance and Growth*. Cambridge, Mass.: Harvard University Press.

Kozul, Jean-Pierre. 1970. "American Banks in Europe." In *The International Corpora-*

tion: a Symposium, C.P. Kindleberger, ed. Cambridge, Mass.: M.I.T. Press, pp. 273–89.

Levy, Walter J. 1982. *Oil Strategy and Politics, 1941–1981*. Melvin A. Conant ed. Boulder, Col.: Westview Press.

Moser, Justus. 1969. "Some Thoughts about the Decline of Commerce in Inland Towns." In *European Society in the Eighteenth Century*, Robert and Elborg Forster, eds. (translated by Gerhard Stalling). New York: Walker & Co., pp. 185–189.

Parker, Geoffrey. 1974. "The Emergence of Modern Finance in Europe, 1500–1730." In *The Fontana Economic History of Europe, Volume 2, The Sixteenth and Seventeenth Centuries*, Carlo M. Cipolle, ed. Glasgow: Collins/Fontana.

Price, Jacob M. 1989. "What Did Merchants Do? Reflections on British Overseas Trade, 1660–1770" *The Journal of Economic History* 49, 267–84.

Platt, D.C.M. 1984. *Foreign Finance in Continental Europe and the USA, 1815–1870, Quantities, Origins, Functions & Distribution*, London: George Allen & Unwin.

Sayers, R.S. 1957. *Lloyds Bank in the History of English Banking*. Oxford: Clarendon Press.

————. 1978. Introduction to *The Collected Works of Walter Bagehot*, N. St. John-Stevas, ed., vol. 9. London: *The Economist*.

Snowden, Kenneth A. 1988. "Mortgage Lending and American Urbanization, 1880–1890." *The Journal of Economic History* 4: 273–86.

Tawney, R.H. 1958. *Business and Politics under James I: Lionel Cranfield as Merchant and Minister*. Cambridge: Cambridge University Press.

Terlizzese, Daniele. 1988. "Delegated Screening and Reputation in a Theory of Financial Intermediaries." *Temi di Discussione*, Banca d'Italia, No. 111.

Warsh, David. 1989. "In Defense of Middlemen." *The Boston Globe* (September 3): 33, 38.

CHAPTER SIX

Minsky's "Two Price" Theory of Financial Instability and Monetary Policy: Discounting versus Open Market Intervention

JAN A. KREGEL

Introduction

There are a number of ways that one might characterize Hy Minsky's principal contributions to economic theory and policy. Since "Ponzi finance" has now entered the professional literature, the obvious choice is the "financial instability hypothesis" based on the idea of endogenous instability. In an age in which exogenous shocks have suspended hard analysis, Minsky's idea—that the perfect operation of a competitive economic system should produce internal destabilizing forces which lead to financial crisis—has intrigued many. Yet, I think that we do him a disservice by chatacterizing Minsky's contribution in this way. As it is now widely recognized, nonlinearities in virtually any type of sequential system are capable of producing endogenous instability, irrespective of the system's internal specification. To say that Minsky had discovered nonlinearities in, say, loanable funds functions, would not only belittle his work, it would positively misappropriate his very real contributions to the field.

Others have been drawn to the technical and financial aspects of his work and its clear point of reference to the real interactions between "Wall Street" and "Main Street" in which we actually live. His monitions of imminent financial debacle have made him something of a Cassandra, warning against the excesses of the world of finance. Yet, the mysteries of finance have intrigued the layman and the scholar since at least the sixteenth century.[1] And, at least since that time, attention has been drawn to those who predicted

The author is professor of economics at the University of Bologna, Italy.

the detrimental effects of the dominance of finance over production and the imminent collapse of financial markets. But Minsky provides something more than a thinking-man's Paul Erdman or an upmarket Ravi Batra.

Instead, I would like to suggest that a more important and distinguishing characteristic of Minsky's work is his contribution to the elucidation of Keynes' price theory. This affirmation will surprise many who believe that Keynes' work was devoid of price theory, but Minsky is one of a small group of post-Keynesian economists who has insisted on the importance of the price-theoretic aspects of Keynes' work, and continued to try to develop this aspect of the Keynesian revolution.[2] His work may thus be clearly distinguished from the earlier expositions of Keynes' *General Theory* in terms of either rigid interest rates (the horizontal section of the LM curve), or rigid wages (a horizontal section of the labor supply curve), and prices (either by assumption or via a fixed markup over rigid wages). In the two dimensional IS-LM diagram, financial affairs may be left out of the discussion because, on Keynes' assumption of the savings-investment identity, the "loans market" becomes the nth "aggregate market" which is automatically in equilibrium under Walras' Law. It is against this background that I suggest that Minsky's insistence on the relation between Keynes' theory of prices and financial factors distinguishes his work from traditional approaches to Keynesian macroeconomics.

One consequence of the absence of attention to prices in the mainstream popularization of Keynes' theory, as Minsky has frequently pointed out, has been the dominant belief that economic policy was exhausted by the "fine-tuning" of the economy. If economic policy has its major effects on quantities, rather than on absolute (or relative) prices, then policy should not have any effect on the productive structure of the economy, and consequently, on the financial structure of the economy. Since it is the attention to Keynes' analysis of prices which allowed the development of the concept of financial instability, it is only from this background that it is possible to understand the major policy proposals aimed at dampening financial instability that have emerged from Minsky's work.

Thus the second characteristic aspect of his work, to which I would like to draw attention, is the policy conclusions which he proposes to counter financial instability. There is one area, in particular, on which I would like to focus; the location of the policy intervention of the Central Bank (open market policy versus the discount mechanism). Minsky's declared preference for the latter is directly linked to the way financial prices are determined and their impact on the economy. The role of prices in Minsky's work is also crucial to understanding his policy recommendations.

I will first give a sketch of the relation between financial instability and policy in Minsky's approach. Then I will discuss the origins of financial instability in the theory of prices, and finally the origins of the policy recommendation in the theory of prices.

The Interrelation of Minsky's Approach to
Prices and Policy

Minsky's theoretical explanation of financial instability, and his policy proposals to control it, are to be found in the relation between the "Two Price Systems and Finance." He writes:

> There are really two systems of prices in a capitalist economy—one for current output and the other for capital assets. When the price level of capital assets is high relative to the price level of current output, conditions are favorable for investment; when the price level of capital assets is low relative to the price level of current output, then conditions are not favorable for investment, and a recession—or a depression—is indicated. (1986, 143)

The first price (of current output) represents the "carrier of profits" and the means for validation of debt. Current output prices are determined by investment expenditures and supported by Big Government expenditure flows. Big Government is, in reality, a support system for private sector current output prices and profits.[3] The second system of prices (of capital assets) helps determine the first set through its impact on investment. Since the decision to hold capital assets is also a decision concerning their financing, investment represents a decision about both asset and liability structures. The values attached to the capital assets have an impact on the value of the liabilities created to acquire them. Capital goods prices have an impact on the viability of the balance sheets of both the firm and its bankers.

Minsky argues implicitly against the assumption of informational asymmetry between bankers and entrepreneurs; since both face the same uncertainty over the present value of uncertain future returns from the possession of fixed capital assets, both will tend to "live in the same expectational environment," and their behavior will often be reinforcing. Thus, a change in the expectational environment will have an effect on both the demand prices of capital goods and desired investment, and the willingness and terms at which the banking system is willing to provide financing for the increased investment. As a result, there is an adjustment in both the liability structure of the firm, and in the financial structure of the banking system. While the financial structure may be perfectly rational, and thus perfectly viable for the evolution of current output prices which is expected to prevail, expectations may be wrong.

The endogenous generation of instability is thus built around the linkage between current output prices and the demand for investment and capital goods prices. Expectations of increasing current output prices cause capital asset prices to rise relative to currently prevailing output prices. This, then, leads to an increase in borrowing to fund new investment. The increased borrowing leads to higher interest payments which can only be met if expectations of increased future returns are confirmed. Bankers must share the expectations of the firms if new lending is to be extended. The increased lending is reflected in the firms' liabilities held as assets by the banking system to support its own liabilities, and acquired to fund the lending. The value of these liabilities also depends on the realization of expectations of future profit flows. A sufficiently large fall in capital asset prices may then have an impact on the value of bank liabilities. Uncertainty over the value of a bank's liabilities, i.e., its ability to meet its payments commitments, is the source of financial panic and crisis.[4] For Minsky, Big Government spending can partially offset the fall in profit flows which results from a fall-off in investment or overoptimistic expectations, and in this way, provides support for consumption goods prices. But it cannot directly support the fall in the value of a bank's assets which results from a fall in capital goods prices. This is why Big Government, by itself, is not enough to counter instability. A Big Bank must come in to stabilize the prices of capital assets by indirectly supporting the prices of these assets as they appear on the banks' balance sheets. Thus, in Minsky's "two price" view of the world, two stabilizers are needed: Big Government (BG) and a Big Bank (BB). Minsky's explanation of why the capitalist economy has been able to escape the catastrophic implications of financial instability is based on the belief that these two stabilizers have been sufficiently strong to keep the economy teetering on the brink of collapse.

In contrast to Minsky's account of postwar economic performance based on two targets for stabilization policy (the two prices), and two instruments BG and BB, the monetarist-neoclassical synthesis may be characterized as being based on a single target—either stable prices or full employment output. Monetarists propose the use of a stable monetary growth rule to keep the price of goods stable, and a balanced budget to allow output to reach its natural, stable level. The neoclassical Keynesians assign fine-tuning of both monetary and fiscal policy to keep the growth of output stable at just below full employment; prices are presumed to be stable below this level.[5]

We thus have the fundamental point of difference between the two approaches: Is monetary policy (the Big Bank) to be assigned to control goods prices (monetarist), or aid fiscal policy to control quantities (neoclassical Keynesian); or should it, instead, be directed to stabilize capital asset prices? If the central bank is to support asset prices and the stability of the financial system in general, then is it clear that it will have to be both discretionary in its action and act as a direct participant in the financial markets where the prices of financial assets found on the banks' balance sheets are determined? Minsky's support of discount policy is an attempt to introduce monetary policy at the beginning, rather than at the end, of the process which determines capital asset prices, i.e., at the moment when banks and firms evaluate the future profitability of investment in drawing up lending agreements.

The Origins and Evolution of "Two Price"
Explanations of Fluctuations

There is a long history of "two price" models to explain cyclical fluctuations. In the modern literature they start with Knut Wicksell (1898 in German, 1936 in English) and Irving Fisher and culminate in Keynes' work. Fisher's early analysis[6] identified the impact of an increase in the quantity of money in the rise in the general price level of produced outputs, relative to the price of financial assets represented by the rate of interest. This rise in prices increased profits on projects funded with borrowed funds. This caused investment and borrowing from the banks to increase until the rate of interest increased sufficiently to reverse the situation.

Wicksell identified the difference between the *real* and *nominal* rate of interest as the source of a cumulative process initiated when the former remains fixed while increases (decreases) in money and goods prices cause the latter to decrease (increase). This leads to a cumulative process which need not reverse itself because, unlike Fisher, Wicksell assumed pure credit money. Hawtrey (1913) also produced a theory of fluctuations in which a change in the price level altered the inflation-adjusted cost of borrowing, and influenced production and the holding of working capital.

It was against this background that the young Keynes started lecturing on monetary problems and working on economic fluctuations—his reading lists for 1910–14 expressly cite Fisher (1907, chs. 5 and 14, and 1911). After reading Robertson's Fellowship Dissertation on Industrial Fluctuations, he reports having discovered "a superb theory about fluctuations" which is perhaps his clearest enunciation of what Minsky eventually developed into the "Financial Instability" hypothesis. Keynes was unwilling to accept Fisher's mechanical application of the equation of exchange, and, instead, suggested that the correct explanation of the process—by which an increase in the money supply caused a rise in prices—was to be found in the operation of the banking system.

In "How far are bankers responsible for the alternations of crisis and depression?", written by Keynes in 1913 after reading Robertson's essay, he develops this idea in a simple model in which income is spent on consumption goods, saved in the form of the purchase of financial assets, or held in current accounts in banks to serve as "free resources to be spent or saved according as future circumstances may determine" (vol. 8, 5). If bankers, trying to maximize returns, lend these "free resources," deposited with them to finance entrepreneurs' acquisition of capital goods, then actual investment will run ahead of the public's intended purchases of financial assets as given by the proportion of their income allocated to savings. When banks attempt to maximize their returns and lend the public's current account deposits, they will be using what the public believes to be "free resources" to finance fixed capital investments. When the time comes for the "take out" finance to be arranged (by selling financial assets to the public), planned savings will be insufficient to fund entrepreneurs' investment plans, and "bankers as a whole suddenly find that what looked like liquid assets has turned into assets that are very far from liquid indeed" (ibid). Whether or not this causes the banks difficulties (Keynes suggests it will lower the quality of the assets they hold), they will curtail current lending resulting in a fall-off in funding for new investment projects:

> Let me summarize . . . . What precipitates a reduction of banking facilities and a crisis . . . is not so much the proportion of the bank's commitments to its cash reserves, as the *character* of the commitments. . . . Since some of the old commitments do not clear themselves off, the bank cannot enter into new business. [The result must then be] a slackening of investment . . . . This must necessarily be accompanied by a depression in those industries which are chiefly concerned in the production of capital goods. (Ibid., 9-11)

In the process of adjustment, goods prices rise as the result of the boom caused by the excess of investment over saving. Lending, meanwhile, is curtailed and interest rates are increased. It is the banks who control the divergence between households' planned savings and investment, and it is this relation that produces changes in commodity prices and fluctuations in investment.

In this 1913 version there is no direct recognition of the link between interest rates, capital asset prices, and investment. In the *Tract on Monetary Reform* Keynes continues his pursuit of an explanation of the way the quantity of money affects prices in order to replace Fisher's explanation. Here, we find the clear beginning of an explanation of the way in which interest rates influence capital asset prices, and, thus, investment decisions, in the formulation of the interest rate parity theorem.[7]

This chain of reasoning, from saving-investment balance to prices, reappears in the "Fundamental Equations" of the *Treatise on Money* (the influence of Wicksell now dominating that of Fisher). The price of consumption goods is amplified through the addition of a first term, expressing unit costs of production, to the second term, expressing the excess demand effect caused by the divergence of investment from saving already seen in the 1913 essay. Although there are two fundamental equations, they do not represent the two price levels. There is one equation for the price level of "available output" or current output, and one for output as a whole, i.e., including the price of unavailable output (or capital goods), determined by a quite different process. The banking system is now responsible for the price of current output only indirectly through its influence on the price of assets, and, thus, on investment relative to saving. The price of capital assets, or the rate of interest, is given by the relation between the supply of deposits determined by the banking system relative to the public's demand for them as determined by the balance of bullish and bearish sentiment.

The overall price level, as expressed in the second fundamental equation, is the combination of the price of available goods as determined by the first equation with the price of nonavailable goods as given by the rate of interest which is, itself, determined by the lending and borrowing policy of the banks and the bullish-bearish sentiment of the public.

This approach to the determination of the general price level helps explain what appears to be Keynes' rather ambiguous position with respect to the use of the interest rate as a tool of policy. The two terms of the fundamental equations allowed the definition of two types of inflation: a "profits inflation," due to the divergence of savings and investment in the second term; and an "income inflation," due to changes in unit costs in the first term. The latter relates to the wage-price-productivity nexus and is not directly influenced by interest rates. Interest rates do, however, have a direct impact on the savings-investment relation represented in the second term of the fundamental equation. Thus, monetary policy can only stop an "income inflation" by reducing investment and income sufficiently to cause a slump deep enough to reduce wage rates. Monetary policyis an extremely blunt tool with which to control inflation once a savings-investment imbalance has spilled over into the first term and caused wages to rise; it can do so only indirectly by reducing investment and employment.[8] On the other hand, monetary policy may be more efficient in its effect on the prices of capital goods and, thus, on a profits inflation But even this is an uncertain process since, "strictly, . . . it is the *anticipated* profit or loss which is the mainspring of change, . . . it is by causing anticipations of the appropriate kind that the banking system is able to influence the price level" (vol. 5, 143).

Here we have a fully developed answer to the question posed in 1913 when Keynes challenged Fisher's explanation of the way money influences prices. The operation of the banking system remains at the center of the process, but it must now contend with both the portfolio decisions of the public and of entrepreneurs as determined by each group's anticipations of future returns—the public's anticipations of the prices of financial liabilities issued by banks or by firms, and the entrepreneurs' anticipations which determine the demand prices of capital assets. In an expansion the bankers' anticipations conform to the entrepreneurs', but will diverge in other conditions. When anticipations are changing rapidly, there may be no change in the rate of interest that can influence anticipations in the appropriate way, and monetary policy may be useless.9

We may identify the *Treatise* as a source of Minsky's "two prices" theory. We can also see how this formulation grew out of Keynes' attempt to show how the normal operation of the banking system, in pursuit of maximum profit, produced fluctuations in prices which caused general economic fluctuation. This is the reading of Keynes which escaped the attention of virtually all the major expositors until Minsky's *John Maynard Keynes* appeared in 1975.

Keynes' *Treatise* was substantially complete by the summer of 1929.[10] The analytical framework was available as a vehicle to interpret the Great Crash and the U.S. Depression. This Keynes did in a popular piece that Hy Minsky is fond of quoting, "The Consequences to the Banks of the Collapse of Money Values" (vol. 9, 150–58). In this article Keynes takes up a theme already present in his analysis of the August 1914 London Stock Market crash;[11] the difference between the "productivity" or real value of capital assets, and their nominal or money values as represented by their prices on financial markets.

In 1914 Keynes notes that the "destruction of paper values" due to the threat of war gives a misleading impression of real conditions because the ability of capital goods to produce real output is unimpaired. He writes:

> It is the business of financiers to hold their assets, through the medium of title deeds, bonds, and securities, in the form of goods, partly consumable but mainly fixed; while their liabilities, on the other hand, are in the form of promises to pay out sums of money. If the financiers are called on to fulfill their liabilities at a time when for reasons of prudence or panic people generally do not choose to have more of their resources than they need in the form of fixed capital goods, they are forced at any cost to themselves to turn their assets into money, even though they know well enough that the future money value of their assets is certain to be far higher than the present money value. With a . . . fall in the value of securities, we learn not, as with the destruction of Liège or Louvain, of a loss in the world's real wealth, but only of the financial world's extreme urgency for money. . . . We experience, therefore, a sudden and violent change in our relative valuation of present and future income. (Vol. 11, 268)

After the 1929 Crash and the 1931 Banking Crisis Keynes argued in a similar vein that many of the real assets comprising capital wealth were obtained using borrowed money. According to Keynes, the financing activities of the modern banking system (namely, imposing the guarantee between the bank's depositors and its borrowers) drops a "veil of money" between capital assets and their *nominal* owners. That the owner has a claim only to money and not directly to the capital asset, Keynes argued, is a particular characteristic of the modern economic world, and obscures the issue of real wealth and its ownership (vol. 9, 151).

Keynes then goes on to analyze the effect of a fall in the money value of the real assets—their real productivity unchanged—which exceeds the margin or collateral left with the banks, impairing the banks' willingness to lend. Even if panic has not broken out, bankers' realizations that their margin has "run out" "is likely to have a very adverse effect on new business (ibid., 153–54). For the banks, being aware that many of their advances are in fact 'frozen' and involve a larger latent risk than they would voluntarily carry, become particularly anxious that the remainder of their assets should be as liquid and as free from risk as it is possible to make them. . . . it means that the banks are less willing than they would normally be to finance any project which may involve a lock-up of their resources". Here it is the banks' "urgency for money" which is identified as crucial.

But Keynes goes further in his 1931 analysis and notes that "a decline in money values so severe as that which we are now experiencing threatens the solidarity of the whole financial structure" (ibid., 156) and that "nothing on earth can put the banks in good shape or save them from ultimate default except a general recovery in prices and money-values" (ibid., 157). Thus, a fall in the value of capital assets of a sufficient degree to overcome normal margins of safety will lead to a decline of confidence in the banks' liabilities, and eventually, to a collapse in their value represented by a bank panic and a collapse of the system. Which, in fact, occurred in 1932.

Here the endogenous feedback mechanism, between the structure of banks' balance sheets and the structure of the liabilities of the firms to which they lend, is extended to encompass the difference between the money values of the capital equipment lying behind the banks' assets and the value of their liabilities. The policy prescription is, clearly, to avoid the collapse of confidence in banks' liabilities by supporting the prices of capital assets. This echoes Keynes' (who had been advising the Chancellor, Lloyd George) strong approval of the 1914 reaction of the Bank of England in turning "all bills into money at a very moderate rate of discount" (vol. 11, 250), i.e., supporting prices at par, thereby saving the discounters from capital losses, supporting the prices of their assets, and preventing a collapse in the price of their liabilities and a general collapse of confidence.

It is important to note that the analysis of the stability of the financial structure is determined here by the evolution of two prices—real capital goods' prices and financial liability prices, rather than the price of current output and the price of capital. In conditions of crisis we must add another price duality. Above, it was noted that the role of monetary policy in affecting anticipations would have to deal with two separate sets of anticipations—of the public over financial liabilities, and of entrepreneurs over capital assets.

It is *this* distinction that Keynes had been dealing with, implicitly, in his discussion of financial crisis, but which did not appear, explicitly, until the *General Theory*. At this time, he introduced liquidity preference to deal with the public's anticipations over liability prices[12] and the efficiency of capital to deal with entrepreneurs' anticipations of capital asset prices:

> Whilst liquidity-preference due to the speculative-motive corresponds to what in my *Treatise on Money* I called "the state of bearishness", it is by no means the same thing. For "bearishness" is there defined as the functional relationship, not between the rate of interest (or price of debts) and the quantity of money, but between the price of assets and debts, taken together, and the quantity of money. This treatment, however, involved a confusion between results due to a change in the rate of interest and those due to a change in the schedule of the marginal efficiency of capital. . . . (Vol. 7, 173)

This division was part of the change required by the shift from the *Treatise* definition of income, to that of the *General Theory* where savings and investment were brought into equality by changes in the level of income generated by the multiplier. This has led some to argue that since this left the rate of interest without a role to play, liquidity preference was created as an afterthought. Rather more important is Keynes' desire to clarify the impact of money on prices by separating the determination of the prices of capital assets from the price of debts. Liquidity preference (as bullishness, bearishness, and the policy of the banking system from the *Treatise* is now called) determined the interest rate or the price of debts. It was the marginal efficiency of capital, however, which had to be newly invented to determine the price of capital assets.[13]

Indeed, it is the separation of the determinants of the prices of assets and debts—or the distinction between the marginal efficiency of capital and liquidity preference—which may be called the great innovation of the *General Theory*, a division which grew out of the conundrum that had bothered Keynes since the 1914 crisis, i.e., the difference between the nominal value of capital assets and their ability to produce real output. In rejecting the simple physical ability to produce real output as equivalent to producing income, and introducing the theory of effective demand to determine income, Keynes creates a distinction between production potential and income. It is now the expectation of sales, or the anticipation of profits on the sale of real output (effective demand), which determines the value of capital assets or their demand price as given by the present value and determined by discounting the future incomes at the rate of interest on competing financial assets.[14]

The sharp changes in the money values of assets and liabilities which occur independently of any change in their underlying real productive potential can now be explained via liquidity preference leading to a fall in liability prices as agents shift their holding of financial liabilities to more liquid assets. This, then, spills over into firms' liabilities which are assets for the banks, and leads the banks to reduce accommodation in an attempt to restore the liquidity of their balance sheets. There is a subsequent rise in the interest rate and a fall in the discounted value of anticipated future profits, as well as a downward revision in expectations. Both lead to a revision of capital asset prices represented by a reduction in the marginal efficiency of capital which reduces investment expenditures.[15]

The investment decision is explained by the relation between the interest rate and the marginal efficiency of capital; the rate of return which brings the discounted expected future earnings of the asset into equality with its acquisition costs. As Keynes insists in chapter 11, this can be viewed as either a "two rate" theory or a "two price" theory. It can be presented as either the divergence of the marginal efficiency of capital from the rate of interest, leading to a rise in investment which is balanced by saving through the expansion of output (the simple quantity adjustment process of neoclassical Keynesianism), or as a price adjustment process.

There are two ways of looking at this price adjustment process. In *Treatise* terminology it would represent a divergence of the demand price of capital goods and the supply price or the price of current output of capital goods. In the *General Theory* Keynes is able to characterize this same relationship in terms of the adjustment of asset and liability prices, with investment proceeding until the price of capital assets is driven down to the price of liabilities, in particular money. The multiplier, then, not only operates on the quantity of output, it produces changes that "modify the money prices of other capital assets in such a way as to equalize the attraction of holding them and of holding cash" (vol. 14, 213). In equilibrium demand and supply, prices of capital goods are equal just as the prices of assets and liabilities are driven to equality. This, I have argued elsewhere (Kregel 1988a), shows the unity of the price and quantity adjustment processes in the *General Theory*; a unity which has disappeared in the fix price or fixed quantity expositions.

This is also one of the reasons why Minsky had to go back to the *Treatise* to find the two-price trail. If we look at the *General Theory* as an extension of the price analysis of the former book, rather than the IS-LM no-price model, we can see that there are two levels to the "two prices" approach: The first level, presented in the *Treatise*, distinguishes between the prices of current output and capital goods output; the second level, added in the *General Theory*, distinguishes the prices of new and existing capital assets from the prices of new and existing financial liabilities. The first is sufficient to express the financial instability hypothesis, while the second is necessary to analyze fully how a change in asset prices will affect confidence in bank liabilities and how it may or may not lead to financial panic.

In the *General Theory* presentation, Keynes limits the effects of the needs for liquidity to the price of financial liabilities; that is, the interest rate that is charged for the creation of bank accommodation. The concept of liquidity then becomes linked, not to the rapidity with which one can convert an asset to money by selling it in the open market (in its *marketability* as in the traditional approach), but the price at which someone is willing to lend money in exchange for the asset. The charge for taking an asset onto a balance sheet will be related to the increased risk of insolvency, or the liquidity premium which will express the liquidity preference via the interest rate charged (Kregel 1984). This charge for temporary lending against an asset is normally associated with the process of discounting rather than direct sale of assets in the market.

Thus, the "two level" approach to the "two price" theory makes it easier to see why assigning the Central Bank control of the price of current output (via control of the liabilities of the banking system) may be highly inefficient. As Keynes points out in his 1932 lectures:

> ... the banking system consists of dealers in money and debts rather than consumables and assets. Debts acquired by open-market operations and debts acquired through discounting are the same, though in practice the debts of the first sort are long term. ... The market rate of interest is an expression of the

> terms at which the banking system is able to deal in debts. . . . Bankers and money markets deal in debts and not in terms of capital goods proper. . . . The price of capital assets comes in only indirectly—they are dealt with among members of the public. . . . [the price of capital goods] only affects the rate of interest indirectly. . . . The banking system fixes the ratio between the values of debts and money—that is, the rate of interest. (Rymes 66–70)

Keynes then sets out an explanation of the determination of the prices of "three classes of purchasable things, namely, debts, assets and consumables" (ibid., 76) noting that the quantity of money will first have an impact on debt prices, then on asset prices and only subsequently on consumables.

He also points out that "Money is created when banks buy debts. Money is destroyed when banks get rid of debt, by selling it or having it discharged. Hence there is no distinction between open market operations and discounting or advancing, that is, banks create money [bank deposits] when they buy debt, discount private debt or make loans and/or advances to the community. The main practical point is whether the banking system fixes the prices of all debts (that is, long-term loans) or not" (ibid., 67). Since banks do not deal in commodity markets, they can only have an affect on commodity prices, indirectly, by changing the relation between debt and assets, and then, between capital assets and current output prices. But, the prices of capital assets are determined by two factors: the efficiency of capital, and the rate of discount. The banks only control the second, and there is nothing to guarantee that rises in the former may more than offset rises in the latter in a boom—and vice versa in a slump. This is the crux of Keynes' analysis of fluctuations in volume 2 of the *Treatise*, and in chapter 22 of the *General Theory* dealing with the cycle.

The source of financial instability may thus be found in the interface between the expectations of entrepreneurs of future profits and of the banks of future debt service payments (from a new investment found in the numerator, and the rate of interest set by the banking system found in the denominator of the present value of an investment project representing the demand price of capital goods). When firms and banks share the same expectational environment, the banks will create liabilities in order to lend funds which convalidate the expectations of entrepreneurs represented by capital asset prices. The dilemma of using monetary policy to control such financial instability is that the Central Bank can only deal in financial liabilities, and cannot directly affect the process which determines the prices of capital assets; the process by which the banks evaluate the ability of a project to meet future interest payments.

An Instability Hypothesis for Monetary Policy?

It is because of its indirect impact on asset prices that Minsky has criticized the excessive reliance of the Federal Reserve on open market purchases and sales of government securities to control unborrowed reserves. He also criticizes the fact that it separates the day-to-day operations of affecting bank reserves, from the lender-of-last-resort function. Indeed, it creates a direct conflict between the two for open-market-policy-attempts to influence the banks' volume of lending by influencing holdings of nonbusiness sector assets through price changing which affects the liquidity of the balance sheet. Lender-of-last-resort action, on the other hand, requires "the fixing of a minimum price of some financial instrument or real asset" (1986, 49) and, subsequently, supports the liquidity of the balance sheet. Minsky's policy goal is to try to find a mechanism which eliminates this conflict by providing a more direct method of influencing the value of banks' business sector assets; or, in Keynes' terms above, attempts to influence long-term interest rates, and thus investment decisions, by means of discount policy. Minsky advocates a more extended use of the Fed's discount mechanism in order to not only provide support for asset prices, but also to join it, more directly, to the supervisory function through the reintroduction of a reserve-creation "relationship" between the banks and the Federal Reserve.

The question naturally arises as to how this state of affairs developed. Minsky suggests that it was due to the increased role of government in the 1930s, increasing the supplies of government debt which replaced the "nonspecie reserves" of the banks (1986, 48). We have already noted the use, by a major Wall Street fund manager, George Soros, of an approach very similar to the financial instability hypothesis (Soros 1987). It is interesting to note that Soros considers his approach incomplete without the addition of the direct role played by regulatory policy in the cyclical behavior of the economy. He amplifies his "reflexivity theory" of the credit cycle with a reflexive "regulatory cycle." If the lending relationship between firms and banks gives rise to an endogenous instability, it seems reasonable that a similar process might occur as a result of the lending relationship between the banking system and the Central Bank. Indeed, investigation of the historical record would suggest that the demise of the use of a discount mechanism was not simply caused by government debt "crowding out" discounts as the major source of bank reserves.

The Federal Reserve had been created with the aim of providing an "elastic currency," to be achieved by discounting "eligible" commercial paper which was to be "self-liquidating" against Federal Reserve Notes issued by the Government through the Federal Reserve Banks. Already in the early 1920s, the District Federal Reserve Banks had discovered that they could affect bank reserves via purchases and sales of bank acceptances and Treasury certificates, since these were the assets in which the larger banks invested excess reserves. According to Kemmerer (1951), the Federal Reserve believed that it had discovered a mechanism which could prevent depressions, and their experience in the 1920s supported this belief. Open market policy was used both to control domestic conditions, but also to aid Britain's return to the Gold Standard. But, even in this period, the Fed was limited in its use of open market policy.

As already mentioned, to achieve flexibility of the currency, the Federal Reserve Note issue was to be backed by 40 percent in gold and 60 percent in discounts of commercial paper. Government paper was not included. In 1917 the 40 percent gold backing was set as a minimum. By the beginning of the 1930s, business conditions were such that there was not enough eligible paper and the currency was backed by over 100 percent in gold. This condition was also the result of the Federal Reserve's use of open market purchases of Treasury certificates to increase bank reserves. The banks promptly used these extra reserves, not to lend, but to repay discounts at the Fed, reducing the discount backing and requiring an increase in the gold backing of the note issue. When England went off the gold standard in September 1931, and the market presumption was that the United States would follow suit, this led to a run on the U.S. gold supply at the same time as the U.S. banking crisis was breaking, and the Fed found itself caught between two diverse currents. In order to create Federal Reserve Notes to support the banks, the Fed had to use either gold or rediscounts. The only way that it could maintain the supply of reserve notes and free gold to meet the rising foreign demand was to substitute government securities for discounts, i.e., sell government securities to the banks who would then finance these purchases by discounting eligible assets. But since the banks lacked sufficient eligible assets, and the government securities were not eligible for discounting, the result of the operation would have been increased interest rates and tightened money market conditions in the face of continuing reserve losses due to the domestic run. The Federal Reserve, thus, could not use open market policy since it could neither buy nor sell government securities.

The solution, which gave the Federal Reserve effective freedom to deal in government securities, was the Glass-Steagall Act of 1932 (not the Glass Banking Act of 1933, which legislated the separation of commercial and investment activities of banks) which permitted government securities to be used as the backing for the issue of Federal Reserve Notes for an emergency period of one year. This allowed the Federal Reserve Banks to buy, rather than sell, government securities and reduce interest rates as it increased reserves and the supply of gold available to meet foreign demand.

Thus, the primary use of government securities in open market policy was the result of the Glass-Steagall Act and became institutionalized only with the creation of the Open Market Committee in Marriner Eccles' Banking Act of 1935. The Glass-Steagall provisions became permanent in 1945 and this, as well as the policy of interest rate stabilization during the war, provided the postwar conditions in which government securities became the principle position-making asset for banks when the Fed, once again, started to use active monetary policy.

It was neither the growth of BG (and the associated rise in the quantity of outstanding government debt), nor a policy decision based on theoretical principles, that led to the discounting of eligible paper as the primary source of bank reserves being replaced by open market dealings in government securities. The result was, nevertheless, "that Federal Reserve operations undertaken to affect bank reserves no longer use the same markets and instruments as lender of last resort operations." But, paradoxically, the discounting mechanism had failed to provide an efficient means of supporting the prices of assets on the balance sheets of the banks, mainly because Reserve Banks could not lend against real estate mortgages, installment finance paper, or loans secured by stocks or bonds.[16]

The implications of this separation between reserve policy and the lender-of-last-resort function was not immediately recognized, because the central bank was not required to use the latter in the first two decades of the postwar period. After the 1951 Fed-Treasury "Accord" which released the Fed from supporting the price of Treasury securities, however, the Fed launched a policy of "bills only" open market policy, which was intended to create a "free market" determination of the prices of long-term Treasury issues (cf. Weintraub 1956). It was only in late 1953 that the decision was taken to use open market policy exclusively to affect bank reserves (Anderson, 125). Both of these policy changes increased the price variability, and decreased the liquidity of Treasury's as position-making assets for the banking system. This provides an explanation of the sharp declines in the ratio of protected assets to liabilities in both 1950–51 and 1954–55 (cf. chart 5 of Minsky 1982, 53). Between 1950 and 1955, the ratio of governments to total assets fell from 42.9 percent to 34.5 percent, the largest proportionate decline of the postwar period (cf. Cooper and Fraser 1986, 13). Both the action of the Fed, as well as the banks' changing perception of risk, led to the long-term decline in the ratio of "protected assets" and, in particular, of government securities to long-term liabilities. This decline continued as banks worked off the securities accumulated during the war, and increased their lending activities, leading to further reliance on "market-based" reserves via the Federal Funds market.

This Treasury impulse toward increased "free market" determination of long-term interest rates also produced the shift from asset adjustment (changes in holdings of Treasuries) to liability adjustment (borrowed reserves in the Fed funds markets) by banks to monetary policy. It also changed the efficiency of open market sales and purchases, which no longer had direct effect on the proportions of the asset side of the balance sheet, but led, first, to adjustments on the liability side. Greater changes in interest rates were then required to produce a given impact on bank reserves and on bank lending.

This increased volatility of interest rate movements accentuated the push toward liability management as the banks sought to maintain profitability by adjusting their liabilities in response to reserve deficiencies. The Fed maintained its "bills only" policy until December 1961, when it was again forced by international conditions to use policy for internal and external reasons simultaneously; intervening in foreign exchange markets from 1962 and trying to supply reserves by buying longer term while it supported short-term interest rates in "operation twist" in 1965.

This brief history of open market policy might be described as an endogenous mechanism whereby the Fed's increasing reliance on free market determination of long-term interest rates led to increased volatility and decreased liquidity of such assets. Commercial banks then, substituted position-making assets which had deeper markets and minimum variation in capital value. If changes in interest rates have an impact on asset holdings because they change capital values, this movement toward shorter-term assets, and then to overnight Fed funds, means that interest rates have diminished impact on bank behavior and ever-larger changes in rates are required to have a desired change in lending. This mechanism has produced the perverse result that "interest rate movements are not the key influence on the profits of major financial institutions; rather the primary factor is the volume of loans and investments in their portfolios. Insulated from the impact of interest rate swings, institutions try to maximize profits by growth of assets and liabilities—and therefore growth of debt" (Kaufman 1986, 44). In short, open market policy now no longer has any appreciable affect on the values of banks' assets, nor on their liabilities.

By 1966 this change in liability structure of commercial banks had gone far enough to require changes in interest rates sufficiently large to produce an effect on other financial institutions. The credit crunch of 1966 initiated the retail certificate of deposit (CD), which started the run of deposits from the Savings and Loan banks,[17] as well as triggered the extension of U.S. banks into the Euro-currency markets. The scenario was repeated in 1969, with the collapse of the commercial paper market. But Penn Central was not the most important victim. The movements of funds from the London Eurodollar market, which were un-wound when rates went down in 1970 and 1971, are blamed by many for the collapse of the Bretton Woods System. In both of these episodes, the open market policy required to produce response was so severe that it depressed capital asset prices directly, and had to be abandoned in favor of lender-of-last-resort intervention to support the banks' own liabilities.

The system increasingly came to resemble the bind in which the Fed found itself in 1931, when it wanted to buy government securities, but the only way it could increase reserves was to sell them and increase interest rates and depress asset prices. To stop an expansion requires selling government securities. But this only produces liability innovation by the banks, which, to be stopped, requires interest rates so high that the value of the liabilities is damaged, and the Fed then has to intervene to support asset prices directly, which is precisely the opposite of the initial policy.

Minsky offers a policy recommendation similar to Glass-Steagall by suggesting that the reason for the banks' resistance to open market policy is to be found in the self-reinforcing impact of lending on capital values. If the Fed were to return to creating reserves by discounting against banks' commercial lending, it would be "cofinancing business" and be "participating in and encouraging hedge financing" (1986, 322). Indeed, such a policy would find the Central Bank situating itself at the interface between firms' anticipations of future profits and banks' anticipations of ability to pay interest; the point at which the price of capital assets is determined. It would thus be directly influencing the process of determination of assets prices, and, thereby, investment expenditures. If we accept the "two level/two price" theory explanation, Minsky's proposal is that BG, as the sustainer of the overall level of investment and of current output prices, be joined by the BB, which is capable of supporting investment via the effect of its discounting policy on the price of capital assets. This partnership could support the value of bank liabilities, discourage the generation of instability, and make lender-of-last-resort action less necessary. This is, of course, just the reverse of the change in Fed policy initiated in the 1950s to allow free market determination of long-term interest rates and capital asset prices; a process which, it is argued here, led to a response by the banking system to offset such variability.

It is clear that, first of all, increased use of discount policy would involve making a wider range of assets eligible for discount. Indeed, Minsky suggests that asset eligibility be part of policy discretion.[18] It would also imply a move away from reliance on the money market as the efficient allocator of financial resources and evaluator of capital values. For those who object to this policy as interfering with the efficient operation of the market, Marriner Eccles' observation on the Fed's change of policy in the 1950s may be appropriate: "If the Federal Reserve System discharges its responsibility, there is no such thing as a free market. ... That concept was meant to be discarded when the Federal Reserve System was established in 1913. It is the function of the Federal Reserve System to maintain economic stability so far as that is possible within the scope of monetary and credit management" (Weintraub 1953, 408).

Notes

1. Compare Lodovico Guiciardini writing of the Netherlands in the middle of the sixteenth century, quoted by Ehrenberg (1928, 243): "Formerly the nobles, if they had ready money, were wont to invest it in real estate, which gave employment to many persons and provided the country with necessaries. ... Nowadays ... a part of the nobles and the merchants ... employ all their available capital in dealing in money, the large and sure profits of which are a great bait. Hence the soil remains untilled, trade in commodities is neglected, there is often increase of prices, the poor are fleeced by the rich, and finally even the rich go bankrupt."

2. Rymes (1989, 10) has recently noted that the fact that "Keynes was fundamentally rewriting the theory of value" was not generally appreciated even by his students. Davidson (1978) uses Keynes' Marshallian background to delineate the link between stock and flow supply prices as the organizing feature of a monetary economy.

3. And at the same time a "shield that protects an inefficient industrial structure" (cf. Minsky 1982, 56).

4. This same principle has been used by George Soros in his investment strategy based on the concept of "reflexivity": "loans are based on the lender's estimation of the borrower's ability to service his debt. The valuation of the collateral is supposed to be

independent of the act of lending; but in actual fact the act of lending can affect the value of the collateral. . . . The reflexive interaction between the act of lending and collateral values has led me to postulate a pattern in which a period of gradual, slowly accelerating credit expansion is followed by a short period of credit contraction—the classic sequence of boom and bust. The bust is compressed in time because the attempt to liquidate loans causes a sudden implosion of collateral values" (Soros 1987, 17–18). If we substitute capital asset values for collateral values and changes in these values with "margins of safety," this comes close to Minsky's definition of financial instability.

5. This becomes the natural level unemployment of the monetarists with the addition of the Phillips curve.

6. Fisher (1907), chs. 5, 14; and Fisher (1911) in particular, chap. 4: "Disturbance of Equation and Purchasing Power During Transition Periods."

7. Which has been used as the basis of the interpretation of Keynes' theory given in Kregel (1982).

8. And need not succeed in doing so if it causes productivity to fall by more than wage rates.

9. This is noted in the *Treatise* in the discussion of Hawtrey's theory, and again in the *General Theory* discussion of the trade cycle where Keynes suggests that higher interest rates may even support excessively optimistic expectations of real returns at full employment. The increasingly optimistic expectations of entrepreneurs and bankers are thus self-reinforcing.

10. It was born of the English postwar slump of the 1920s (Keynes published his pamphlet "Can Lloyd George Do It?" in May 1929), but predated the Wall Street Stock Market Crash of October 1929.

11. Which must be supposed to have been based on his 1913 theory of fluctuations.

12. It would seem obvious from the discussion above that the idea of liquidity preference also applied to bankers, although formal discussion of the point is virtually absent from the book.

13. Keynes is quite clear on this in a letter to Harrod where he notes "the discovery of the marginal efficiency of capital looks very slight and scarcely more than formal, yet in my own progress of thought it was absolutely vital" (vol. 13, 549).

14. Natural rates of interest, real rates, marginal physical productivity, and even "smelly" theories to explain the value of capital thus all must be discarded. This helps explain the difference between Minsky's theory and other seemingly similar approaches, such as Tobin's "q theory," which retains a linkage to "real" returns via the marginal productivity of capital. This difference is also revealed in Minsky's acceptance, and Tobin's rejection, of the Cambridge (UK) critique of neoclassical capital theory.

15. In chapter 22 Keynes links the fall in capital asset prices to a fall in prices in the stock market which further increases liquidity preferences and causes a fall in the propensity to consume which then reinforces the fall in the marginal efficiency of capital.

16. Lending against such assets is expressly encouraged in Minsky's policy recommendations.

17. A process whose implications for the S&L's are only being fully recognized today.

18. Recall that a too restricted range of eligible discounts was the main reason for its demise in 1931.

References

Anderson, B.M. 1979. *Economics and the Public Welfare: A Financial and Economic History of the United States, 1914–1946* first edition [1949]. Indianapolis: Liberty Press.

Anderson, C.J. *A Half-Century of Federal Reserve Policy Making, 1914–1964*. Philadelphia: Federal Reserve Bank.

Cooper, K. and Fraser, D.R. 1986. *Banking Regulation and the New Competition in Financial Services*. Cambridge, Mass.: Ballinger.

Davidson, P. 1978. *Money and the Real World*, second edition. London: Macmillan.

Ehrenberg, R. 1928. *Capital & Finance in the Age of the Renaissance*. London: Jonathan Cape.

Fisher, I., 1907. *The Rate of Interest*. New York: Macmillan.

———, 1911. *The Purchasing Power of Money: Its Determination and Relation to Credit, Interest and Crises*. New York: Macmillan.

Hawtrey, R.G., 1913. *Good and Bad Trade*. London: Constable.

Kaufman, H. 1986. *Interest Rates, the Markets, and the New Financial World*. New York: Times Books.

Kemmerer, D.M. 1951. "The Federal Reserve System." *American Financial Institutions*, H.V. Prochnow, ed. New York: Prentice Hall.

Keynes, J.M. *The Collected Writings of John Maynard Keynes*, Vols. 5–6, *A Treatise on Money* [1930], 1971; Vol. 7, *The General Theory of Employment, Interest and Money*, [1936], 1973; Vol. 9, *Essays in Persuasion* [1931], 1972; Vol. 11, *Economic Articles and Correspondence, Academic*, 1983; Vol. 13, *The General Theory and After, Part I: Preparation*; Vol. 14, *The General Theory and After, Part II: Defence and Development*. London: Macmillan.

Kregel, J.A. 1982. "Money, Expectations and Relative Prices in Keynes' Monetary Equilibrium." *Economie Appliquee* 36, 3: 449–65.

———. 1984. "Monetary production economics and monetary policy." *Economies et Societés*, Serie MP. 17 (1): 4.

———. 1988a. "The Multiplier and Liquidity Preference: Two Sides of the Theory of Effective Demand." In *The Foundations of Keynesian Analysis*, A. Barrere, ed. London: Macmillan.

———. 1988b. "Irving Fisher, Great-Grandparent of the General Theory: Money, Rate of Return over Cost and Efficiency of Capital." *Cahiers d'Economie Politique* (Nos. 14–15).

Minsky, H.P. 1975. *John Maynard Keynes*. New York: Columbia University Press.

———. 1982. *Can "It" Happen Again: Essays on Instability and Finance*. Armonk: New York: M.E. Sharpe.

———. 1986. *Stabilizing an Unstable Economy*. New Haven, Conn.: Yale University Press.

Rymes, T. 1989. *Keynes's Lectures, 1932–35*. Ann Arbor, Mich.: University of Michigan Press.

Soros, G. 1987. *The Alchemy of Finance*. New York: Touchstone.

Weintraub, S. 1953. "The New Monetary Policy." *Social Research* 20.

Weintraub, S. 1956. "Postscript on Monetary Policy." *Review of Economics and Statistics*, 228–29.

Wicksell, K. 1965. *Interest and Prices*, [1898] German edition, [1936] English edition. New York: Kelley Reprint.

CHAPTER SEVEN

From Business Cycles to the Economics of Instability

PIERO FERRI

1. A Post-Keynesian Paradigm of Research

The occasion of this conference provides me with the opportunity to explore some of Hyman Minsky's ideas on business cycles. I first met Hyman Minsky in Bergamo, Italy, in 1978 where his book on Keynes was so warmly received. He was then about to work on a new book that synthesized his research on analytical tools, institutions, and economic policy.[1]

At that time, I was working on the dynamics of the labor market. I was an Oxford D.Phil who had worked under the scientific direction of John Hicks. It appeared natural to start discussing the business cycle, and since labor and capital markets occupy a strategic position in Keynes' *General Theory*, this fact also contributed to strengthen the links between us. Since then, I have had the privilege of working on these topics with Minsky practically uninterruptedly. So I feel particularly well-situated to describe his scientific itinerary in these matters, which can be epitomized in the title given to this paper.

Minsky's contributions to business cycle theory, which belong to his earliest scientific production, are probably not as well known as his later work on the interpretation of Keynes, on financial instability, and on monetary institutions. Yet, they represent a fundamental step in his theory of economic dynamics, which, according to Minsky, should be at the core of any post-Keynesian research agenda. As summarized in Ferri-Minsky (1989, 124), this agenda should attempt to:

> 1. ... understand the dynamics of an accumulating capitalist economy,

The author is professor of economics at the University of Bergamo, Italy. I wish to thank Hyman Minsky for a scientific collaboration that has lasted since the late seventies. I also wish to thank Steven Fazzari and Edward Greenberg for comments and suggestions. A contribution from the Italian Ministry of University and Scientific Research is acknowledged.

with complex and evolving financial, product and labor markets, where the dynamics may lead to explosive growth, implosive decline, or complex business cycles rather than sustained exponential growth and

2. develop policies to sustain and to thwart such disruptive dynamics. . . . To Post-Keynesian economists the subject is always a capitalism with complex financial structures, product markets and labor organizations: Keynes's theory is interpreted as a Special Theory of Capitalism, where institutional arrangements are not a veil: they affect the behavior of the economy.

The effort to bridge the initial works, essentially formulated in dynamic terms, to the later studies on financial fragility, a dynamical problem studied in static terms, is at the heart of attempts, in recent years, to reach a synthesis. These attempts can be ascribed to the post-Keynesian scientific research program. It goes without saying that this research agenda owes much of its intellectual debt to such authors as Simons, Fisher, Kalecki, Keynes, and Schumpeter.

In the present paper, I shall study Minsky's efforts to fulfill this research agenda. In particular, after having sketched the different levels of investigation that must be considered in order to compare various contributions (section 2), I review Minsky's analysis of the theory of piecewise linear business cycles (section 3). Some criticisms and developments of this approach will be touched upon in sections 4, 5 and 6. In section 7, it will be shown how an extended model, with its interplay of free and constrained dynamics, can be interpreted as a metaphor for the working of complex economies where the presence of institutions can constrain the results of market forces (section 8). Concluding remarks will be put forward in the final section.

2. Three Levels of Investigation

To study Minsky's contribution to the theory of business cycles and economic instability, it is important to consider three levels of analysis. These levels of investigation, although closely related, will be dealt with separately for convenience. We refer to: (1) the general view on the working of the economic system, (2) the technicalities by which a cycle is generated, and (3) the analytical aspects at the root of the basic model. Each of these levels proves useful to understanding Minsky's contribution and for providing a taxonomy for classifying the various criticisms.

As far as the first aspect is concerned, it is worth noting that there have always been two views of economic dynamics.[2] One view is that the endogenous process of the economy generates an equilibrium. This view does not explain business cycles. In the work of Slutsky (1937) and Frisch (1933)—as well as Friedman (1968) and Lucas (1987)—the economy is a mechanism that transforms random shocks into business cycles.[3]

In the second view, business cycles are the natural and inherent consequence of behavior motivated by self-interest in complex, sophisticated economies. Moreover, in this view, economic growth is endogenously explained as the result of cyclical processes where trends in growth emerge as a consequence of time spent in expansion and contraction.[4] The "business cycle" view enables its practitioners to contemplate decline as well as growth, and to envisage the consequences of changes in the structure of institutions. Minsky's contribution definitely belongs to this class of models which he enriched at other levels of investigation. In fact, this dichotomy in the vision of the system strongly influences, and at the same time is deeply influenced by, the other two levels of analysis mentioned above. Take, for instance, the relationship among the mathematical tools that provide the technicalities for explaining a cycle. As we shall see in the next section, Minsky's interpretation of piecewise models are very important in this regard.

Current economic theory is often mathematical in its language. The mathematical formulation constrains the theorems that can be demonstrated. It is agreed that an economy is a multidimensional system. It has long been known that well-behaved, linear n-dimensional systems can be solved; they are mathematically tractable. In fact, given this mathematical knowledge, by specifying an n-dimensional linear system as a representation of the economy, it is possible to consider the solution as an equilibrium. Furthermore, it is important to stress that this linear world disturbed by shocks can be conveniently studied with econometric tools. The success of this research agenda, which was partly due to the nice functioning of the economy, contributed to the decline of the endogenous view of cycles.[5]

But recent events, particularly the turbulence of the seventies, suggest that the world is more complicated than what is implied by simple linear systems. To study accumulation, the system has to be time-dependent. If the system is capitalist, then monetary and financial considerations cannot be ignored, and these factors introduce nonlinearities. The mathematical model of such systems becomes multidimensional, time-dependent, and nonlinear. The mathematically relevant question is "What do we know about complex, multidimensional, time-dependent and nonlinear systems?"

A partial answer to these questions is given by the new developments in the mathematics of nonlinear systems, which have contributed to a revival of the endogenous explanation of economic fluctuations.[6] In general, the patterns studied by these theories are neither tractable nor nice. We must, therefore, understand the relationships between these new tools and the old ones utilized to generate endogenous cycles. In so doing, we shall be obliged to consider also the analytical aspects that have accompanied these changes.

3. Minsky's Contribution to Linear Piecewise Models

The endogenous explanation of the business cycle, which has a long tradition, received a mathematical statement in Samuelson's (1939) formalization of the interaction of the accelerator and multiplier as a second-order linear difference equation.

As is well known, the unconstrained version takes the form:[7]

(1) $C(t) = a\ Y(t-1)$
(2) $I(t) = b\ [Y(t-1) - Y(t-2)]$
(3) $Y(t) = C(t) + I(t)$

where $Y(t)$ denotes the net national product in period t, while $C(t)$ and $I(t)$ represent, respectively, consumption and net investment. By substituting and rearranging, one obtains:

$$(4)\ Y(t) = A(1)\ m(1)^t + A(2)\ m(2)^t$$

where $m(1)$ and $m(2)$ are derived from the parameters a and b, while $A(1)$ and $A(2)$ are derived from the initial conditions. This equation can give rise to a variety of patterns according to the values of the parameters.

There is a conflict between the possibility of generating business cycles, on the one hand, and the necessity of endowing parameter values with empirical meaning, on the other.[8] A sufficiently high value for the accelerator parameter, for example, is capable of generating an explosive pattern.

Hicks (1950) suggested a way out of this dilemma by introducing ceilings and floors. The presence of ceilings and floors can constrain the dynamic pattern of the variables and, at the same time, widen the range of dynamic possibilities. By enriching Hicks's contribution, Minsky (1957, 1959) developed a technique by which the presence of ceilings and floors imposes new initial conditions so that the constrained pattern differs from the endogenous one. For this purpose it is important to stress that to determine the two initial conditions, it is necessary to know the actual incomes at two dates, $Y(0)$ and $Y(1)$, so that:

(5) $Y(0) = A(1) + A(2)$
(6) $Y(1) = A(1)\ m(1) + A(2)\ m(2)$

If we call m the actual rate of growth of income, which implies that $Y(1) = m\ Y(0)$, it follows that:

$A(1) = [m - m(2)] \ / \ [m(1) - m(2)]\ Y(0)$
$A(2) = [m(1) - m] \ / \ [m(1) - m(2)]\ Y(0)$

Since we assume the values of a and b such that $m(1) > m(2) > 1$, it follows that if

$m(1) > m(2) > m$, then $A(1) < 0$ and $A(2) > 0$,

whereas if

$m(1) > m > m(2)$, then $A(1) > 0$ and $A(2) > 0$.

These different ranges of the values of $A(1)$ and $A(2)$ are very important for understanding the actual path generated by the system. For example, let us consider the growth rate of the ceiling; suppose that it is equal to $m(g)$. Then if $m(1) > m(g) > m(2)$, both $A(1)$ and $A(2)$ are positive, and a steady-state solution can be generated.[9] If, on the other hand, $m(1) > m(2) > m(g) > 1$, then $A(1) < 0$ and $A(2) > 0$. In this case, the initial conditions will determine a negative coefficient for the dominant root, and income will bounce off the ceiling. This implies that a turning point can be generated. If $m(g) > m(1)$, then the ceiling never becomes operative, and the time series is an unconstrained explosive accelerator model that migrates to a growth rate given by $m(1)$. (*Mutatis mutandis*, the same observations will be true for the floor.)

It follows that we could "conceive" of the dynamic processes as "one-step-at-a-time" processes in which the recent values of the variable are initial conditions for the next value of the variable. A process can be said to be "unconstrained" when the initial conditions for the "next step" are generated by the process and "constrained" when the initial conditions for the "next step" differ from those that the process would have generated. This method brings about nonlinearity in the system by using functions defined piecewise which undergo a change when new initial conditions are defined.

As we shall see later on, this type of process can be generalized beyond the domain of the particular model that we have examined.

4. Some Criticisms

Before illustrating the richness of this approach, let us consider some of the criticisms that were made of it by various authors at various times. For this purpose, one must distinguish between criticisms within the model and criticisms that favored alternative approaches. For the first category, it is worth stressing that the economic meaning of ceilings and floors has been questioned on several grounds. For instance, ceilings have been questioned because the checking of an expansion by physical constraints does not seem to fit the facts. Many cyclical turning points occur before full employment is reached.[10] These objections can be overcome, however, if one supposes that the ceiling is not necessarily determined by full employment or by the capacity of the investment goods industry.

As Minsky (1957) has shown, it can be determined by a quantity-of-money constraint on money income, given a limited ability of change in velocity to finance investment.[11] In this way, the possible integration of dynamics in real and monetary terms was open. The problem is to understand why it did not happen, and why research programs took a different path.

This leads us to consider the other set of criticisms, which can be classified by the three levels of investigation mentioned in section 2.

As far as the nature of the dynamic process is concerned, econometric evidence seemed to support an exogenous view of the business cycle, which contributed to the rejection of an endogenous approach to economic fluctuations. As Baumol and Benhabib (1989) point out, interest in the endogenous approach waned after the 1950s. Strong business cycles did not appear, and the apparent emergence of rather steady growth made it plausible to assume that the observed fluctuations could best be interpreted as transformations of stochastically determined deviations from a growth path.

From a technical point of view, there have been criticisms of piecewise models. A more general nonlinear process could have the parameters of the model—the a and b of equation (5)—vary with system behavior or with some external constraint. Starting with a contribution to the accelerator-multiplier with (floors and ceilings) literature, Goodwin (1951, 1967) developed nonlinear models. These models could generate closed orbits and, under some changes in the original hypotheses, limit cycles toward which all possible paths of the variable converge.[12] This result was insightful, though unsatisfactory, because, asymptotically, the path of the variables was too regular. This approach has been recently enriched, as we shall see later, by new developments in the theory of nonlinearity that allow for more complex behavior.

Finally, the model itself was criticized. Initially, the criticism was advanced from the same macroeconomic perspective. For instance, the Goodwin models were not only nonlinear, but stressed the impact of income distribution on the dynamics of investment. Later developments in pure theory brought about a strong attack on traditional macroeconomic theory and reinforced the abandonment of the fully endogenous determination of business cycles. Within the New-Classical macroeconomics perspective, any traditional macroeconomic model was declared to be "ad hoc," and its contribution to the endogenous explanation of the cycle was bound to be considered irrelevant. In this perspective, a macro cycle, such as that obtained by the traditional endogenous view, could be anticipated by rational agents who could destroy it. If this did not happen, it was only because agents were supposed to behave irrationally, looking backward.

5. The Econometric Evidence

Each of these criticisms must be carefully examined to evaluate their impact on the approach that we are considering. We start from a reconsideration of the empirical evidence. The econometric evidence in favor of linear models disturbed by external shocks played a very important role in freezing the development of endogenous explanations of economic fluctuations. It is worth discussing this point in more detail. Several econometric models have been found to be generally noncyclical in the absence of outside disturbances in simulation studies.[13] But random shocks applied to the more recent quarterly models proved insufficient to generate movements with the observable cyclical properties. To induce realistic fluctuations in these models, it was necessary to use serially correlated disturbances. Moreover, even the best simulations show only residual cyclical elements, much weaker than those found in the historical series used to estimate the models. This could be due to errors in either the structure of the models, the disturbances, or both. In any case, one can say that the models, estimated with data from periods with mild business cycles, are unable to reproduce fluctuations as violent as those of the 1930s.

The validity of the evidence from macroeconometric models that appears to refute the endogenous cycle and favor the random-shock theory is, according to Blatt (1978), open to question. Blatt showed how a system whose endogenous reactions yield incoherence—in his case explosive cycles—can be constrained to generate values, which if analyzed econometrically, lead to the proposition that the endogenous relations are "damped," i.e., tend toward an equilibrium value. Blatt set up an accelerator-multiplier model, whose parameters are known to yield an explosive time series, along with well-behaved floors and ceilings. He allowed the endogenously explosive accelerator-multiplier, and the ceilings and floors, to generate a time series. He then used these numbers to estimate the parameters of an accelerator-multiplier model. Instead of recapturing the parameters of the true model that led to the known explosive interactions, Blatt's econometrics yielded a set of parameters that generated a damped cycle.

Further, Blatt (1980) argued that the random shock theory is inconsistent with the evidence that the deviation of many economic time series from smooth, long-term trends shows a pronounced asymmetry; the increases tend to be longer than the declines, and the increases proceed at a slower rate than the declines. It follows that if the world being analyzed is known to be endogenously explosive with constraints that contain the tendencies to explode, the econometrics may nevertheless indicate that the world tends toward an equilibrium.

The method followed by Blatt is not beyond criticism.[14] Econometrics is not yet capable of discriminating among the various alternatives. To meet the challenge posed by Blatt's demonstration, new techniques for the analysis of economic time series are necessary. A start has been made on this problem by Brock (1986), who has developed a set of tests that can, in principle, distinguish between data generated by deterministic cycle models and data that are genuinely stochastic. The results are far from being definitive. One can say, however, that there is enough evidence to make nonlinear models worth pursuing. It is not important to ascertain whether or not these models are truly deterministic. In fact, they have both stochastic and deterministic elements. What matters is to identify particular kinds of nonlinearities capable of generating cycles, even in the absence of exogenous shocks.

6. New Developments

New developments in the mathematical tools have affected the sophistication of the models. The dynamic pattern can be so complex, that the term "fluctuations" is more appropriate than "business cycles." Processes of this type do not generate time series that fall into the categories of damped expansion, exponential growth, or cyclical patterns that linear systems generate. Such systems generate time series that can be identified as chaotic. In particular, there are two aspects that characterize these patterns. The first is that they are extremely sensitive to initial conditions. The second is that, although extremely irregular (or aperiodic), these fluctuations remain within a bounded region (in other words, they are dominated by a strange attractor).

Although there are many examples of studies that apply the new technique to the traditional macroeconomic models,[15] it is undoubtedly true that most efforts have been devoted to showing how "self-sustaining deterministic fluctuations, either periodic or chaotic can occur as a perfect-foresight equilibrium phenomenon in well-formulated models of competitive economies" (Woodford 1989, 309).

These kinds of approaches, therefore, use sophisticated nonlinear tools in some type of general equilibrium analysis, which is microfounded, but where imperfections are present. They can sometimes generate Keynesian results, and for this reason they are often called New-Keynesian.[16] For instance, Woodford (1989) presents a model capable of producing complex dynamic patterns because of asymmetry in the access to credit by households and firms.

There are two shortcomings that should be stressed. First, all the various examples seem to reduce to the same quadratic equation, which takes the form

$$y(t+1) = w\, y(t)\, [1 - y(t)]$$

(where w is a parameter), so that it is doubtful that general conclusions have been reached. Second, the most important theorems are stated for low-dimensional systems. For higher dimensions there is much work to be done.[17]

On the whole, one can say that these models have, undoubtedly, contributed to the revival of interest in the endogenous explanation of economic fluctuations. Furthermore, by making forecasts a difficult task, they help to overcome the criticisms raised against macroexplanations. It remains to be seen whether the fact that the time series remain within a bounded region makes the ceiling and floor approach an obsolete tool of analysis.

7. A Metaphor for Economic Instability

The developments just discussed do not exhaust the possibilities for reviving discussion of endogenous explanations for macroeconomic phenomena. Another approach reinterprets the models with ceilings and floors. If one views ceilings and floors as constraints that belong to the institutional sphere, then it is possible to maintain that the insight of that model is still worth considering. In other words, it is possible to talk about an endogenous instability process that is thwarted by the presence of institutional constraints. The impact of such constraints can be modeled through: Regime switching techniques (see Ferri and Greenberg, 1989)[18]; or new initial conditions, as in the accelerator-multiplier model previously discussed.[19] In this case, the simple accelerator-multiplier models, with constraints that reflect endogenously determined economic relations, are primitive examples that are valid only as illustrations or "metaphors" of what is at issue, namely the behavior of complex dynamic systems. These systems are dominated by the interplay between unconstrained and constrained processes.

These reflections characterize Minsky's latest research agenda, which can be summarized by the following points.[20]

Dynamics

Accumulation is a time-dependent process. This dependence goes both forward and back in time. Expectations-determined conjectures drive current commitments even as today's outcome either fulfills or fails to fulfill commitments made in the past. These linkages were considered in a reduced-form sense by models that studied linear endogenous deterministic business cycles.

Money

Monetary and financial considerations cannot be ignored for capitalist economies. This integration not only put Minsky's previous work on financial instability into a new perspective, it introduces new nonlinearities. Furthermore, innovation and technical change are economic phenomena that feed back upon asset values and affect production possibilities and investment decisions.

Thwarting Systems

Mathematically a model of such systems will be multidimensional, time-dependent, and nonlinear. In such complex structures a semblance of coherence can be achieved by appropriate interventions that can be interpreted mathematically as imposing new initial conditions or as changing parameters. Legislated or evolutionary changes in institutional arrangements can alter the reactions or parameters of these models. Incoherence can be thwarted by apt interventions and institutional structure.

Microfoundations

The formal proofs that there exists a competitive equilibrium that is Pareto optimal made it possible to insist upon microeconomic foundations for a macroeconomic model that generated a growth path. In this context, lack of microeconomic foundations becomes a defamatory charge. According to Weintraub (1979, 161), "there should be little argument about the proposition that some sort of revived, reconstituted general equilibrium theory is the only logically possible general link between microeconomics and macroeconomics. Those who argue that the analysis at present prejudges the issue fail to appreciate the variety of modern general equilibrium theory." From this perspective, any traditional macroeconomic model was declared "ad hoc," and its contribution to the endogenous explanation of the cycle was bound to be considered irrelevant.

To this criticism, one can say that microeconomic behavior does not necessarily mean neoclassical microeconomic behavior. One can consider microeconomic behavior in which economic agents are rational, but they recognize that the world they live in may not be fully rational. In particular, they seek their gains, not by maximizing genetically determined preferences with given technologies, but by using resources to affect technology, knowledge and preferences. Also the reliance on general equilibrium theory can be questioned. It cannot be considered as the "theory" par excellence. It is a copy of various modes of thinking in physics. Walras was quite clear that he was following the physics model, and the biological analogy of Marshall fell by the wayside. It follows that it is not necessarily true that every model other than one with a neoclassical microfoundation is an "ad hockery." In the context of endogenous preferences and technical change, it should be remembered that the fundamentals of most general equilibrium models are arbitrary themselves.

8. Market Forces and Institutions

In the "metamodel" we have been discussing, there are several points that merit further consideration. First, in the system there are "multipliers" and "absorbers," the former tending to create instability, and the latter favoring a tendency toward stability. Among these, particular emphasis has been placed on policies and institutions. One should not, however, neglect the role of prices,[21] in particular, and of markets, in general, in facilitating the working of the economy with some price flexibility.[22]

Second, even though the thwarting processes are analogous to homeostatic mechanisms, which may prevent a system from exploding, they are not mechanical. It follows that they differ among economic systems and change in time.[23]

Third, it seems obvious that if the economy is truly nonlinear and endogenously unstable, policy based upon the assumption that the economy is linear and endogenously stable is likely to be inept. The message is that a transitory semblance of stability is achieved by policy interventions and institutionally constrained behavior. However, units learn how policies and institutions affect the outcomes of their actions and try to adjust their behavior in the light of what they think they know.[24] The result is that the economy evolves, not in the great stages of Marx, but from one form of capitalism to another.

Fourth, thwarting mechanisms, which were devised to operate under certain circumstances, can contribute to create new instability. Economic instability as the normal condition of an economy implies that markets and institutions are, to use a phrase of Wesley Mitchell (1913), subject to stresses and strains. Furthermore, the opportunities open to agents change as such an economy transits through time. But stresses, strains, and changing opportunities imply that institutions evolve. Institutional evolution implies an irreversibility in economic processes; economies exist in historical time.

From the above it follows that:

> (a) political processes generate and sustain an economy's structure of intervention and containment; (b) the effectiveness of an institutional structure is likely to attenuate through time as agents learn how to evade and avoid the constraints and as the incentives to behave well become less powerful; (c) new institutional structures of containment and intervention are necessary periodically. (See Ferri and Minsky 1989, 138)

9. Concluding Remarks

The endogenous instability view of the economy in which institutional structures and interventions stabilize a potentially unstable world stands Lucas on his head.[25] It follows from this view that the dynamics of endogenous nonlinear systems lead to poor system performance. Apt intervention and institutional structures are necessary for market economies to be successful.

According to Minsky, this view is consistent with history, for essentially laissez-faire capitalist economies were failures almost everywhere in the 1930s, whereas the post–World War II capitalist economies that have been successful are big government interventionist economies in which market dynamics are often dominated by the impact of government.

What remains to be deepened is the relationship between these institutional changes and the problems now facing the world economy; namely the speed of technical progress, the inefficiency of state-run sectors or economies, and world imbalances, all of which necessitate dealing with a richer analytical framework capable of investigating them.

Notes

1. The book was *Stabilizing an Unstable Economy*, which appeared in 1986. This delay, among other things, has been underlined by Tobin's (1989) review of the book.

2. For a discussion of the two views, see Zarnowitz (1985).

3. This also holds true for the so-called real business cycle theories, which stress technological shocks. For a review, see Plosser (1989). For criticisms of these theories, see Mankiw (1989) and Henin (1989).

4. The necessity of linking growth and cycles belongs to the classical tradition and to Schumpeter. This necessity has been recently recognized also by real business cycle supporters. See, for instance, Plosser (1989). For a review of modern theories of endogenous growth, see Romer (1989).

5. *Is the Business Cycle Obsolete?*, edited by Bronfenbrenner (1969), represents the intellectual atmosphere about business cycles during the golden age growth years experienced by Western economies.

6. For an economic review of these theories, see Grandmont and Malgrange (1986). For more recent developments, see Barnett, Geweke, and Shell (1989). For a mathematical review for economists, see Baumol and Benhabib (1989). See also Gabisch and Lorenz (1987) and Ferri and Greenberg (1989).

7. In this formalization, we are following Minsky (1959), whose model is slightly different from Samuelson's (1939) original version. In this paper, we put the equilibrium solution equal to zero by dropping the constant in the consumption function. It is worth pointing out that in Minsky (1959) this constant could change according to financial considerations. This was yet another channel in which financial aspects could interact with real aspects.

8. In this model, the only possibility of obtaining harmonic oscillations is the presence of complex roots, which, however, imply unrealistic parameter values.

9. See Minsky (1959) where all the possible cases are explained in detail.

10. See Matthews (1959). The floor concept is even more debatable, both on empirical and theoretical bases. Furthermore, it has been demonstrated that either a ceiling or floor is enough to produce a nonlinearity. See Goodwin (1950) and Medio (1979).

11. It is important to stress that, according to Hicks's last book (1989), the old trade cycle (i.e., those crises that happened prior to the Great Depression) was a financial phenomenon where the Gold Standard provided a monetary ceiling to expansion.

12. For a discussion, see the essays edited by Goodwin, Kruger, and Vercelli (1984). It is important to stress that Minsky (1959) considered the possibility of developing a nonlinear model. For instance, if hitting the ceiling increases b, it can be shown that the minor root of the solution equation decreases, and this makes the conditions for steady growth easier.

13. See Adelman and Adelman (1959). The approach of linear models plus random shocks has been recently stressed by Gordon (1986).

14. For a discussion, see Brock (1988)

15. See, for instance, Day and Shafer (1986).

16. For this definition, see, for instance, Greenwald and Stiglitz (1987). For a discussion, see also Mankiw (1989).

17. Baumol and Benhabib (1989) examine difficulties of obtaining clear results for higher order and multivariate systems.

18. For a definition of regime, see Leijonhufvud (1987). The regime switch can be triggered by a threshold measured either in quantities (e.g., a level of employment) or in values (e.g., a real wage value.) For an example of the latter type, see Minsky and Ferri (1984).

19. There is a strict link between the various methods indicated. Jumps induced by changes in the prevailing regime fulfill the role of establishing new initial conditions. Regime switching, therefore, implies both changes in the initial conditions and in the values of the parameters. They can be considered a particular case of bifurcation theory, which can produce irregular dynamic patterns. Whether one should utilize these modern developments in the theory of nonlinearity or some indirect forms of nonlinearity is a matter of convenience. Furthermore, one can also introduce changes in the initial conditions with the use of nonlinear equations.

20. Some of these aspects have been developed in Ferri and Minsky (1989b).

21. The interaction between price and quantity adjustments and their impact on the stability of the system can be considered both in a classical framework (where it is called cross-dual dynamics) or in a Keynesian setting (where it is called dual dynamics). For a discussion of these points, see Flaschel and Semmler (1990).

22. According to Zarnowitz (1989, 2), " ... business cycles coexist with a broad range of behavior in labor and product markets, though they may influence, and be influenced by changes in that behavior. It is these interactions that should ultimately be of primary interest to students of macroeconomic performance and policy, not a postulated dichotomy of flexprice and fixprice models."

23. Some French economists have discussed "regulation." This concept, translated as "socioeconomic tuning," is defined as "covering the whole set of institutions, of private behaviors and of actual functioning of the various markets which channel the long term dynamics and determine the cyclical properties of the economy during an historical period for a given society" (R. Boyer and J. Mistral 1984). For further discussion, see also Piore (1987) and Ferri and Minsky (1990).

24. These remarks are the same as those made by Lucas in his critique of econometric models based upon traditional formulation of expectations. See Lucas (1987).

25. Minsky (1986) makes the same points without reference to the mathematical properties of nonlinear systems and within a specific model of profit generation in which profits are determined by the structure of demand.

References

Barnett, W.A., J. Geweke, and K. Shell. 1989. *Economic Complexity*. New York: Cambridge University Press.

Baumol, W.J. and J. Benhabib. 1989. "Chaos: Significance, Mechanism, and Economic Applications." *Journal of Economic Perspectives* 3: 77–106.

Blatt, J.M. 1978. "On the Econometric Approach to Business Cycle Analysis." *Oxford Economic Papers* 30: 292–300.

———. 1979. *Dynamic Economic Systems*. Armonk, New York: M.E. Sharpe.

———. 1980. "On the Frisch Model of Business Cycles." *Oxford Economic Papers* 32: 469–79.

Boyer, R. and J. Mistral. 1984. *The Present Crisis. From An Historical Interpretation To A Prospective Outlook*. Paris: Cepremap.

Brock, W.A. 1986. "Distinguishing Random and Deterministic Systems: Abridged Version." *Journal of Economic Theory* 40: 168–95.

———. 1988. "Hicksian Nonlinearity." Mimeo, Bologna, Italy.

Day, R.H. and W. Shafer. 1986. "Keynesian Chaos." *Journal of Macroeconomics* 7: 277–95.

Ferri, P. and E. Greenberg. 1989. *The Labor Market and Business Cycles*. New York: Springer Verlag.

Ferri, P. and H.P. Minsky. 1989. "The Breakdown of the IS-LM Synthesis: Implications for Post-Keynesian Economic Theory." *Review of Political Economy* 1: 125–43.

———. 1990 "Market Processes and Thwarting Systems." Mimeo, University of Bergamo, Italy.

Fisher, I. 1933. "The Debt-Deflation Theory of Great Depressions." *Econometrica* 1: 337–57.

Flaschel, P. and W. Semmler. 1990. "On Composite Classical and Keynesian Microdynamic Adjustment Processes." Mimeo. Workshop on Convergence to Long-Period Positions. University of Siena.

Friedman, M. 1968. "The Role of Monetary Policy." *American Economic Review* 58: 1–17.

Frisch, R. 1933. "Propagation Problems and Impulse Problems in Dynamic Economics." *Economic Essays in Honor of G. Cassel*. London: Allen and Unwin.

Gabisch, G. and H.W. Lorenz. 1987. *Business Cycle Theory*. Berlin: Springer Verlag.

Goodwin, R.M. 1950. "Non-Linear Theory of The Cycle." *Review of Economics and Statistics* 32: 316–20.

———. 1967. "A Growth Cycle." In *Socialism, Capitalism and Economic Growth*, C. Feinstein, ed. Cambridge: Cambridge University Press, pp. 54–58.

Goodwin, R.M., M. Kruger and A. Vercelli. 1984. *Non Linear Models of Fluctuating Growth*. Berlin: Springer Verlag.

Grandmont, J.M. and P. Malgrange P. 1986. "Nonlinear Economic Dynamics: Introduction." *Journal of Economic Theory* 40: 3–12.

Gordon, R.J. ed. 1986. *The American Business Cycle*. National Bureau of Economic Research. Chicago: University of Chicago Press.

Greenwald, B. and J.E. Stiglitz. 1987. "Keynesian, New Keynesian and New Classical Economics." *Oxford Economic Papers* 39: 119–132.

Henin, P.Y. 1989. "Une Macroeconomie sans Monnaie pour les Annees 90? Revue Critique des Travaux Theoriques et Empiriques sur les Cycles Reels." *Revue d'Economie Politique* 99: 531–596.

Hicks, J.R. 1950. *Trade Cycle*. Oxford: Clarendon Press.

———. 1989. *A Market Theory of Money*. Oxford: Clarendon Press.

Keynes, J.M. 1936. *The General Theory of Employment, Interest, and Money*. London: Macmillan.

Leijonhufvud, A. 1987. "Whatever Happened to Keynesian Economics—and Does it Have a Future?" Mimeo, presented at a conference in Siena, Italy.

Lucas, R.E. 1972. "Expectations and the Neutrality of Money." *Journal of Economic Theory* 4: 103–24.

———. 1987. *Models of Business Cycles*. Oxford: Basil Blackwell.

Mankiw, N.G. 1989. "Real Business Cycles: A New Keynesian Perspective." *Journal of Economic Perspectives* 3: 79–90.

Matthews, R.C.O. 1959. *The Trade Cycle*. Cambridge: Cambridge University Press.

Medio, A. 1979. *Teoria Non-Lineare del Ciclo*. Bologna: Il Mulino.

Minsky, H.P. 1957. "Monetary Systems and Accelerator Models." *American Economic Review* 37.

———. 1959. "A Linear Model of Cyclical Growth." *Review of Economics and Statistics* 41: 137–145.

———. 1975. *John Maynard Keynes*. New York: Columbia University Press.

———. 1982. *Can "It" Happen Again?* Armonk, New York: M.E. Sharpe.

———. 1986. *Stabilizing the Unstable Economy*. New Haven: Yale University Press.

Minsky, H. P. and P. Ferri. 1984. "Prices, Employment and Profits." *Journal of Post Keynesian Economics* 6: 489–99.

Mitchell, W.C. 1913. *Business Cycles.* Berkeley, California: University of California Press.

Piore, M. 1987. "Historical Perspectives and the Interpretation of Unemployment." *Journal of Economic Literature* 25: 1834–50.

Plosser, C.I. 1989. "Understanding Real Business Cycles." *Journal of Economic Perspectives* 3: 51–78.

Romer, P. 1989. "Increasing Returns and New Developments in the Theory of Growth." National Bureau of Economic Research. Working paper, no. 3098.

Samuelson, P.A. 1939. "Interaction Between the Multiplier Analysis and the Principle of Acceleration." *Review of Economics and Statistics* 21: 75–78.

Schumpeter, J.A. 1939. *Business Cycles: a Theoretical, Historical, and Statistical Analysis of the Capitalist Process.* New York: McGraw Hill.

Slutsky, E. 1937. "The Summation of Random Causes as the Source of Cyclic Processes." *Econometrica* 5: 105–46.

Smith, A. 1776. *An Inquiry into the Nature and Causes of the Wealth of Nations.* E. Cannan, ed. (Reprinted 1961) London: Methuen.

Tobin, J. 1989. Review of Minsky's "Stabilizing an Unstable Economics." *Journal of Economic Literature* 27: 105–8.

Vercelli, A. 1987. *Keynes dopo Lucas.* Roma: La Nuova Italia.

Woodford, M. 1989. "Imperfect Financial Intermediation and Complex Dynamics." In *Economic Complexity*, W. Barnett, J. Geweke, and K. Shell, eds. New York: Cambridge University Press.

Zarnowitz, V. 1985. "Recent Work on Business Cycles in Historical Perspective: A Review of Theories and Evidence." *Journal of Economic Literature* 23: 523–580.

———. 1989. "Cost and Price Movements in Business Cycle Theories and Experience: Hypotheses of Sticky Wages And Prices." National Bureau of Economic Research, Working paper, no. 3131.

CHAPTER EIGHT

Keynesian Theories of Investment and Finance: Neo, Post, and New

STEVEN FAZZARI

Investment theory has long been the subject of much economic research and a corresponding amount of controversy. One of these controversies centers on whether financial factors that are independent of the real productivity of an investment project influence the decision to undertake the project. The issue addressed in this paper concerns the relationship between new developments in research on the link between finance and investment, and the views advanced by traditional post-Keynesian and neo-Keynesian schools. In particular, do developments in what has come to be called the "new" Keynesian approach represent a convergence in any meaningful sense between post-Keynesian views and the mainstream intellectual progeny of the neo-classical synthesis in macroeconomics? Also, have the developments in new Keynesian economics advanced the post-Keynesian approach, or is the mainstream just rediscovering in a limited way what the post-Keynesians have known all along? We also shall speculate on what is yet to be learned from the various approaches that may advance their respective research programs.

A Brief Intellectual History of the Link between Investment and Finance

In the *General Theory*, John Maynard Keynes emphasized the central role of investment in the theory of aggregate output and employment. His ideas differed from traditional views at the time, and mainstream views that persist today in two fundamental ways. First, the importance of investment, not only resulted from its long-term effect on capital stock growth, but from Keynes' focus on investment as the driving force of aggregate demand and short-run fluctuations in economic activity. Second, Keynes rejected microfoundations of investment that were based exclusively on technological conditions of capital productivity by stressing uncertainty, finance, and monetary factors as fundamental determinants of investment.

The author is associate professor of economics at Washington University, St. Louis. He thanks Edward Greenberg for helpful comments.

121

One of Keynes' fundamental contributions was to develop conditions under which "money," broadly conceived, mattered for the real performance of the macroeconomy. This objective is evident in the theory of investment, in which financial and monetary conditions affect firms' capital spending. These insights spawned a rich theoretical and empirical literature in the decades following the publication of the *General Theory*. In particular, this work has been carried forward in the writings of Hyman Minsky, who has led what might be called the "financial Keynesian" school for about three decades.[1] This work emphasizes the essential role of financial influences on investment. According to this perspective, one could not hope to understand investment and, at the same time, abstract from the analysis of investment finance.

These ideas, however, have been much debated. In particular, economists working primarily in the neoclassical tradition have questioned whether purely financial factors can have an impact on a "real" phenomenon like investment. Such a result seems to contradict the optimizing foundations for microeconomic decision-making that characterizes the neoclassical perspective. The most prominent work on this approach is associated with Dale Jorgenson and his collaborators.[2] It grounds desired capital accumulation, and hence optimal investment, in the fundamental preferences and technology that characterize the economy. Purely financial conditions do not affect investment. Indeed, Jorgenson bases his results on the Miller-Modigliani theorem that shows the independence of real and financial decisions under some conditions.[3] Jorgenson's work also dismisses the financial effects found in other empirical research as spurious because of correlations between financial variables and neoclassical determinants of investment.

This view had important implications for the emerging synthesis of Keynesian results with neoclassical microfoundations. For if stable tastes and technology ultimately determined investment, one could dismiss much of the volatility of aggregate demand predicted by Keynes; Keynes' colorful concepts like "animal spirits" no longer played a useful role in understanding aggregate fluctuations. Under these circumstances, fluctuations in aggregate output were more likely to be predictable and they could be better offset by enlightened stabilization policy.

In the 1960s and 1970s, views about the links between finance and investment bifurcated into distinct schools of thought. The "post-Keynesians" maintained that the original insights of Keynes remained valid; instability in financial relations could cause volatility in investment and the macroeconomy. The more formal "neo-Keynesian" approach rested on optimizing models derived from neoclassical "first principles" that did not allow important links between finance and investment.[4] During this period, there was little common ground between the two schools of thought.

In the 1980s, however, a new and distinct macroresearch program emerged. It has become known, somewhat unfortunately, as the "new Keynesian" economics. The roots of this work lie, at least partially, in both the success and failure of the new classical macroeconomics of the seventies. On the one hand, the new classical approach places special emphasis on building models from first principles, consistent to the greatest possible degree with neoclassical optimization. This characteristic has been retained in most of the new Keynesian research. On the other hand, the implications of the new classical theories did not fare well empirically, leading some economists to resurrect Keynesian ideas in the mainstream that many new classical economists thought should be completely abandoned at the height of the rational expectations revolution.

The new Keynesian approach changes the environment in which agents optimize. The models explicitly recognize features of decentralized market activity that prevent the system from attaining the efficient general equilibrium results that characterize most of the new classical macromodels. The analysis goes beyond the sticky nominal wages or systematically biased expectations that underlie much of the neo-Keynesian view by examining more fundamental problems of market economies. Many of the problems center on asymmetric information between buyers and sellers in markets that prevents some of the efficient exchanges that would occur in equilibrium if all agents were fully informed.[5] These problems are sometimes referred to as "market imperfections." To the extent that this term connotes a secondary importance, *a priori*, of the problems addressed in the new Keynesian economics, it is misleading. One can judge the significance of these issues only after they have been subjected to serious theoretical and empirical scrutiny. Rather than being small flaws in an otherwise smoothly functioning system, these "imperfections" may be basic aspects of decentralized market economies that alter the operation of the economy in fundamental ways, an issue we shall return to later.

One of the most fruitful applications of these ideas has been to the study of credit markets. When agents have asymmetric information, many nontraditional results arise even though all agents act as neoclassical optimizers. For example, credit may be rationed, and interest rates may not equate the supply and demand for loans. Agents' access to funds may depend on their financial circumstances. More specifically, the ability of a firm to undertake an investment project may depend not only on the fundamentals of the project under consideration, but also on the firm's financial condition. Projects, in which firms would invest if they had sufficient internal funds, might not be undertaken if the firm must raise external funds to finance the project. These ideas provide a new foundation for links between financial structure and real activity.[6] This research program has led recently to new empirical work that reexamines the importance of finance for investment.[7] This approach has resurrected, at least in a limited way, Keynes' and Minsky's original view of investment and finance that had disappeared from mainstream neo-Keynesian research.

Aspects of the Keynesian Theory of Investment
and Their Emergence in New Keynesian Research

The theory of investment, regardless of one's perspective, is a rich and diverse subject. Therefore, to keep the topic manageable, the focus here is on two major aspects of the determinants of investment emphasized in post Keynesian research: lenders' risk and borrowers' risk. The following considers the way in which they have been addressed in the new Keynesian research to assess the degree of convergence between the post- and new Keynesian theories, and to suggest the direction of further developments. This focus is appropriate to the task at hand, although it necessarily abstracts from a large number of potentially interesting issues.[8]

Lenders' Risk

Keynes claimed that as investment spending rises, lenders become more reluctant to finance marginal projects. According to Minsky (1975), this risk is characterized as an increase of the marginal supply price of investment to firms—that is, the effective cost of investment includes not only the purchase price of capital goods, but it also incorporates the present value of the debt service commitments set up to finance the investment project. As the cost of external finance rises, the supply price rises.[9] Minsky argues that this kind of risk actually "shows up in contracts" when borrowing increases in the form of higher interest rates, collateral requirements, or other restrictive covenants in debt contracts.

On the surface, these phenomena look like risk-averse behavior on the part of providers of external funds. But, from a neoclassical perspective, the problems could be overcome by diversification if the only difficulty were risk aversion. Each lender should have only a small exposure to the idiosyncratic risk of any borrower. Individual firms should face an infinitely elastic supply of external finance at an interest rate determined in centralized securities markets. Firms, then, should undertake any positive net present value investment project, regardless of the mix of internal and external funds required to finance it. Financial conditions and investment are independent, consistent with the spirit of the Miller-Modigliani theorem.

This argument has received close scrutiny in recent literature. The financial irrelevance result rests fundamentally on the assumption that both borrowers and lenders have full information about the quality of the project and the character of the borrower. Suppose, on the contrary, that information is asymmetric and the quality of projects and borrowers is variable. If the same general equilibrium interest rate that cleared the market for external finance in the full information case were to prevail with asymmetric information, borrowers with poor-quality projects could behave opportunistically. They could obtain loans that they would not have been able to get if the lenders could determine the true probability of default. Lenders recognize this incentive, and, therefore, they charge a higher rate of interest to borrowers of all qualities when information is asymmetric.[10]

These circumstances forge a link between a firm's financial structure and its investment. Firms face a higher cost of external capital than their opportunity cost of using internal funds, because the cost of external funds includes a premium to compensate lenders for the risk of inadvertently funding bad projects. This premium creates a preference for internal funds, and firms may not invest in projects that require borrowing or new equity issues even though they would undertake them if they had sufficient internal cash flow.

It is important to note that this result requires more than just risky returns on investment. If projects are risky, but borrowers and lenders are symmetrically informed about the distribution of returns, expected profit-maximizing lenders would still finance all projects that have an expected positive net present value. As mentioned above, problems with risk aversion could be handled by diversification. Therefore, risk alone does not explain why financial structure is important for investment, in the sense that inadequate finance will prevent firms from undertaking otherwise desirable projects. Put another way, *imperfect* information (in the sense of uncertainty) does not provide adequate foundations for financial constraints; one needs *asymmetric* information. The latter provides the opportunity for borrowers to take advantage of lenders' information disadvantage, leading lenders to charge a premium for external finance.

This result is fundamentally different from predictions of the neoclassical theory predicated on the independence of real and financial decisions. One cannot understand real investment as ultimately determined by exogenous tastes and technology alone. It is possible that two firms with access to identical investment opportunities, from a technological standpoint, will reach different decisions about whether or not to invest in the projects depending on the firms' financial structure.[11] Despite the nonneoclassical characteristics of the results, however, the models developed in this literature retain the optimizing approach that is associated with neoclassical research.

Are these results Keynesian? Does this more formal (and more limited) approach add to the research on the investment-finance link in the post-Keynesian tradition? The answer is not obvious. But while many of the rich insights associated with the idea of lenders' risk may not be captured by these new models, I believe the problem of asymmetric information in markets for external capital is an essential element in the story. Furthermore, this problem is not an arbitrary "imperfection" tacked on to an otherwise standard model. Rather, it represents a fundamental characteristic of decentralized market economies.

Lenders' risk, unless it is an empirically trivial concept, involves an unwillingness of lenders to finance investment that a firm wishes to undertake. To assume, therefore, that such a risk arises when both borrowers and lenders have identical information about the profitability of investment implies that either the borrower wants to go ahead with a money-losing deal or the lender systematically forgoes what it knows are money-making opportunities.[12] Neither alternative seems to capture post-Keynesian ideas. Rather, an interesting theory should explain why it is fully rational for a firm to seek finance for investment, but for the providers of finance to refuse the request or charge a premium over their market cost of funds. A theory based on asymmetric information does so.

A legitimate criticism, however, of most existing models of credit markets under asymmetric information is that they do not adequately explain the sources of the asymmetry. Probably for this reason, participants from both sides of the debate question the relevance of the results. Those who criticize the new approach from the neoclassical "tastes and technology" perspective of financial irrelevance, claim that the basic assumption of asymmetric information is "ad hoc," with no foundation, itself, in optimizing behavior. On the other hand, from the post-Keynesian perspective, asymmetric information may seem to be no more than a minor flaw, incapable of supporting the pervasive critique of orthodoxy associated with the Keynesian revolution.

It is clear, however, that asymmetric information problems are likely to be fundamental, and empirically significant, in market economies. The inherent structure of decentralized markets includes the separation of agents and the lack of institutional structures that consciously coordinate the diverse activity of isolated individuals. Agents specialize in particular economic activities, and their informational advantages are specific to their circumstances. Indeed, some neoclassical economists argue most strongly that a great virtue of market organization arises from the fact that agents with different specialties need not be informed about the details of others' activities.[13] In a market system, we do not need to know the details of how wheat or cars or toasters are produced. We only need to know the market prices of these goods and the way these commodities satisfy our preferences.

Consider, however, the implications of specialization and information isolation for the functioning of financial markets. Entrepreneurs have informational advantages in developing new technologies and marketing new goods and services. Bankers and financiers specialize in financial intermediation. If an entrepreneur seeks funds from an intermediary to finance an investment project, the natural starting assumption to make is that the entrepreneur has more information about the project's prospects than the banker. The banker may be able to obtain some information from independent sources, but this activity is costly. The fact that intermediaries evaluate creditworthiness at all is evidence of asymmetric information. By specializing in these activities, intermediaries can reduce the extent of information problems between the primary borrowers and lenders—but at a cost. And there is no reason to believe that the information gap can be eliminated. To become fully informed would require that the banker become an entrepreneur, a condition that would undo the specialization that is fundamental to the productivity of the system.[14]

The upshot of these ideas is that financiers will be able to get full information about the projects they are financing only if the investor voluntarily reveals it. But it is impossible for this to happen because borrowers have an incentive to present their situation in the best possible light. This incentive is well understood by the lenders, and it leads to a rational skepticism that results in a wide variety of institutional features designed to safeguard the lenders' interests. These may take the form of equity participation arrangements, collateral requirements, restrictive covenants, or simply a premium charged for external funds that increases the cost to investors of external finance compared to the opportunity cost of internal cash flow. Any one of these outcomes links real investment to the structure of finance; they all indicate that Keynesian lenders' risk is evident as a result of asymmetric information. These asymmetries are not just minor wrinkles in an otherwise smoothly functioning system, nor are they arbitrary, "ad hoc" assumptions. They are inherent characteristics of decentralized market production.

Borrowers' Risk

Lenders' risk may be the most obvious manifestation of the intrusion of financial effects on real decision-making. Hyman Minsky has argued that lenders' risk can be directly observed in the characteristics of real-world financial arrangements. But the Keynesian and post-Keynesian view of the investment-finance link also encompasses a different and more subjective channel through which financial conditions have an impact on real decisions—borrowers' risk. Minsky describes this risk as "doubts in the mind of the entrepreneur," and argues that this is the only relevant financial factor if "a man ventures his own money" (1975, ch. 5). Similar ideas have entered the post-Keynesian literature through Michal Kalecki's (1937) "principle of increasing risk." This idea explains an increase in the marginal opportunity cost of investment, or, equivalently, a reduction in the marginal demand price for investment goods, "because the more of one's wealth tied up in a particular fixed investment, the more danger one was exposed to in the event of failure [or] . . . in case of a sudden need for liquidity" (Mott 1985, 7).

Again, while these ideas are intuitive and seem to characterize real-world phenomena, their significance is apparently reduced in a neoclassical environment. If borrowers' risk arises from entrepreneurs' risk aversion, then diversification seems to provide the obvious solution. Systemic, undiversifiable risk may affect the return that investors require to undertake projects. But the desire to avoid undiversifiable risk is ultimately rooted in exogenous preferences, and therefore does not change the tastes and technology view of neoclassical thought.

The insights of the new Keynesian approach, however, lead to different conclusions about borrowers' risk. We can demonstrate that the original Keynesian insight can be sustained in an optimizing framework without arbitrarily assuming that agents ignore opportunities to diversify their risks. The lack of diversification emerges as an optimal response to a realistic economic environment.

Much of the groundwork for this analysis has been laid in the previous section. The key insight again springs from asymmetric information between borrowers and lenders. As discussed above, this circumstance prevents external funds from perfectly substituting for internal funds. External finance will be more costly, if it is available at all. Therefore, to undertake a profitable investment project a firm's insiders may have to commit more of their own capital, either as a direct means to finance the project, or as collateral to obtain outside funds. This requirement forces entrepreneurs to forgo diversification opportunities if they want to invest. The more committed they become to particular fixed capital, the greater their exposure and the greater their risk.

This problem leads directly to "borrowers' risk" or Kalecki's "increasing risk" as a limitation on the expansion of investment. The limitation is not technological, but inherently financial. It can be overcome by increased availability of internal finance independent of changes in the technological characteristics of the project.

Conclusion: An Opportunity for Convergence?

Are the new Keynesian models just another entry in a line of "imperfection" theories that attempt to reduce Keynesian macroeconomics to a special case of neoclassical general equilibrium theory? The answer to this question is not clear. There is no doubt that the new Keynesian models share methodological features with mainstream neoclassical research. On the surface, this fact may not seem to further the influence of the Keynesian school. But the similarities between the new Keynesian approach and models of the "new classical" macro or "real" business cycle theory have more to do with form than substance. The new Keynesian theoretical models attempt to ground macroeconomic results in formal optimizing models. But Keynes and his more prominent followers never denied that agents optimize. The debate has focused, correctly in my view, on the environment in which optimization occurs.

At this level, the new Keynesian models, I believe, are more consistent with the views of post-Keynesians than anything that has come along in mainstream macro for decades. Whether one labels the information asymmetries that generate Keynesian results "imperfections" seems purely a matter of semantics. The important point is that these problems are pervasive in decentralized market economies, and that they give rise to fundamentally Keynesian results—financial relations matter for real economic activity.

The view of investment that emerges from these new models is unmistakably Keynesian in its empirical implications. Information asymmetries lead to a preference for internal funds over external finance. Since the most important determinant of fluctuations in internal cash flow and liquidity is undoubtedly the aggregate business cycle, these models immediately suggest a link between investment and the cycle unlike anything that comes out of the "tastes and technology" microfoundations of the neo-Keynesian synthesis. These insights may lead to more rigorous foundations for the accelerator, a much maligned, but empirically successful investment model. Of course, models with accelerator features return the multiplier concept to the mainstream and open the door to the possible need for stabilization policy. On a more theoretical level, these models explain aggregate fluctuations as an inherent aspect of market economies that is not tied to their technological characteristics, e.g., as in real business cycle theory. Fluctuations, rather, result from the economic structure of production.

Is there then some possibility for convergence between the bifurcated schools of thought? There are important aspects of the post-Keynesian approach that have yet to find their way into the mainstream thinking represented by the new Keynesian macroeconomics. For example, the fundamental role of uncertainty in the determination of investment is just beginning to appear in the mainstream literature. Yet, the ideas still remain somewhat removed from the view of chapter 12 of the *General Theory*.[15] Therefore, I would not claim that the new models incorporate the whole Keynesian story; much is yet to be rediscovered in the mainstream.

At the same time, I believe the post-Keynesian approach can gain insights from these new developments. The central role of information structure, for example, is implicitly in Keynesian and much post-Keynesian research. The new models emphasize and explore this issue and motivate new empirical research. The result has been a more convincing case for the proposition that financial influences on investment are of central importance. This cannot help but bolster a Keynesian world view validating the deep insights of economists such as Hyman Minsky who has refused to sacrifice reality to find a comfortable niche in orthodoxy.

These observations make the case that there is a basis for discussion between at least two of the three species of Keynesians: the "new" and the "post." There is reason to hope that the intersection of post-Keynesian interests and real-world empirical observation with the analytical and empirical tools developed primarily in mainstream neoclassical analysis can lead to important new insights into how the macroeconomy behaves. Both schools of thought have much to gain by taking the work of each other seriously.

Notes

1. These ideas are developed in a number of Minsky's writings. See, in particular, Minsky (1975, ch. 5). Other significant contributions in this area include Gurley and Shaw (1955), Meyer and Kuh (1957), Davidson (1972), and Eisner (1978).

2. Well-known papers include Jorgenson (1963), Hall and Jorgenson (1967), and the survey in Jorgenson (1971).

3. There are a number of reasons why the assumptions of the Miller-Modigliani theorem would be violated in realistic economic circumstances; e.g., nonneutral taxation. But these problems did not seem, at the time, to explain the kind of links between investment and finance emphasized in the work of Keynes, Minsky, and others in this tradition.

4. Further developments in macro theory pushed this conclusion even further. In the "new classical" macroeconomics, the nominal rigidities that gave rise to short-run Keynesian results in the neoclassical synthesis disappeared as a result of the combined assumptions of market clearing and model-consistent (rational) expectations. Of course, the new classical models maintained the tastes and technology approach already evident in Jorgenson's work. Therefore, investment continued to be understood in this approach as a real phenomenon, independent from financial influences.

5. Akerlof (1970) is a seminal paper in this literature, although his ideas were not applied to macro issues until later.

6. Representative papers include Stiglitz and Weiss (1981), Myers and Majluf (1984), Blinder and Stiglitz (1983), and Bernanke and Gertler (1990). A more detailed survey of these ideas which develops their particular relevance for investment, can be found in Fazzari, Hubbard , and Petersen (1988).

7. See Fazzari and Athey (1987), Fazzari, Hubbard, and Petersen (1988), and Kashyap, Hoshi , and Scharfstein (1991).

8. For example, I do not address the importance of volatile long-term expectations as emphasized in chapter 12 of Keynes's *General Theory*.

9. See also the discussion in Fazzari and Mott (1986).

10. This environment is similar to the conditions that can result in "credit rationing" in the model of Stiglitz and Weiss (1981). The particular approach described here is drawn from the formal presentation in Myers and Majluf (1984). The ideas are extended and many additional references are provided in Fazzari, Hubbard, and Petersen (1988).

11. The relevant aspects of "financial structure" go well beyond the availability of internal funds. Bernanke and Gertler (1990) emphasize the importance of "internal net worth" or "collateral" as theoretical determinants of a firm's access to investment finance. Various problems with debt finance and restrictive debt covenants are discussed by Fazzari, Hubbard, and Petersen (1988). Fazzari and Petersen (1990) show the empirical importance for investment of firms' stock of liquid assets. Minsky (1975) emphasizes the importance of "cash commitments" related to debt service as a limiting factor in obtaining external funds for investment. This idea is examined empirically by Fazzari and Mott (1986) and Fazzari and Athey (1987).

12. Two qualifications to this statement are in order. First, transaction costs might give rise to some preference for internal versus external sources of finance, but this is not the kind of problem that either the post-Keynesian or new Keynesian schools have in mind. Second, one might explain credit limitations on the basis of systematic differences in risk preferences between borrowers and lenders. But, as already discussed, it is hard to understand why diversification would not solve this problem, at least when transaction costs are low.

13. See, for example, Friedman and Friedman (1979).

14. See Bernanke (1983) and Calomiris, Hubbard, and Stock (1986) for related discussion.

15. Bernanke (1983) and Jones and Ostroy (1984) present models in which uncertainty about economic structure has real effects. Also see Ferderer (1988). A recent paper by Scharfstein and Stein (1988) models the "herd behavior" Keynes discussed in a formal optimizing model.

References

Akerlof, George A. 1970. "The Market for 'Lemons': Qualitative Uncertainty and the Market Mechanism." *Quarterly Journal of Economics* 85: 488–500.

Bernanke, Ben S. 1983a. "Irreversibility, Uncertainty, and Cyclical Investment." *Quarterly Journal of Economics* 98: 85–106.

————. 1983b "Nonmonetary Effects of Financial Crises in the Propagation of the Great Depression." *American Economic Review* 73: 257–276.

Bernanke, Ben S. and Mark Gertler. 1990. "Financial Fragility and Economic Performance." *Quarterly Journal of Economics* 105: 88–114.

Blinder, Alan S. and Joseph E. Stiglitz. 1983. "Money, Credit Constraints, and Economic Activity." *American Economic Review* 73: 297–302.

Calomiris, Charles, R. Glenn Hubbard, and James H. Stock. 1986. " The Farm Debt Crisis and Public Policy." *Brookings Papers on Economic Activity*, no. 2, 441–79.

Davidson, Paul. 1972. *Money and the Real World*. New York: John Wiley and Sons.

Eisner, Robert. 1978. *Factors in Business Investment*. Cambridge, MA: Ballinger.

Fazzari, Steven M. and Michael J. Athey. 1987. "Asymmetric Information, Financing Constraints, and Investment." *Review of Economics and Statistics* 69: 481–487.

Fazzari, Steven M., R. Glenn Hubbard, and Bruce C. Petersen. 1988. "Financing Constraints and Corporate Investment." *Brookings Papers on Economic Activity*, no. 1: 141–195.

Fazzari, Steven M. and Tracy L. Mott. "The Investment Theories of Kalecki and Keynes: A Study of Firm Data 1970–82." *Journal of Post Keynesian Economics* 9: 171–187.

Fazzari, Steven M. and Bruce C. Petersen. 1990. "Investment Smoothing with Working Capital: New Evidence on the Impact of Financial Constraints." Washington University Working Paper no. 149.

Ferderer, J. Peter. 1988. "Aggregate Parameter Uncertainty and Economic Fluctuations: An Empirical Analysis." Unpublished Ph.D. dissertation. Washington University, St. Louis, Missouri.

Friedman, Milton and Rose Friedman. 1979. *Free to Choose*. New York: Harcourt, Brace, Jovanovich.

Greenwald, Bruce, Joseph E. Stiglitz and Andrew Weiss. 1984. "Information Imperfections in the Capital Market and Macroeconomic Fluctuations." *American Economic Review* 74: 194–99.

Gurley, John G. and E.S. Shaw. 1955. "Financial Aspects of Economic Development." *American Economic Review* 45: 515–38.

Hall, Robert E. and Dale W. Jorgenson. 1967. "Tax Policy and Investment Behavior." *American Economic Review* 57: 391–414.

Hoshi, Takeo, Anil K. Kashyap and David Scharfstein. 1991. "Corporate Structure and Investment: Evidence from Japanese Panel Data." *Quarterly Journal of Economics* 106: 33–60.

Jones, Robert A. and Joseph M. Ostroy. 1984. "Flexibility and Uncertainty." *Review of Economic Studies* 51: 13–32.

Jorgenson, Dale W. 1963. "Capital Theory and Investment Behavior." *American Economic Review* 53: 247–259.

————. 1971. "Econometric Studies of Investment Behavior." *Journal of Economic Literature* 9: 1111–47.

Kalecki, Michal. 1937. "The Principle of Increasing Risk." *Economica* 4 (new series): 440–447.

Keynes, John Maynard. 1936. *The General Theory of Employment Interest and Money*. London: Macmillan.

Meyer, John and Edwin Kuh. 1957. *The Investment Decision*. Cambridge, MA: Harvard University Press.

Minsky, Hyman P. 1975. *John Maynard Keynes*. New York: Columbia University Press.

Myers, Stewart C. and Nicholas S. Majluf. 1984. "Corporate Financing and Investment Decisions When Firms Have Information That Investors Do Not." *Journal of Financial Economics* 13: 187–221.

Mott, Tracy L. 1985. "Kalecki's Principle of Increasing Risk and Keynesian Economics." Mimeo (September).

Scharfstein, David S. and Jeremy C. Stein. 1990. "Herd Behavior and Investment." *American Economic Review* 80: 465–79.

Stiglitz, Joseph E. and Andrew Weiss. 1981. "Credit Rationing in Markets with Imperfect Information." *American Economic Review* 71: 393–410.

CHAPTER NINE

Imperfect Information, Corporate Finance, Debt Commitments, and Business Fluctuations

DOMENICO DELLI GATTI AND MAURO GALLEGATI

1. Introduction

The influence of financial factors on investment and output is not emphasized in traditional macromodels implicitly rooted in the Arrow-Debreu general equilibrium framework. The Modigliani-Miller irrelevance theorem (Modigliani and Miller, 1958) provides a rationale for this modeling procedure by showing that internal and external funds are perfect substitutes in investment financing. This result, however, is valid if and only if markets are competitive, transaction costs are negligible, and information is freely available to all market participants. As Miller has recently pointed out:

> The view that capital structure is literally irrelevant or that "nothing matters" in corporate finance, though still sometimes attributed to us (and tracing perhaps to the very provocative way we made our point) is far from what we ever actually said about the real world applications of our theoretical propositions. Looking back now, perhaps we should have put more emphasis on the other, upbeat side of the "nothing matters" coin; showing what *doesn't* matter can also show, by implication, what *does*. (Miller 1988, 100)

If some sort of market imperfection exists, such as transaction costs or asymmetric information, the irrelevance theorem no longer holds, and financial factors occupy a central place in investment and income determination.

Dipartmento di Scienze Economiche, Universita' Cattaolica, Milan, Italy and Istituto di Scienze Economiche, Universita' di Urbino, Italy. We are indebted to Olivier Blanchard, Ben Bernanke, Steve Fazzari, Charles Kindleberger, Hyman Minsky, Franco Modigliani, and Lance Taylor for helpful comments and criticisms on the basic structure of the model presented here. Of course, the usual disclaimer applies. Domenico Delli Gatti wrote sections 1, 3, 5, 7, and 9 while Mauro Gallegati wrote sections 2, 4, 6, 8, and 10.

The relationship between a firm's liabilities structure and its investment decisions ranked high in the macroeconomic research agenda of the late fifties (Meyer and Kuh 1957; Duesenberry 1958). Since the early sixties the widespread acceptance of the Modigliani-Miller proposition has inhibited further research on this theme—shifting focus from the financial to the real determinants of investment activity, and laying the foundations of the neoclassical theory of investment e.g., co-authors Hall and Jorgenson (1967).

In the seventies, only the so-called "debt-deflation" school, rooted in the seminal contribution of Fisher (1933), and expanded by Kindleberger (1978), and Minsky (1975, 1982, 1986), has emphasized the role of financial factors in business fluctuations, implicitly discarding the Modigliani-Miller theorem. By working out his financial instability hypothesis based upon the changing weights of hedge, speculative, and Ponzi units in the financial structure of the economy during the business cycle, Minsky has outlined the analytical framework capable of supporting the historical evidence provided by Kindleberger.

The Fisher-Kindleberger-Minsky line of thought has represented the minority view for a long time in the profession. It is worth noting, however, that research interest in the macroeconomic effects of credit availability has somehow survived even outside the debt-deflation school. A case in point is Brunner and Meltzer's version of monetarism. In their analysis, a monetary shock sets off a process of portfolio substitution which is not limited to money, bonds and real assets as in the Friedmanian framework, but works its way through the whole range of financial assets. In particular, credit is not a perfect substitute for other securities and, therefore, has a specific role to play in portfolio adjustment. Focusing on the role of credit in portfolio adjustment, however, Brunner and Meltzer do not seem to recognize and fully appreciate the effects of credit on corporate investment and business fluctuations; i.e., through its impact on the financial balance sheet of the business sector which is the central tenet of the Fisher-Kindleberger-Minsky line of thought.

In the 1980s a considerable amount of research work has been devoted to the real effects of the changing financial structure of the economy. Suffice it to mention the work by Bernanke and Blinder (Bernanke 1983; Blinder 1987; Bernanke and Blinder 1988). This renewed attention has been fostered by the burgeoning literature on market imperfections and asymmetric information which has highlighted the weaknesses of the Modigliani-Miller irrelevance proposition (Fazzari, Hubbard, and Petersen 1988).

The macroeconomic implications of imperfections in the goods, labor and capital markets are of central importance in the "new Keynesian" research agenda (for surveys see Stiglitz, 1987; Romer 1988; and Rotemberg 1987). Menu costs (Mankiw 1985) and near-rationality (Akerlof and Yellen 1985) are basically responsible for price rigidities which can explain the amplitude and persistence of business fluctuations. In the literature on efficiency wages (Shapiro and Stiglitz 1984; Katz 1986) asymmetric information about the quality of labor services is at the root of the gap between the optimal wage for the representative firm and the market clearing wage. This information, therefore, explains wage rigidity and excess supply of labor at the same time. Finally, asymmetric information on the quality of borrowers is the reason for the gap between the optimal interest rate for the representative bank and the market clearing interest rate, and accounts for both interest rate rigidity and excess demand for loans, that is, credit rationing (Stiglitz and Weiss 1981).

So far, the new Keynesian approach has provided deep insights into the macroeconomic implications of nominal rigidities within a partial equilibrium framework. No attempt has been made, however, to build a full-fledged macromodel capable of retaining the basic results of the new Keynesian literature, with the notable exception of Greenwald and Stiglitz (1988a). In this paper, we outline a macroeconomic model whose fundamental relations have a distinct New Keynesian mark. In particular, financial variables, such as retained earnings and debt commitments, play a prominent role in investment determination due to the uneven distribution of information about the reliability of borrowers, and the performance of managers among participants in the credit and stock market, respectively.

General equilibrium in the markets for goods, bank loans, and equities leads to the definition of a dynamic path for the stock of debt, which, in turn, provides the endogenously determined dynamics for the level of output, the rate of interest and the price of capital assets. In other words, starting from the assumption of asymmetric information on the credit and equity markets, we are naturally led to link the endogenous dynamics of the system to the accumulation of debt. This approach bears a close resemblance to the theoretical perspective on business fluctuations of the debt-deflation school. By working out the implications of asymmetric information on capital markets, the new Keynesian literature can be used to resurrect the idea of financially determined, endogenous dynamics of the economy, typically stressed in the Fisher-Kindleberger-Minsky line of thought.

The paper is organized as follows. We will present the stylized balance sheets of the three types of agents in the economy (households, firms, and banks) and outline the basic structure of the model. Then we will focus on goods, equities, and credit markets respectively. Next we will derive the fundamental difference equation that describes the dynamic path of corporate debt, and provides the endogenous dynamics of income, the price of capital assets, and the rate of interest. That will lead us to examine a benchmark version of the model characterized by debt neutrality. From there, we relate the changing nature of the equilibrium dynamic path of corporate debt to changing values of the propensity to invest. Finally, we will provide some conjectures on the nature of business fluctuations, summarize the model, and draw some conclusions.

2. Agents, Assets, and Liabilities

We consider a closed economy with three types of agents: households, firms, and banks. Households demand consumption goods, money (deposits) and securities

Table 1

Sectoral Balance Sheets

Households		Firms		Banks	
Assets	Liabilities	Assets	Liabilities	Assets	Liabilities
M	W	K	L	L	M
EV			EV	R	

Note: M = deposits, E = equities, V = price of capital assets, W = wealth, K= nominal value of physical capital, L = bank loans, R = bank reserves.

(equities), and they are labor services. Firms supply (consumption and investment) goods, bank assets and equities, and they demand labor services and investment goods. Banks supply money and demand bank assets. For the sake of simplicity we do not consider taxation and government expenditure. The public sector, therefore, coincides with the central bank, which supplies bank reserves, the only type of high-powered money in the model. In the following analysis, wages and prices will be considered constant—an assumption that we would like to relax in subsequent refinements of the present work.

Our economy consists of five markets: goods, labor, deposits, bank loans, and equities. As usual in Keynesian macromodels, the labor market is "residual." Employment is a positive function of output, which, in turn, is determined by effective demand. In this framework, the real wage has no equilibrating role to play—we rule out full employment and assume that an excess supply of labor always prevails. Therefore, we will leave the labor market in the background and ignore it in the formal analysis which follows.

Thanks to Walras' law, in equilibrium we can neglect one of the remaining four markets. Contrary to the usual procedure, we will abstract from the market for money. Therefore, we are left with three markets: goods, equities, and credit. This modeling procedure aims at bringing the financial decisions of the firms to the fore. The key role played by decisions over the firms' liability structures in investment and income determination is ultimately rooted in the presence of asymmetric information in capital markets.

The balance sheets of the three sectors of the economy are represented in Table 1.

Households' portfolio consists of two assets (deposits and equities) so that portfolio choice depends upon the expected return on equities, the interest rate on deposits being nil by definition. This assumption is not restrictive. We could easily account for other private debt instruments in households' portfolios (e.g., short- and long-term debentures), and impose equalization of the rates of return by an appropriate arbitrage procedure. Since the final outcome of the analysis would not be dramatically affected, we will keep the analysis of portfolio choice as simple as possible.

As far as investment financing is concerned, we drop the traditional assumptions of perfect substitutability between internal and external funds and between bank loans and securities. Following Fazzari, Hubbard, and Petersen (1988), who, in turn, refer to the burgeoning literature on asymmetric information in the capital markets, we assume a "financing hierarchy" exists in which internal finance has a cost advantage over bank loans and the issue of new equities.

Investment expenditure is financed primarily through the flow of retained earnings that signals the performance of the representative firm, and makes the access to capital markets easier. For the sake of simplicity, we rule out the issue of new equities as a viable means of financing investment so that the need for external funds can be satisfied only through bank loans. This assumption is fairly restrictive, but can be justified as a consequence of equity rationing on the stock market (Myers and Majluf 1984; Greenwald, Stiglitz, and Weiss 1984). Due to asymmetric information between managers and external investors about the quality of firms, potential shareholders require a "lemons premium" to purchase the new equities of relatively high-quality firms to offset the losses they will face from supplying funds to low-quality firms (lemons). Of course, the lemons premium raises the cost of equity financing for good firms. By ruling out the issue of new equities, we are implicitly assuming that the lemons premium is prohibitively high, forcing firms to bypass the stock market and ask for bank loans to fund investment.

Moral hazard and adverse selection also occur in the credit market, due to asymmetric information on the quality of borrowers between banks and firms. Following the "new Keynesian" literature on asymmetric information in the credit market, we consider banks primarily as social accountants and screening institutions; that is, lending institutions specialize in monitoring borrowers through customer relationships. To stress this social function, we make the simplifying assumption that banks do not take part in the market for equities; that is, the asset side of their balance sheet consists solely of reserves and loans. In our framework, both the volume of bank loans and the interest rate are endogenously determined. We cannot rule out, however, the possibility of a credit crunch or, more generally, of credit rationing, which occurs when the banking system restrains credit availability due to a discrepancy between the optimal rate for the representative bank and the market-clearing interest rate.

3. The Goods Market

Consumption expenditure *(C)* depends upon current income *(Y)* and wealth *(W)* according to the life-cycle/permanent-income hypothesis. Wealth, in turn, is positively influenced by the price of equities *(V)*. Investment expenditure depends upon the price of equities, according to Tobin's q theory, and the flow of internally generated funds (IF), that is, retained profits net of interest payments. For the sake of simplicity, retained profits are considered a constant proportion θ of income (between zero and one), while debt commitments are the product of the (current) interest rate (r) times the stock of debt inherited from the past (D_{t-1}). The flow of internal finance, therefore, is defined as:

$$IF = \theta Y - rD_{t-1}.$$

In sum, aggregate demand is determined by the price of capital assets, current income, and debt commitments. An increase in the price of equities boosts aggregate demand through Tobin's q effect on investment expenditure and the wealth effect on consumption expenditure. For the sake of simplicity, and without any loss of generality, in the following we will overlook the wealth effect and assume that consumption depends solely upon current income.

An increase in income stimulates not only consumption, as usual in traditional macromodels, but also investment through the associated increase in retained earnings. Finally, other things being equal, an increase in debt commitments depresses investment by reducing the flow of internal funds available for expenditure on capital goods.

Adopting a linear functional form, we can write the consumption function as follows:

(1) $C = C_0 + cY \quad C_0 > 0, 1 > c > 0$

where:

$c \; = c_w(1-\pi) + c_d \pi(1-u)$
c_w = propensity to consume out of the wage bill
$\pi \;$ = profit share in national income
c_d = propensity to consume out of dividends
$u \;$ = retention ratio

In sum, the marginal propensity to consume out of current income (c) is a polynomial of parameters describing consumption patterns out of different types of income (c_w, c_d), income distribution π, and corporate financial strategy (u). The ratio of retained earnings to national income, denoted by θ, is the product of the retention ratio times the profit share in national income: that is, $\theta = u\pi$; while the ratio of dividends to national income, d, is the product of the payout ratio times the profit share; that is,

$d = (1-u)\pi$, so that $\pi = \theta + d$.

Table 2

Signs of the Coefficients of the GG Locus

	a_0	a_1	a_2
$s > i$	+	+	−
$s < i$	−	−	+

For the sake of simplicity, we assume that consumption patterns do not vary across different types of income; that is,

$$c_w = c_d = c'$$

Therefore, the expression for the aggregate marginal propensity to consume simplifies to:

$$c = c'(1-\theta).$$

The investment function is:

$$(2)\, I = aV + b(\theta Y - rD_{t-1})\quad a > 0, b > 0, 1 > \theta > 0$$

Therefore, corporate financial policy, as captured by θ, provides a link between the consumption and investment functions. Substituting equations (1) and (2) in the equilibrium condition:

$$(3)\, Y = C + I.$$

And rearranging terms, we get:

$$(GG)\, Y = a_0 + a_1 V + a_2\, rD_{t-1}$$

where :

$$a_0 = C_0 / (s-i)$$
$$a_1 = a / (s-i)$$
$$a_2 = -b / (s-i).$$

For notational convenience s stands for $1 - c$ and represents the marginal propensity to save, while i stands for $b\,\theta$, and represents the marginal propensity to invest.

Let (GG) denote the locus of the equilibrium triples (Y, V, r) for the goods

Figure 1. **The GG Curve**

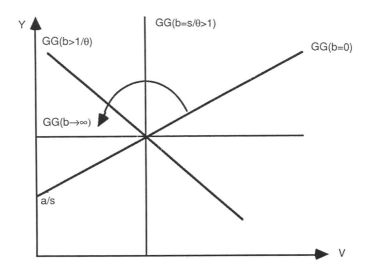

market. The signs of the coefficients of the (GG) equation depend upon the relative magnitude of the propensity to save (s), and the propensity to invest (i, see Table 2). The relationship between s and i depends upon the value of the parameter b; $s > i$ if $b < s/\theta$ and vice versa.

We can represent the (GG) curve on a (Y,V) plane by considering debt commitments (rD_{t-1}) as a shift parameter. When $s > i$ (that is, $b < s/\theta$), the GG curve is positively sloped. Other things being equal, an increase in V induces an excess of investment with respect to saving and therefore must be associated with an increase in output to keep equilibrium on the goods market. This increase in output stimulates investment less than saving and wipes out excess investment. This assumption is currently adopted in macromodels of the neoclassical-Keynesian synthesis, in which the income elasticity of investment expenditure is zero by definition; that is, $b = i = 0$ and therefore $s > i$.

Symmetrically, when investment is more income-elastic than saving (that is: $i > s$ or $b > s/\theta$), the GG curve is negatively sloped. An increase in V produces an excess investment and must be associated with a decrease in output to keep equilibrium on the goods market. An increase in output would stimulate investment more than saving, widening the gap between the former and the latter.

When $b = 0$, the GG curve has a positive slope equal to a/s. Given the marginal propensity to save, and the share of retained profits in national income, an increase in the income elasticity of investment (as captured by b) rotates the GG curve counterclockwise as shown in Figure 1.

We will define a situation in which $s > i$ as "normal times" or a "tranquil" era. By strengthening (weakening) saving more than investment, the process of income creation (destruction) set off by a demand shock converges; that is, the change in income resulting from the shock is finite—the system has a built-in self-stabilizing mechanism. On the contrary when $i > s$, an increase (decrease) in income following a demand shock feeds on itself in a spiralling boom (depression). Excess investment (excess saving) gets larger, magnifying the effect of the demand shock on output. In this case, destabilizing forces are at work—the system enters periods of "boom and bust." This source of instability is well-known in the Kaleckian literature, and has been repeatedly stressed by Minsky in his financial instability hypothesis (e.g., papers by Taylor and Semmler in Semmler 1989).

Of course there is no watertight separation between normal times and a period of boom and bust. On the contrary, the transition from the former to the latter (and vice versa) is essential to the development of business fluctuations. In our framework we cannot model a smooth transition between the two periods. In our section on business fluctuations, we will describe a stylized transition (given the propensity to save) by means of a jump from a relatively "low" to a sufficiently "high" propensity to invest, which, in turn, will be rooted in a change of the income-elasticity of investment activity.

4. The Stock Market

The demand for equities (E^d) is an increasing function of the expected return on equities. This is defined as the sum of dividends and expected appreciation. The flow of dividends is a constant proportion of income (dY), while expected appreciation is simply the difference between the expected and the current stock price $(V^e - V)$. As a first approximation, price expectations are assumed constant, an assumption that we plan to relax in future research. The expected stock price can be thought of as a weighted average of individual expectations over the future stock price. Households adopt a naive portfolio diversification strategy according to which the share of equities in total wealth is proportional to the sum of dividends and the expected capital gain; i.e., it increases (decreases) with income and decreases (increases) with the current stock price, and is expressed as:

$$(4)\ E^d = e(V^e - V + dY)\ \ e > 0.$$

Since households' portfolio consists solely of money (deposits) and equities, the portfolio choice sketched above implies that the share of money in total wealth decreases (increases) with income and increases (decreases) with the current stock price.

Equation (4) implicitly embodies a negative relationship between income and the demand for money, and a positive relation between the current stock price and money demand. An increase in income strengthens the flow of dividends and makes portfolio composition change in favor of equities, so that the demand

Figure 2. **The EE Curve**

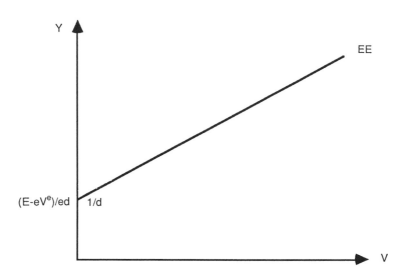

for money decreases. This is basically Blanchard's (1981) "good news effect." In our rationalization of the demand for money, therefore, the positive relationship between income and the demand for money arises because the transactions motive is weak enough to be offset by the good news effect, and, therefore, the monetary feedback effect is negligible.

As a consequence of the equity rationing assumption, we take the supply of equities (E^s) as given and constant:

(5) $E^s = E$.

Substituting equations (4) and (5) in the equilibrium condition:

(6) $E^d = E^s$,

and rearranging, we get:

(EE) $Y = b_0 + b_1 V$

where:

$b_0 = (E - eV^e)/ed$ and $b_1 = 1/d$.

Equation (EE) gives the locus of the equilibrium pairs (Y,V) for the stock market. The (EE) curve is positively sloped; an increase in the current stock price produces an excess supply of equities, and, therefore, must be associated with an increase in income. This in turn, stimulates demand to maintain equilibrium on the stock market (Figure 2).

In a regime of perfect foresight $(V = V^e)$, the demand for equities is a positive (linear) function of dividends (income):

$$E^d = e(dY).$$

Equilibrium in the stock market is brought about by a unique level of national income:

$$Y = E / ed.$$

The (EE) curve is perpendicular to the Y-axis on the (Y,V) plane.

When price expectations are given, investors stick to their expected future price no matter what happens to the current stock price. The simplest alternative modeling procedure links expectations formation to movements of the observed market price; that is,

$$V^e = V_0 + vV, \quad V_0 > 0, v > 0.$$

In this case the (EE) curve must be rewritten as:

$$Y = b_0' + b_1' V,$$

where:

$$b_0' = (E - eV_0)/ed \text{ and } b_1' = (1-v)/d.$$

If v is greater than 1, the (EE) curve is negatively sloped. An increase in the current stock price boosts price expectations and makes the expected capital gain larger. This stimulates demand so that income (and the flow of dividends) must fall to restore equilibrium on the stock market. In this case the expected future stock price overreacts to the current price. The mechanism of expectations formation rules out a capital loss in the future. Every increase in the current price is offset by a larger increase in the expected price so that a capital gain is expected in the future. The stock market is dominated by bulls and can well be characterized as euphoric. When $v = 1$, we are in the regime of perfect foresight discussed above. It is worth noting that when v is unity or larger—since capital losses are ruled out by the assumptions of euphoric expectations or perfect foresight—there is no rationale for "hoarding"; that is, for keeping money in households' portfolio in excess of a limited amount held for precautionary motives.

When v is less than one, expectations are essentially adaptive. The future expected stock price can be conceived of as a weighted average of the current and past values of the actual stock price. The parameter $v < 1$ is the weight of the current stock price, while V_0 stands for the weighted sum of past values of the actual stock price, with geometrically declining weights. In this case the (EE) curve is positively sloped. To simplify the analysis, in the following we will suppose that expectations are exogenously given. But the argument could be recast in terms of adaptive expectations and yield essentially the same results. Of course, both constant and adaptive expectations are inconsistent with stock market efficiency. Inefficiency is due not only to the uneven distribution of relevant information on the fundamental value of corporations listed on the stock exchange, but also to investors' short-sightedness in forming their price expectations.

5. The Credit Market

The demand for bank loans (L^d) is the sum of the stock of debt lagged one period (D_{t-1}), and the need for external finance (EF), defined as the difference between planned investment expenditure (I) and internal finance (IF). Equity rationing prevents firms from issuing new equities to fund their investment.

Internal finance, in turn, is equal to retained earnings (RE), less interest payments (IP). Therefore:

$$EF = I - IF = I - RE + IP = NEF + IP$$

where NEF (net external finance) is equal to external finance, less interest payments:

$$NEF = I - RE = EF - IP.$$

Following the definitions above, the demand for bank loans is:

$$(7)\ L^d = D_{t-1} + EF = D_{t-1} + aV + (b-1)(\theta Y - rD_{t-1}).$$

Given the stock of debt inherited from the past, the (flow) demand for bank loans (EF) is a function of the price of capital assets, income and the rate of interest. While a change in the price of capital assets brings about a change in the same direction of the demand for bank loans ($\partial L^d/\partial V = a > 0$), the income and interest rate elasticities of the demand for bank loans can be either positive or negative:

$$\partial L^d/\partial Y = \partial NEF/\partial Y = (b-1)\theta = i - \theta,$$

or

$$\partial L^d/\partial r = \partial NEF/\partial r + \partial IP/\partial r = -bD_{t-1} + D_{t-1} = (1-b)D_{t-1}.$$

The signs of the partial derivatives above crucially depend upon the value of b (see Table 3).

Table 3

Signs of the Partial Derivatives of L^d

	$\partial L^d/\partial Y$	$\partial L^d/\partial r$
$b < 1$	−	+
$b > 1$	+	−

Table 4

Signs of the Coefficients of the (LL) Locus

	g_1	g_2	g_3	g_4
$\theta > i$	+	+	+	−
$\theta < I$	−	−	+	+

Income affects the demand for bank loans through its impact on net external finance. An increase in income has a negative direct impact on *NEF* through the larger flow of retained earnings, and a positive indirect effect through the propensity to invest. When $b < 1$, the direct impact predominates: a change in income brings about a change of opposite sign in the demand for bank loans. Of course, just the opposite is true when $b > 1$.

The rate of interest affects the demand for bank loans through its impact not only on net external finance, but also on interest payments. An increase in the rate of interest has an ambiguous impact on *NEF*; it slows down investment activity, but it increases interest payments. When $b < 1$, the latter prevails over the former so that a change in the rate of interest brings about a change of the same sign in *EF*, hence in the demand for bank loans. Of course, just the opposite holds true when $b > 1$.

A well-behaved credit demand function shows a negative elasticity to income. In the traditional view, therefore, the propensity to invest is so low ($b < 1$) as to guarantee that $\partial L^d/\partial Y$ is negative. Firms are cautious and responsible borrowers—reducing their demand for bank loans when income goes up, that is, during the ascending phase of the business cycle (and vice versa).

In Minsky's terminology, the traditional view would predict reduced "financial fragility"—that is a decline of the relative weight of speculative and Ponzi units with respect to hedge units—during prosperous times. As is well known, with his financial instability hypothesis, Minsky conjectures the opposite; i.e., that financial fragility escalates during the ascending phase of the business cycle. Firms (and households as well) are bold and sanguine borrowers, whose finan-

Figure 3. **The Supply of Bank Loans**

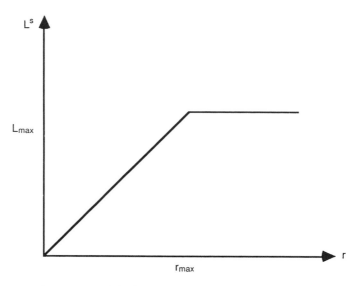

cial exposure is aggravated during the boom because prosperity boosts the entrepreneurial animal spirits and strengthens business confidence in the possibility of repaying their debt in the future.

Minsky's view translates into a "perverse" credit demand function characterized by positive $\partial L^d/\partial Y$. In our framework, this is the case when $b > 1$. Since b can be conceived of as a confidence parameter for the business sector, $b > 1$ is a clear symptom of an optimistic and confident attitude toward the future.

The supply of bank loans is an increasing function of the interest rate:

$$(8)\, L^s = R\, l\, r,$$

where R is the supply of bank reserves on the part of the central bank and $l\, r$ is the credit multiplier. Since banks' excess reserves are negatively related to the rate of interest on loans, the credit multiplier is a positive function of the rate of interest. For the sake of simplicity, we have represented this function by a linear approximation. The credit multiplier is bounded by the reserve requirements established by the central bank; that is, $l\, r < l_{max}$, where l_{max} stands for the credit multiplier when banks' reserves coincide with required reserves. This condition implies that the rate of interest is bounded; that is, $r < r_{max}$, where $r_{max} = l_{max}\, /\, l$. When the credit multiplier is l_{max}, the supply of bank loans is $L_{max} = R\, l_{max}$ (Figure 3).

Equilibrium in the credit market implies:

$$(9)\, L^d = L^s.$$

Substituting (7) and (8) in (9), and rearranging, we get:

(LL) $Y = g_1 V + g_2 D_{t-1} + g_3 r D_{t-1} + g_4 r$

where:

$g_1 = a / (\theta - i)$
$g_2 = 1 / (\theta - i)$
$g_3 = 1 / \ \theta = b / i$
$g_4 = -R \ 1 / (\theta - i)$

Equation (LL) gives the locus of the equilibrium triples (Y, V, r) for the credit market. It can be represented as a curve on the (Y, V) plane, provided we consider r and D_{t-1} as shift parameters. The LL curve can be either positively or negatively sloped, depending upon the relative magnitude of the parameters θ and i (see Table 4). These are, in turn, linked to the value of b. If $b < 1$, then $\theta > i$ and vice versa.

Other things being equal, an increase in the current stock price stimulates investment and creates an excess demand for bank loans. If $\theta > i$, to restore equilibrium in the credit market, income has to increase. In this case, in fact, since retained earnings are more income-elastic than investment, excess demand for loans will be reduced. Just the opposite holds true, of course, if $\theta < i$. Then, income must decrease to restore equilibrium on the credit market. In this case, in fact, an increase in income would strengthen investment more than the flow of internally generated funds, widening the gap between demand for and supply of loans. When $b = 0$, the slope of the (LL) curve is positive and equal to a/θ. Other things equal, an increase in b makes the (LL) curve move counterclockwise as shown in Figure 4.

A situation in which $\theta > i$ is "financially sound." By strengthening retained earnings more than investment, an increase in income reduces the demand for bank loans, and therefore, is beneficial to the financial situation of the firms. On the contrary, a situation in which $i > \theta$ is "financially fragile." In this case, in fact, an increase in income would boost the demand for bank loans by stimulating investment more than the flow of internal funds.

Because $\theta < 1$, it follows that $s = 1 - c'(1-\theta) > \theta$. Therefore, when $\theta > i$, it must be true that

$s > \theta > i.$

In this case both the (GG) and (LL) curves are positively sloped and the former is less steep than the latter. For the sake of symmetry, we will assume that if $\theta < i$, then

$\theta < s < i.$

In this case both the (GG) and (LL) curves are negatively sloped and the former is steeper than the latter. Therefore, normal times on the market for goods can be charac-

Figure 4. **The LL Curve**

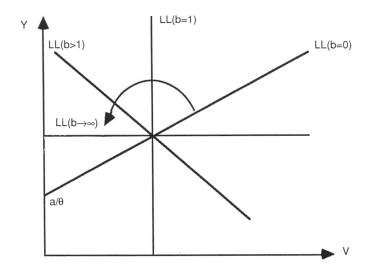

terized as financially sound from the viewpoint of the market for bank loans. On the
other hand, a period of boom and bust on the goods market is also financially fragile. In
other words, when a self-stabilizing mechanism is at work on the goods market, tranquil-
lity also prevails on the credit market. On the contrary, when destabilizing forces dominate the goods market, the credit market is prone to financial turbulence.

6. Macroeconomic Equilibrium and Debt Accumulation

The solution of the system given by the equations (GG), (EE), and (LL)
yields the equilibrium values of the endogenous variables (Y,V, r)—which
will be denoted by stars—given the stock of debt inherited from the past. The
triple $Y^*(D_{t-1})$, $V^*(D_{t-1})$, $r^*(D_{t-1})$ is the general equilibrium solution for the
goods, equities, money, and credit markets.

   In equilibrium, the law of motion of debt can be written as follows:

$$D_t = D_{t-1} + EF = D_{t-1} + aV^*(D_{t-1}) + (b-1)[\theta Y^*(D_{t-1}) - r^*(D_{t-1})D_{t-1}]$$

or, more simply,

$$D_t = R \, l \, r^*(D_{t-1}),$$

since the feasible debt of the corporate sector is equal to the credit supply. The
solution to this difference equation describes the dynamic path of corporate debt.
We can plug it into the general equilibrium triple (Y^*,V^*, r^*) to determine the
endogenous dynamics of income, the price of capital assets, and the rate of

interest. In our framework, therefore, the accumulation of debt is ultimately responsible for the equilibrium dynamics of each and every endogenous variable.

Following the procedure outlined so far, and after a little algebra, we end up with a nonlinear first-order difference equation:

$$(10) \; D_t = (d_2 + d_0 D_{t-1})/(d_0 + d_1 D_{t-1})$$

where

$$d_0 = R \, l \, e \, [(s-i) - ad]$$
$$d_1 = e[s(b-1) + ad]$$
$$d_2 = R \, l \, \{C_0 e \, [(\theta-i) - ad] - (s-\theta)a(E - eV^e)\}.$$

Solving equation (10) for $D_t = D_{t-1}$ yields the steady state solution:

$$D^* = (d_2/d_1)^{1/2}.$$

The dynamic path of debt accumulation converges to the steady state (either monotonically or through damped oscillations)—that is, the system is stable—if the absolute value of dD_t/dD_{t-1} is less than unity (in the steady state), where:

$$dD_t/dD_{t-1} = (d_0^2 - d_2 d_1)/(d_0 + d_1 D_{t-1})^2.$$

Otherwise, the system is unstable; the dynamic path of debt accumulation diverges from the steady state (either monotonically or with explosive oscillations).

Equation (10), therefore, has essentially the same set of solutions as a linear first-order difference equation. The nonlinearity of equation (10) is not sufficient to bring about a richer set of solutions. This result is partly due to the restrictive assumptions we made to keep the model as simple as possible. First, we have linearized some inherently nonlinear relationships (see the credit multiplier, for instance). Second, to speed up the solution of the system we have defined interest payments as the product of the current interest rate times the stock of debt of the previous period. The relaxation of these simplifying assumptions would presumably generate a richer set of dynamic paths, but would also blur the basic results of the model.

7. Debt Neutrality

When the Modigliani-Miller irrelevance proposition holds true, there is no financing hierarchy. The flow of internally generated funds does not impinge upon investment activity. In our framework, this is the case when $b = 0$, which implies that $I = aV$; investment activity is entirely explained by Tobin's q theory.

When $b = 0$, the (GG) curve becomes:

(GG) $Y = a_0 + a_1 V$,

where

$a_0 = C_0/s$, and
$a_1 = a/s$.

The parameter b does not affect the (EE) curve, which is here reproduced for convenience:

(EE) $Y = b_0 + b_1 V$,

where

$b_0 = (E - e V^e)/ed$, and
$b_1 = 1/d$.

Finally, the market for bank loans is in equilibrium if:

(11) $R \, l \, r = D_{t-1} + aV - \theta Y + r D_{t-1} = (1+r) D_{t-1} + NEF$

where $NEF = aV - \theta Y$. By algebraic manipulation of equation (11) we get the (LL) curve:

(LL) $Y = g_1 V + g_2 (1+r) D_{t-1} + g_4 \, r$

where

$g_1 = a/\theta$,
$g_2 = 1/\theta$, and
$g_4 = -Rl/\theta$.

The system (GG), (EE), and (LL) is now block-recursive. Equations (GG) and (EE) form an independent subset of equations which can be solved for the equilibrium values of income and the price of capital assets. The pair (Y^*, V^*) that clears the goods, equities, and money markets is not affected by developments on the credit market (unless a credit crunch occurs, see below). This is a regime of debt neutrality.

Of course the converse is not true. Developments on the goods, equities, and money markets do have effects on equilibrium in the market for bank loans. In fact, the equilibrium pair (Y^*, V^*) is necessary to solve equation (11) for the

Figure 5. **Equilibrium in the Goods, Equities, and Money Markets when b=0**

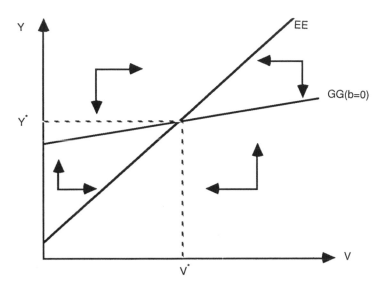

equilibrium interest rate (r^*), and determine the endogenous dynamics of debt. At first sight, equation (11) seems a superfluous extension of the (GG) and (EE) subset of equations, which is a self-contained static model of the goods, equities, and money markets. In our framework, however, equation (11) plays the crucial role of disclosing the hidden dynamics of debt embedded in traditional macromodels, which is clearly at odds with their static nature.

Solving (GG) and (EE) for Y and V, we get the equilibrium values of income and the price of capital assets:

$$Y^* = [C_0e - a(E - eV^e)]/(s - ad)$$
$$V^* = [C_0ed - s(E - eV^e)]/(s - ad).$$

It can be easily ascertained that to guarantee stability of equilibrium, the marginal propensity to save must be high enough; that is, $s > ad$. Otherwise the equilibrium is a saddle point. Geometrically, the (EE) curve must be steeper than the (GG) curve, both curves being upward sloping (see Figure 5). In the following we will assume that this stability requirement is always fulfilled.

The equilibrium pair (Y^*, V^*) determines the equilibrium volume of net external finance (NEF^*):

$$NEF^* = [C_0e(ad - \theta) - (E - eV^e)(s-\theta)]/(s - ad).$$

We can then plug NEF^* into equation (11) and solve for the rate of interest:

$$r^* = (NEF^* + D_{t-1})/(R! - D_{t-1}).$$

Figure 6. **Phase Diagram of Equation (10) when b=0**

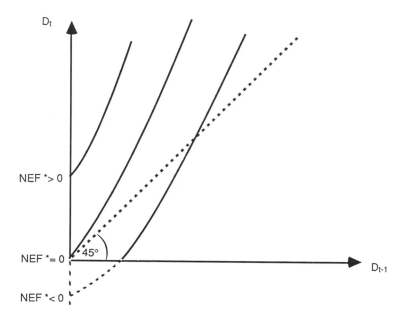

The law of motion of debt, therefore, becomes:

(12) $D_t = R \, l(NEF^* + D_{t-1})/(R \, l - D_{t-1})$.

The phase diagram of equation (12) is shown in Figure 6. A steady state can be computed only if $NEF^* < 0$ (that is, investment expenditure is smaller than the flow of retained earnings), but it is unstable. If $NEF^* \geq 0$, an explosive growth of debt occurs which the banking system accommodates through a parallel increase of the interest rate on loans until excess reserves are available. When the required stock of debt exceeds the maximum credit supply ($L_{max} = R \, l_{max}$), a credit crunch occurs which will force firms to revise their investment plans to take into account the available sources of funds. Of course, in this case, the interest rate has also reached its maximum.

In this case the flow supply of external finance provided by the banking system is given by:

$L_{max} - D_{T-1}$

where T is the time period in which the credit crunch has occurred. Firms cannot carry out investment expenditure in excess of the sum of the internally generated cash flow and the fixed flow supply of bank loans. Hence, the investment equation must be rewritten as follows:

$(2') \, I = (\theta Y - r_{max}D_{T-1}) + (L_{max} - D_{T-1}) = \theta Y + L_{max} - (1 + r_{max})D_{T-1}$.

Figure 7. **Equilibrium in the Goods, Equities, and Money Markets when a Credit Crunch Occurs**

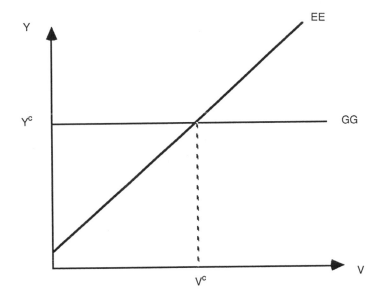

Substituting (1) and (2′) in (3) we get equilibrium income:

$$Y^c = [C_0 + L_{max} - (1 + r_{max})D_{T-1}]/[1 - (c + \theta)].$$

The expression above can be thought of as the equation of the (GG) curve in a credit crunch, which is a straight line perpendicular to the Y-axis. The (EE) curve can then be used to determine the equilibrium value of V (Figure 7):

$$V^c = (d/e) Y^c + V^e - (E/e).$$

8. The Propensity to Invest and the Nature of Equilibrium

In our framework when $b = 0$, the goods, equities and money markets are locked in a static equilibrium, while an explosive growth of debt occurs with no effects on the real side of the economy—until a credit crunch occurs. This representation of the macroeconomic system is implausible, but consistent with a benchmark configuration of behavioral parameters according to which firms do not look at their balance sheets when planning their investments and banks do not care about the reliability of their customers and are eager to accommodate the required stock of corporate debt.

When $b > 0$, the Modigliani-Miller irrelevance proposition no longer holds true. Firms take their liability structure into account as they choose their investment expenditure. When the propensity to invest is close to zero, firms' financial

Table 5

Signs of the Coefficients of Equation (10)

	d_0	d_1	d_2	Dynamics
$0 < b < 1-ad/\theta$	+	−	−	Unstable S.S.
$1-ad/\theta < b < 1-ad/s$	+	−	+	Explosive
$1-ad/s < b < (s-ad)/\theta$	+	+	+	Stable S.S.
$(s-ad)/\theta < b$	−	+	+	Unstable S.S

awareness is insufficient to stabilize the growth of debt; that is, to reverse the nature of the endogenous dynamics of debt accumulation with respect to the benchmark configuration of parameters examined in the previous section. In fact, when

$$0 < b < 1-ad/s,$$

the signs of the parameters of equation (10) are such that its solution yields an unstable steady state (the dynamic path diverges—either monotonically or by means of explosive oscillations—from the steady state) or describes an explosive growth of corporate debt.

When the propensity to invest is not "too low," firms pay enough attention to their balance sheets and ease the demand pressure on the market for bank loans slowing down the growth of debt. In fact, when

$$1 - ad/s < b < (s - ad)/\theta,$$

the dynamic path converges—either monotonically or by means of damped oscillations—to the following (positive) steady state:

$$D^* = R\, l\{-(s-\theta)a(E - eV^e) + C_0 e[(i-\theta) + ad]\}/e[s(b-1) + ad].$$

When the propensity to invest becomes "too high," the stabilizing effect of an increasing financial awareness is bound to be reversed. Firms' investment expenditures overreact, so to speak, to the flow of internally generated funds. In fact, when $b > (s-ad)/\theta$, the solution of equation (10) yields an unstable steady state or describes an explosive growth of corporate debt (Table 5).

9. Some Conjectures on Business Fluctuations

The set of solutions of equation (10) is not apt to mimic the stylized dynamics of the business cycle. In particular, it is not suitable to model and endogenously explain the turning points of the cycle. Nevertheless, it can help in forming some useful conjectures about the nature of business fluctuations.

Figure 8. **Effects of a Decrease in Debt Commitments ($r_2D_1 < r_1D_0$)**
when $1 - (ad/\theta) < b < (s\text{-}ad/\theta)$

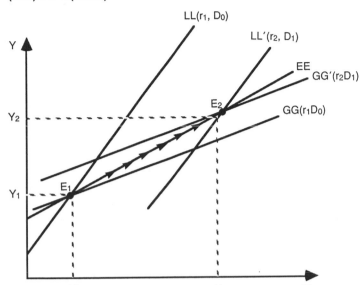

During a period of growing investment, income increases through the usual Keynesian multiplier. The growth of income boosts retained profits which, in turn, have a positive feedback on investment. If the configuration of behavioral parameters, however, describes a tranquil and financially sound era ($s > \theta > i$), retained earnings and households' savings increase more than investment expenditure, reducing the need for external finance. A decrease of the interest rate ensues, and the burden of debt commitments becomes lighter. As far as the market for equities is concerned, the positive impact of the increase in dividends on the return on equities pushes up demand and the price of capital assets.

This scenario describes a virtuous circle in which the growth of investment, income, cash flow, and the price of capital assets is paralleled by the decline of the interest rate, the stock of debt, and debt commitments. We will label this situation a *safe expansion*. Geometrically, the dynamic process is represented by the arrows in Figure 8. When b is neither too low nor too high,

$$(1 - ad/\theta < b < (s - ad)/\theta),$$

then the (LL) curve is steeper than the (EE) curve, which, in turn, is steeper than the (GG) curve, all the schedules being upward-sloping. A decrease in debt commitments can be captured by an upward shift of the (GG) curve and a downward shift of the (LL) curve, the (EE) schedule being unaffected by changes in interest payments. The equilibrium point moves northeast along the (EE) curve. From a quick inspection of Table 5, we infer that the dynamic process (in the chosen range of values) is explosive if the propensity to invest is relatively low,

1 − ad/θ < b < 1 − ad/s,

while it converges to the steady state if the propensity to invest is relatively high,

(1 − ad/s < b < (s − ad)/θ).

Inasmuch as the increasing cash flow stimulates investment expenditure, we can determine a transition to a different structure of parameters, which characterizes a financially fragile boom: $i > s > θ$. In other words, we imagine a jump in the sensitivity of investment to cash flow, measured by our parameter b. Income keeps going up through the ever-increasing excess investment in a spiraling boom of profits and capital accumulation. Therefore, the need for external finance goes up, and the same is true of the interest rate. Moreover, the booming price of capital assets strengthens investment and the demand for bank loans. This scenario describes a vicious circle of growing indebtedness paralleling the growth of investment, income, and the price of equities, which will be labeled *fragile expansion*. Note that a fragile expansion is the counterpart in a fix-price framework of the "credit-inflation," discussed at length in the monetary literature on business fluctuations of the 1920s and 1930s, whose roots are to be found in Wicksell's pioneering work on the credit cycle.

Geometrically, the dynamic process is represented by the arrows in Figure 9. When b is greater than $s/θ > 1$, both the (GG) and (LL) curves are negatively sloped, and the former is steeper than the latter. An increase in debt commitments can be captured by an upward shift of both the (GG) and (LL) curves along the (EE) schedule. The equilibrium point moves northeast along the (EE) curve. From Table 5 we know that, in this case, the steady state is unstable.

When the flow of retained earnings does not succeed in catching up with the growing burden of debt commitments, a turning point in the business cycle is likely to occur. If the euphoric and financially fragile structure of parameters $(i > s > θ)$ remains unaffected by the change in the nature of the fluctuation, the recession will be the mirror image of the fragile expansion; that is, it will be characterized by the decline in investment, income, the price of capital assets, and debt—a situation that we can label a *safe recession*. It is worth noting that the decreasing volume of debt commitments is a common feature of both a safe recession and a safe expansion. A safe recession, however, is brought about by a euphoric and financially fragile structure of parameters, while a safe expansion is associated with a tranquil and financially sound configuration of parameters.

It seems likely that after the turning point of the cycle has been passed, a pessimistic change will occur in the entrepreneurial state of confidence, which can be captured by a drop in our parameter b and, eventually, by a change in the structure of parameters. If this is the case, the recession will be characterized by the tranquil and financially sound structure of parameters: $s > θ > i$. This change in the mood of entrepreneurs would have far-reaching and paradoxi-

Figure 9. **Effects of an increase in Debt Commitments ($r_2 D_1 > r_1 D_0$)
when $b > s/\theta > 1$**

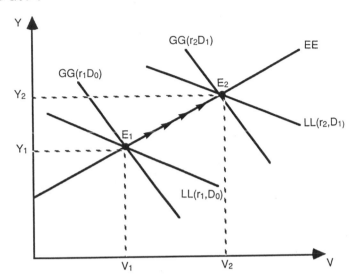

cal implications. The decline of income, in fact, would bring about a greater decrease in retained earnings than the decline in investment and would, therefore, increase the need for external finance.

In other words, by adopting a more cautious investment strategy to reduce indebtedness, entrepreneurs would worsen the financial situation of their firms. This is clearly a metaphor for the process of "selling positions in order to make positions," repeatedly described by Minsky. This scenario describes what could be called a *fragile recession*. It is worth noting that the increasing volume of debt commitments is a common feature of both a fragile recession and a fragile expansion. A fragile recession, however, is brought about by a tranquil and financially sound structure of parameters, while a fragile expansion is associated with a euphoric and financially fragile structure of parameters. A fragile recession is the counterpart in a fix-price framework of the "debt-deflation" discussed by Fisher (1933).

Only when the (declining) investment expenditure falls short of the (declining) internal funds will the lower turning point of the cycle occur. It goes without saying that, during the recovery, the macroeconomic system will feature a safe expansion and, subsequently, will pass through the stages of the business cycle discussed so far and summarized in Table 6.

This analysis holds true when both the interest rate and the supply of credit and money are endogenously determined. If asymmetric information prevails, the optimal interest rate for the banking system may be different from the market-clearing interest rate, and, therefore, the demand for bank loans can exceed the optimal supply. In this case the system is locked in a credit-rationing trap, which can be formally dealt with along the lines of the credit crunch discussed in section 6.

Table 6

A Taxonomy of Business Fluctuations

Stage	Structure of Parameters
Safe Expansion (Recovery)	Tranquil and Financially Sound: $s > \theta > i$
Fragile Expansion	Euphoric and Financially Fragile: $i > s > \theta$
Safe Recession	Euphoric and Financially Fragile: $i > s > \theta$
Fragile Recession (Depression)	Tranquil and Financially Sound: $s > \theta > i$

10. Conclusions

In this paper we have analyzed the structure and the dynamic behavior of a macroeconomic model with asymmetric information and imperfect competition. While the latter is responsible for the stickiness of wages and prices, the former determines a financing hierarchy which plays a crucial role in investment and income determination.

The law of motion of corporate debt provides the endogenous dynamics of the values of income, the price of capital assets, and the rate of interest which simultaneously clear the goods, equities, and credit markets. We can figure out a benchmark model, characterized by zero income-elasticity of investment, in which the Modigliani-Miller irrelevance proposition holds true and debt is neutral. It is easy to show that, in this case, the system is dynamically unstable.

The same conclusion holds if the propensity to invest is positive but extremely low; that is, relatively close to zero. There is a range of values of the propensity to invest, however, which stabilizes the growth of debt: if the propensity to invest is neither "too low" nor "too high," the dynamic path of debt converges to a long-run equilibrium position. Finally, if the propensity to invest becomes too high, a regime switch occurs: the system becomes dynamically unstable as it was when the propensity to invest was too low.

The nature of business fluctuations is determined by the interaction between retained earnings and debt commitments. We have devised a tentative taxonomy of business fluctuations in which a safe recovery is followed by a financially fragile boom, and a safe recession is followed by a financially fragile depression. Further research should be devoted to the implications of stochastic shocks to aggregate demand. The model features the "infinite memory" property which characterizes, for instance, real business cycle models, but for eminently different reasons. In our model, a typically financial process (the accumulation of corporate debt), embodies the history of the macroeconomic system, while in the real business cycle models, the infinite memory property is rooted in technological change.

Our analysis of business fluctuations is based upon the lack of a central coordinating mechanism capable of preventing the rate of debt accumulation from overcoming that of capital. In this context, income and unemployment fluctuations cannot be conceived of as the reaction of a system—otherwise stable—to exogenous impulses. On the contrary, they are the normal way of functioning for a decentralized economy with capital and debt accumulation.

References

Akerlof, George and Janet Yellen. 1985. "A Near-Rational Model of the Business Cycle with Wage and Price Inertia." *Quarterly Journal of Economics* 100: 823–38.

Ball Lawrence, N.Gregory Mankiw, and David Romer. 1988. "The New Keynesian Economics and the Output-Inflation Trade-off." *Brookings Papers on Economic Activity* no. 1, pp. 1–65.

Bernanke, Ben. 1983. "Nonmonetary Effects of the Financial Crisis in the Propagation of the Great Depression." *American Economic Review* 73: 257–76.

Bernanke, Ben and Alan Blinder. 1988. "Credit, Money and Aggregate Demand." *American Economic Review* 78: 435–39.

Blanchard, Olivier. 1981. "Output, the Stock Market and Interest Rates." *American Economic Review* 71.

Blanchard, Olivier and Stanley Fisher. 1989. *Lectures on Macroeconomics*. Cambridge, Massachusetts: MIT .

Duesenberry, James. 1958. *Business Cycles and Economic Growth*. London: McGraw Hill.

Fazzari, Steven, R. Glenn Hubbard, and Bruce Petersen. 1988. "Financing Constraints and Corporate Investment." *Brookings Paper on Economic Activity* no. 1, pp. 141–95.

Fisher, Irving. 1933. "The Debt-Deflation Theory of Great Depressions." *Econometrica* 1: 337–57.

Greenwald, Bruce and Joseph Stiglitz. 1988a. "Imperfect Information, Finance Constraints, and Business Fluctuation." In *Finance Constraints, Expectations and Macroeconomics*, M. Kohn, and S. Tsiang, eds. Oxford, England: Oxford University Press.

———. 1988b. "Money, Imperfect Information and Economic Fluctuations." In *Finance Constraints, Expectations and Macroeconomics*, M. Kohn, and S. Tsiang, eds. Oxford, England: Oxford University Press.

———. 1988c. "Financial Market Imperfections and Business Cycles." National Bureau of Economic Research. Working Paper no. 2494.

Greenwald, Bruce, Joseph Stiglitz, and Andrew Weiss. 1984. "Informational Imperfections in the Capital Market and Macroeconomic Fluctuations." *American Economic Review* 74.

Hall, Robert and Dale Jorgenson. 1967. "Tax Policy and Investment Behaviour." *American Economic Review* 57: 391–414.

Katz, Lawrence. 1986. "Efficiency Wage Theories: A Partial Evaluation." *Macroeconomics Annual*. Cambridge, Massachusetts: National Bureau of Economic Research.

Kindleberger, Charles. 1978. *Manias, Panics and Crashes*. New York: Basic Books.

Kohn, M. and Tsiang, S. 1988. *Finance Constraints, Expectations and Macroeconomics*. Oxford, England: Oxford University Press.

Mankiw, N. Gregory. 1985. "Small Menu Cost and Large Business Cycles: A Macroeconomic Model of Monopoly." *Quarterly Journal of Economics* 100: 529–39.

Meyer, John and Edwin Kuh. 1957. *The Investment Decision: An Empirical Study*. Cambridge, Massachusetts: Harvard University Press.

Miller, Merton. 1988. "The Modigliani-Miller Propositions After Thirty Years." *Journal of Economic Perspectives* 2: 99–120.

Minsky, Hyman. 1975. *John Maynard Keynes*. New York: Columbia University Press.

———. 1982. *Can "It" Happen Again?* Armonk, New York: M.E. Sharpe.

———. 1986. *Stabilizing an Unstable Economy*. New Haven, Connecticut: Yale University Press.

Modigliani, Franco and Merton Miller. 1958. "The Cost of Capital, Corporation Finance and the Theory of Investment." *American Economic Review* 48: 261–98.

Myers, Stewart and Nicholas Majluf. 1984. "Corporate Financing and Investment Decisions When Firms Have Informations that Investors Do Not Have." *Journal of Financial Economics* 13: 187–220.

Rotemberg, Julio. 1987. "The New Keynesian Microfoundations." *Macroeconomics Annual*. Cambridge, Massachusetts: National Bureau of Economic Research.

Semmler, Willi, ed. 1989. *Financial Dynamics and Business Cycles*. Armonk, New York: M.E. Sharpe.

Shapiro, C. and Joseph Stiglitz. 1984. "Equilibrium Unemployment as a Discipline Device." *American Economic Review* 74: 433–44.

Stiglitz, Joseph. 1987. "The Causes and Consequences of the Dependence of Quality on Price." *Journal of Economic Literature* 25: 1–48.

Stiglitz, Joseph and Andrew Weiss. 1981. "Credit Rationing in Markets with Imperfect Information." *American Economic Review* 71: 393–410.

CHAPTER TEN

Minsky's Financial Instability Hypothesis and the Endogeneity of Money

L. RANDALL WRAY

There is a vision of the economy, which runs throughout the works of Minsky, that is based on profit-seeking entrepreneurs, a financial theory of investment, innovations, and endogenously created instability. While Minsky's financial instability hypothesis and his financial theory of investment are well known by post-Keynesians, his theories of money and of banking have received less attention. In fact, however, Minsky's vision requires a sophisticated analysis of the endogenous creation of money to finance spending, and of the endogenous determination of interest rates over the course of the business cycle.

In this paper I will argue that Minsky adopted an endogenous approach to money in his early work, and that this approach is consistent with his financial instability hypothesis. While post-Keynesians have lately come to accept the endogenous approach to money, they have generally ignored Minsky's early insights.[1] I will identify two major strands within the endogenous money approach: that which adopts an exogenously determined interest rate, and that which adopts an endogenously determined interest rate. I will argue that Minsky adopts the second strand within his endogenous money approach and within the financial instability hypothesis. Finally, I believe that this approach is more appealing than the exogenous interest rate approach adopted by "horizontalists" like Moore and Kaldor. The horizontalists are forced to abandon liquidity preference theory and many other Keynesian insights. In contrast, Minsky's integration, which incorporates an endogenous money supply, endogenous instability, and an endogenous interest rate, retains the revolutionary nature of Keynesian theory.

The author is assistant professor of economics at the University of Denver. An earlier version of this paper was presented at a special session in honor of Hyman Minsky during the Twenty-Fifth Annual Conference of the Missouri Valley Economic Association, February 23-25, 1989, in Kansas City, Missouri. The author would like to thank Hyman Minsky and Gary Dymski for valuable comments.

Before proceeding, I want to emphasize that this paper presents an interpretation of Minsky rather than a detailed exegesis of his ideas. Minsky has always avoided arguments over "what the great man really said," preferring, instead, to present an interpretation. This paper follows the practice of "standing on the shoulders of giants," which Minsky prefers.

Minsky's Theory of Money, Banking, and Economic Activity

In 1957, when orthodox "Keynesians" were fine-tuning IS-LM analysis with a fixed money supply and dichotomized real and monetary sectors, Minsky related institutional innovation to profit opportunities and showed how financial innovation allows business activity to expand even without an expansion of bank reserves. Specifically, he showed how the development of the federal funds market allows a given level of aggregate reserves to support a greater expansion of deposits, and how repurchase agreements allow a given volume of demand deposits to support a greater quantity of bank loans (Minsky 1957).

Minsky also related innovation to tight monetary policy. If a business expansion causes the monetary authorities to fear inflation, they institute tight monetary policy which can push up interest rates. Tightness in the money market does not, however, immediately reduce the demand for loans. If interest rates rise, liquid balances are reduced to take advantage of profit opportunities so that velocity of liquidity increases. Furthermore, financial institutions also want to take advantage of the new higher interest rates and, so, find new ways of meeting loan demand. Innovations result in a shift of the relation between velocity and interest rates: a higher velocity will be associated with each interest rate. Thus, central bank restraint raises interest rates and induces innovations, both of which increase velocity (of both high-powered money and narrowly defined money). Monetary policy will not be effective in constraining monetary aggregates unless it decreases aggregate reserves sufficiently to compensate for the rise in velocity (ibid).

Kaldor and the Radcliffe Committee (1959) had argued that the velocity of money is infinitely elastic so that monetary policy would have no direct effect on spending. If the central bank slowed the growth of the money supply, velocity would merely rise as interest rates rose. In this case, the quantity of money was taken as an exogenous variable under the control of the central bank, but velocity was endogenously determined by spending, which was a function of interest rates. Critics of Keynesianism believed that if they could show that velocity is reasonably stable, then Keynesianism would be defeated and the quantity theory of money would be validated (see Wray 1990). Indeed, Friedman and Schwartz (1963) were able to show that the evidence did not appear to support the Radcliffe Committee's supposition that velocity would be unstable.

Minsky's approach would prove to be far more robust. He had adopted an upward-sloping velocity function: as interest rates rose, banks would expand credit in response to profit opportunities. Thus, any given quantity of money, narrowly defined, could permit more spending as credit is created. Furthermore, innovations can shift the velocity-interest rate function so that velocity might increase even without rising interest rates. Similarly, revisions of commonly accepted views regarding appropriate levels of leverage allow banks to expand portfolios without raising interest rates. That is, banks would make loans by issuing liabilities, raising asset-to-reserve ratios and loan-to-equity ratios through reserve-economizing behavior. This action would increase riskiness by decreasing liquidity of bank balance sheets and by leveraging equity. Eventually, however, financial institutions will come up against the maximum "prudent" leverage ratio. Another innovation, or a revision of standards, will again allow expansion without a rise in interest rates. In the meantime, however, only an increase in the liquidity premium would induce banks to expand loans further. That is, velocity is an upward-sloping step function relative to interest rates in the presence of innovations. Beyond some point, expansion of bank balance sheets requires rising interest rates even though there is no strict quantity constraint on bank lending.[2]

Because he focuses on balance sheets and profit-seeking behavior of banks, Minsky's analysis would survive the attack by the quantity theorists. As bank liabilities expand when banks make loans, and as many of their liabilities are counted as part of the money supply, it is not surprising to find that the money supply will expand as loans are extended to finance spending.

Thus, stable velocity of, say, M1 would be consistent with Minsky's approach. As banks expand their balance sheets while financing spending, the money supply is increased and interest rates rise to compensate for rising risk. Innovations, however, can allow expansion of balance sheets without pressure on interest rates. Thus, the money supply curve would be an upward-sloping step function of interest rates. In turn, the velocity of high-powered money would also be an upward-sloping step function as innovations or revisions of rules of thumb permitted expansion of the money supply and of spending even with a given quantity of bank reserves.

To his credit, Minsky correctly predicted the extensive innovations and rising velocity which would begin a decade after his seminal 1957 paper, and which would thoroughly discredit the quantity theory of money. Furthermore, his approach could survive the attack by quantity theorists which doomed the Radcliffe Committee—for while Minsky predicted rising velocity, his theory did not require it. Money and spending could maintain a fairly stable relation for a number of years because banks expand the money supply as they finance spending. The highly liquid balance sheets held by banks during the 1950s and through the mid-1960s enabled them to expand the money supply with little effect on interest rates.

The banking system emerged from each World War with portfolios full of government bonds. Minsky argues that each postwar expansion was financed as banks gradually replaced liquid balance sheets with illiquid portfolios by taking positions in private assets (Minsky 1984). As Goodhart (1989) notes, banks could subvert tight money policy after World War II by selling government bonds whenever reserves were needed to cover deposit withdrawals which would occur as market interest rates rose above legislated deposit rate ceilings. As Minsky argues, banks were forced to find another method of evading tight policy by the early 1960s because their secondary reserves of government bonds had been depleted.

Thus, banks learned to "operate on liabilities" so that they could meet loan demand or deposit withdrawals by expanding their liabilities. Banks that experienced a deficiency of reserves would normally purchase funds (expand liabilities) rather than sell assets because the private information involved in loan-making activities limited the extent of secondary markets for bank assets. (During the 1970s, however, securitization of loans greatly expanded secondary markets and revolutionized financial sectors, as will be discussed in a moment.) A bank that needed reserves would turn to the Fed funds market, to repurchase agreements, to certificates of deposit, to international liquidity markets, or, if all else failed, to the discount window of the Federal Reserve Bank (Fed).

Minsky does not present a strict dichotomy between "banks" and "financial institutions," nor between financial institutions and nonfinancial institutions. All types of economic institutions engage in balance sheet operations, and any economic institution can create money. As Minsky says, the problem lies in getting it accepted (Minsky 1986b, 228). Liabilities finance positions in assets, and represent a "money now for money later" proposition. A wide variety of balance sheet items enables one to spend now and pay later (ibid).[3] As banks take positions in assets, they create money as they accept the liabilities of borrowers.

In Minsky's analysis, money and economic activity must be linked, and money cannot be neutral. Banks arrange funding so agents may take positions in assets which are expected to generate cash flows (Minsky 1986a). Money transfers purchasing power across time from the future to the present, enabling agents to spend now on the basis of a promise to pay later. Money is necessary in a capitalist economy precisely because it enables one to purchase capital today which can be operated to produce goods and services which can be sold later. Production always involves a "money now for money later" proposition. Thus, money cannot be neutral in any economy in which production takes time, in which production is for the market, and in which existential uncertainty exists.

Commercial banks typically establish relations with customers to reduce the uncertainty involved in making loans. Once a bank has entered into a relationship with a customer, it has strong incentives to meet the demands of that customer. As Minsky says,

> Because bankers live in the same expectational climate as businessmen, profit-seeking bankers will find ways of accommodating their customers. . . .

Banks and bankers are not passive managers of money to lend or to invest; they are in business to maximize profits. They actively solicit borrowing customers, undertake financing commitments, build connections with business and other bankers, and seek out funds. (Minsky 1986b, 228–30) [4]

Thus, money creation arises naturally out of the profit-maximizing behaviors of banks and their customers.

Certain liabilities of financial institutions also circulate as media of exchange and means of payment. The extent to which a "monetary asset" will circulate depends on a variety of factors. Demand deposits circulate as a medium of exchange because (1) they have bank equity behind them, (2) banks diversify assets, (3) the government is willing to guarantee that demand deposits will exchange at parity with government debt, and (4) debt commitments are normally written in terms of demand deposits (ibid). While orthodoxy begins with money operating as a medium of exchange, Minsky rightly focuses on the creation of money as positions are taken in assets. This is not to say that the medium of exchange function of money is not important, but that the essential characteristics of a capitalist economy are not apparent in exchanges, but in the profit-seeking entrepreneurial activity that creates capital.

Minsky argues that innovations are undertaken to earn monopoly rents, which accrue to those firms that capture market power (Minsky 1986a). Thus, the drive to market power is a fundamental determinant of innovation. As Schumpeter (1951) emphasized, banks are also entrepreneurial firms that innovate to earn profits. As financial institutions innovate, the financial system evolves, finding new ways to finance the profit-seeking behavior of other institutions. Innovators who develop new financial instruments, new financial practices, and new financial institutions, are rewarded with monopoly rents that are only dissipated as the innovations spread. Innovators who stretch liquidity and revise rules of thumb regarding appropriate leverage ratios are able to provide more finance of accepted practices or to provide finance in areas which were previously unacceptable. Thus, the drive for monopoly rents continually stretches the bounds of financial practices. For example, the development of the leveraged buy-out has resulted in substantial fee income and capital gains for innovators.

Another such innovation is securitization, which has shifted the initiative for arranging funding away from financial institutions and toward financial markets (Minsky 1987, 2). A security is merely the "prior allocation" of cash flows expected to be generated by income-creating activities. Typically, an investment banker creates the portfolio which will be securitized, provides bridge financing, sells the securities (commonly to pension funds, mutual funds, and insurance companies), and selects a trustee to act in the interests of the security owners. Securitization is an "off-balance sheet operation" which compromises neither the equity nor the reserves of the bank that intermediates (Minsky 1988b, 24–26). The trend toward securitization is a response to a variety of factors, including:

technological advances which have lowered transactions costs; too tight money policy, which raised market interest rates far above regulated deposit rates; changing rules of thumb regarding appropriate liquidity ratios; pressure by the Fed to increase bank capital ratios; and, perceived dimunition of the quality of bank balance sheets due to the third world debt crisis, the energy loan crisis, and the collapse of real estate markets in certain regions of the country.[5]

Minsky (1989) has also attributed the recent phenomenal rise of nonbank funding capability to the rise of "money-manager capitalism" during the past two decades. Minsky argues that the absence of a generalized debt deflation since World War II has permitted the accumulation of vast financial wealth in the form of pension funds, insurance funds, money market mutual funds, and bank-managed trust funds. These funds are characterized as "active money," managed by professionals in pursuit of short-term asset appreciation and short-term yields. Money-manager capitalism enhances the globalization of world financial markets and greatly restricts the range of alternative policies open to central banks. Virtually any loan or other liability can already be securitized. Minsky predicts that in the near future, bearer liabilities that appreciate to face value will be issued to finance a portfolio of assets, with these bearer securities serving as money. Such securities can be issued in any currency and can finance a portfolio of assets of any nationality. As will be discussed below, financial globalization has decreased the central bank's ability to constrain financial markets.

In conclusion, credit creation gives purchasing power to entrepreneurs so they may finance capital accumulation. As Minsky argues, the markup in the consumption goods industry guarantees that workers in the investment goods industry can obtain consumption goods, while spending on investment goods generates a surplus over labor income.[6] Minsky calls this "gross capital income," out of which profits are realized and interest commitments are met. Money is created in the process of financing investment and forces the surplus which is necessary to allow capital accumulation. More fundamentally, credit creation is the means by which society ensures that the workers cannot purchase the total product. Thus, money creation is intimately tied to the essential feature of capitalism—capital accumulation. The money thus created fulfills two other important functions: it serves as a medium of exchange, and it can be held as insurance against an uncertain future. The quantity of money can't be exogenously determined as it is created as a result of private profit-seeking behavior. Neither can money be neutral since its creation is "tied up with the process of creating and controlling capital assets . . . " (Minsky 1986b, 223).[7]

Minsky's Financial Instability Hypothesis

Financial innovations are related to what has come to be known as Minsky's financial instability hypothesis (FIH). "(E)very institutional innovation which results in both new ways to finance business and new substitutes for cash assets decreases the liquidity of the economy" (Minsky 1957, 184). Innovations allow an existing quantity of high-powered money to support greater expenditures. Innovations allow "a pyramiding of liquid assets" as illiquid assets replace cash, government bonds, or short-term bank debt in portfolios. This increases the instability of the system since failure by only a few large firms (financial or nonfinancial) to meet debt commitments can lead to a cascade of failures as assets are written-down.[8]

In Minsky's analysis, investment spending is a fundamental determinant of aggregate effective demand, while investment is substantially determined by expected future aggregate demand. As Minsky puts it, investment this period is only forthcoming if investment is expected to take place next period since future investment will determine future aggregate demand and, thus, the aggregate profits which are necessary to validate investment projects undertaken this period. Each firm must weigh the supply price of capital against its demand price. The supply price will be a function of current production costs plus finance costs, including "lender's risk" if the project requires external finance. The demand price will be a function of the expected stream of returns to be generated over the life of the asset, discounted to take account of "borrower's risk." If the demand price exceeds the supply price, investment can proceed (Minsky 1975).

Any given investment good will have a demand price which varies over time. The demand price will also vary across firms by degree of market power since market power is a fundamental determinant of the stream of returns that can be generated by any asset (Minsky 1986a). Furthermore, borrower's risk will fluctuate depending on the balance sheet position of the borrower and on the degree of confidence the borrower places on the estimated returns. Thus, a rise of optimism, a fall of desired liquidity ratios, or an increase in the quantity of liquidity available, will all tend to raise the demand price of assets.

Similarly, the supply price of assets can vary over time. A rise in current production prices (for example, due to rising wages or finance costs) will tend to increase the supply price of capital assets. A fall of liquidity preference, or a rise in the quantity of liquidity, will tend to reduce supply prices as lender's risk falls.

Finally, financial market behavior influences the incentive to innovate by affecting asset prices and generating monopoly rents (ibid). The banking system is able to directly or indirectly influence the price system for assets either by purchasing them or by providing the finance which is necessary for their purchase. Thus, financial institutions innovate and reward innovation as they permit a boom to generate capital gains when asset prices are driven higher. In this way, rising prices of financial assets can stimulate innovation in search of market power which will generate capital gains. On the other hand, "speculation" can take the place of "enterprise" since innovations need not be in the area of production of real goods and services. Thus, financial markets may operate to reward speculation—leading to a speculative boom.

A crisis can occur if finance costs rise, if liquidity preference rises, or if income flows turn out to be less than expected. Endogenous processes tend to ensure that one of these (or all three) will, in fact, occur. As an expansion proceeds, falling unemployment will tend to raise wages and cause capital asset supply prices to rise. As discussed above, Minsky argues that as bank balance sheets expand, there is upward pressure on interest rates because banks are concerned with leverage ratios. Furthermore, the central bank often attempts to constrain the growth of reserves at the peak of an expansion, which reduces bank liquidity (the ratio of cash assets to liabilities) and also tends to raise interest rates (Fazzari and Minsky 1984). Rising interest rates increase the portion of income flows which firms must commit to debt payments (firms must roll over some of the debt since construction projects take real time).[9] As interest rates rise, "present value reversals" occur, which reduce planned investment, and may even cause some projects to be abandoned (Minsky 1978, 16–17; and 1986b, 195). Thus, current output prices and lender's risk tend to rise during an expansion, setting the stage for crisis by inhibiting investment.

Just as supply prices tend to increase over the course of an expansion, demand prices will eventually fall. In an expansion, rising investment and appreciating asset prices generate aggregate profits, which tend to encourage both borrowers and lenders to accept liability structures in which payment commitments become closely articulated to receipts from assets (Minsky 1989). That is, debt commitments increase faster than the ability to pay. If a few large agents have second thoughts about their leverage ratios, or if a few expectations are disappointed, expected profits are reevaluated downward, and liquidity preference is increased. This process then reduces the demand price of capital assets below the supply price, so that investment falls. However, falling investment reduces aggregate profit flows so that profit expectations continue to fall and liquidity preference rises. This might cause a run to liquidity: firms that cannot meet payment commitments out of income flows or through borrowing must liquidate assets.[10] However, asset liquidation under these circumstances requires devaluation and capital losses.

As assets are devalued, and as falling investment reduces profit flows, debts eventually are repudiated. Debt repudiation will reduce leverage ratios and the depression eventually sets the stage for the next expansion because interest rates will come down after balance sheets are liquidated through default. Furthermore, supply prices will tend to fall as rising unemployment reduces labor costs.

Today, however, government deficits place a floor to the level of profit flows and to wages and current output prices by maintaining aggregate demand as investment falls. Furthermore, central bank intervention as a lender-of-last-resort places a floor to the value of bank assets and liabilities (Minsky 1978, 17). Thus, depression and debt deflation are avoided as the government constrains deflationary behavior which is endogenously created by capitalist systems. The combination of big-government deficits and lender-of-last-resort intervention validate profit expectations (and cause asset price appreciations) and lend an inflationary bias to an economy precisely because debts and interest payments continue to climb: As interest payments must be included in the markup to obtain the surplus, rising indebtedness places pressure on prices. Thus, proper monetary and fiscal policy should also place ceilings on asset prices and profit flows. Floors and ceilings provide coherence to a capitalist system which is endogenously unstable—but might also enhance instability over time as private agents adapt their behavior to take account of these institutional constraints. This point will be discussed in further detail in the final section.

As mentioned above, the central bank's policy increasingly becomes endogenously determined. Its lender-of-last-resort function is continually extended to new institutions and instruments.[11] In the late 1960s, the Fed was forced to intervene to protect the municipal bond market. In 1970, it was forced to guarantee the commercial paper market. And in the 1980s it was forced to intervene during the Hunt silver speculation fiasco, during the foreign debt crisis, during the failure of Continental Illinois, and during the stock market crash. In each of these cases, the Fed provided liquidity and was forced to validate, to some extent, various financial practices. New innovations, such as securitization and other off-balance sheet operations, will test the Fed's continuing willingness to expand its coverage to other instruments. Increasing globalization of financial markets will test the Fed's willingness to expand its coverage to foreign-based institutions and instruments.[12] When these new innovations do encounter crisis, the Fed's hand will be forced due to the interlocking nature of balance sheets—the alternative is simply not acceptable.

The Endogenous Approach to Money

Post-Keynesians have come to accept the endogenous money approach.[13] At the most general level, endogeneity implies that the supply of money is not independent of demand. Often, however, the exogeneity-endogeneity distinction has referred to the ability of the central bank to control the money supply. As Cooley and LeRoy (1981) have argued, exogeneity in the control sense does not imply that the money supply is independent of money demand if the central bank either accommodates money demand or leans "against the wind." In other words, if the central bank's reaction function includes any variables which are influenced by money demand, then the money supply is not statistically exogenous. While most orthodox economists believe that the money supply is exogenous in the control sense, few would argue that it has been statistically exogenous in the past.

Desai (1989) has distinguished between weak exogeneity and strong exogeneity of money. If money at time t is statistically independent of spending at time t, but is not independent of past spending, then money can be said to be weakly exogenous. This would be the case, for example, if the money supply is exogenous in the control sense, but where the central bank accommodates changes in the demand for money induced by previous changes in income. However, if money is independent of even past values of spending, then it can be taken as strongly exogenous. On the other hand, if money at time t depends on spending at time t, money is an endogenous variable.[14]

Post-Keynesians do not accept money exogeneity, even in the control (or weak exogeneity) sense, however. Some, like Moore (1988), emphasize the necessity of accommodative policy by the central bank. Indeed, Moore often argues as if the central bank always supplies reserves on demand. As discussed above, Minsky also acknowledges the necessity of lender-of-last-resort operations by the central bank. He argues, however, that the central bank does use quantity constraints to influence credit markets, rather than passively supplying reserves on demand. Only when a crisis threatens is the central bank forced to accommodate. (The distinction between Moore and Minsky will be clarified below.)

Post-Keynesians have also emphasized the ability of financial institutions to economize on reserves and to innovate to escape attempts by the central bank to use quantity controls. As discussed above, Minsky made this argument as early as 1957, and Rousseas emphasized the importance of financial innovations in 1960 (Rousseas 1989). While Moore has also mentioned reserve economization and innovation as factors that reduce the central bank's ability to control monetary aggregates, they do not seem to play an essential role in his analysis. In contrast, these activities play a central role in Minsky's FIH (as discussed above), for they contribute to the transition from a robust financial system to a fragile one in which liquidity has become stretched.

Returning to the exogenous approach, orthodoxy argues that the central bank can, and should, control the money supply. Actually, however, the central bank cannot implement Monetarist policy. There are two main reasons why a "constant growth rate rule" for money is not feasible. First, as argued above, the rule will have to be abandoned if it is effective in constraining the growth of reserves. As leverage ratios increase, the system becomes unstable and increases the probability of a run to liquidity. If this occurs, the central bank will have to step in and provide reserves to prevent debt repudiation. That is, the central bank reaction function must contain variables which indicate the performance of the economy. Second, if the central bank targets a monetary aggregate, e.g., M1, profit-seeking behavior and private initiative ensure that banks and other financial institutions will innovate to circumvent constraints to meet creditworthy demand. Thus, forms of money not included in the target will grow to accommodate demand.[15] Furthermore, innovations such as securitization and globalization of financial markets further increase the endogeneity of central bank behavior and expand the areas in which intervention may become necessary.

The endogeneity of money has often been linked to the "reverse causation" argument: spending causes money (Davidson and Weintraub 1973; Rousseas 1989). This argument does not necessarily imply that changes in spending must precede changes in the money supply, as Rousseas (1989) erroneously assumes.

For example, if the demand for finance is a function of planned spending, and if credit demand is met by an increase in the money supply, then the money supply will expand as planned expenditures rise and before the spending actually occurs. In contrast, in the exogenous approach to money, an exogenous increase in the money supply either directly increases spending (Monetarists), or lowers interest rates and indirectly induces spending (orthodox Keynesian IS-LM analysis). That is, money causes spending.

Similarly, the exogenous approach to money has been summarized as the assumption that "reserves cause money," while the endogenous approach has been summarized as "money causes reserves" (Lavoie 1985). In the exogenous approach, the central bank injects reserves into the system (or lowers the required reserve ratio), or the public deposits cash, either of which will increase excess reserves and cause an increase in the money supply through the "deposit multiplier." In the endogenous approach, financial institutions increase the supply of money as they extend loans to creditworthy customers. Reserves lost through the clearing facility must be recaptured as deposits, or purchased in wholesale markets. If required reserves rise, banks must economize on reserves or purchase them. In practice, even with contemporaneous reserve accounting, banks have several weeks to come up with required reserves (Wray 1990).

This does not mean, however, that the central bank has no influence over the rate of growth of the money supply. Injections of reserves will tend to lower wholesale interest rates and encourage more loans, while tighter monetary policy will tend to have the opposite effect. Given the high inelasticity of the demand for loans with respect to interest rates that post-Keynesians generally expect, tight money policy will probably have little short-run effect on the growth of the money supply even if it succeeds in slowing the growth of reserves and raising interest rates.

It might be useful to think of a continuum of possibilities, with strict exogeneity at one extreme and strict endogeneity at the other. In the case of strict exogeneity, the money supply curve would be vertical in interest-money space. Moore (1988) has called this the "verticalist" approach. Although this is the way the money supply curve is often drawn in orthodox textbooks, even most orthodox economists admit that the central bank accommodates shifts in money demand to prevent wide fluctuations of interest rates. Some orthodox economists would admit that banks will respond, to some extent, to rising interest rates by reducing excess reserves. As it is often presented in texts, the central bank can either target monetary aggregates or can peg interest rates by fully accommodating money demand. Thus, the extreme verticalist position is, at best, meant to indicate "what ought to be" rather than "what is."[16]

At the other extreme lies complete endogeneity, where money supply completely accommodates money demand as the Fed pegs the interest rate. This is the "horizontalist" position which has been adopted by Kaldor and Moore: The money supply curve is horizontal at any interest rate determined by central bank policy, and a shift of the money demand curve will raise the equilibrium quantity of money, but not interest rates.[17] Therefore, the money supply is endogenous and passively adjusts to money demand, but interest rates are exogenously determined by central bank policy (Moore 1988, 127–30). If the central bank sets the rate too low, inflation will result from excess demand. If the rate is set too high, unemployment results. Thus, by fine-tuning interest rates, the authorities can maintain full employment and stable prices.

Finally, according to the horizontalist approach, private banks passively supply credit money at any short-term interest rate established by the central bank's discount and open market policies. They are able to meet any level of credit demand since they can always obtain reserves from the central bank at the discount rate. Thus, Moore's analysis relies critically on the role of the central bank as the ultimate provider of liquidity, albeit at a price chosen by the authorities. In his model, banks, other financial institutions, and financial markets play a passive role. The Fed determines the price, and borrowers determine the quantity of loans. There is no room in his model for liquidity preference, for entrepreneurial financial institutions, for market power, or for credit rationing and quantity constraints (Wray 1990).

A horizontal money supply curve requires one of the following conditions: either financial institutions do not care about their balance sheet position, or at least one financial institution stands ready to buy offered assets at a pegged price by issuing liquid liabilities which are always in demand. If banks are indifferent to liquidity ratios, they will stand ready to make loans at a fixed interest rate regardless of the ratio of loans to safe assets (or equity) held. Thus, the supply of credit would be infinitely elastic at a given interest rate. Alternatively, if banks do care about their balance sheet position, then a horizontal credit supply curve can be maintained only if banks can always achieve desired liquidity ratios by selling illiquid assets to a financial institution which stands ready to buy them at a pegged price. For example, a central bank can peg any asset price by purchasing it at the administered price through expansion of bank reserves. In this way, private banks can always achieve desired leverage ratios by selling assets to the central bank.

Alternatively, the central bank could supply reserves by opening the discount window and passively lending on demand. This, however, might not prevent interest rates from rising (and asset prices from falling) if banks are concerned with various liquidity ratios in addition to the ratio of reserves to total assets or liabilities. For example, if banks are concerned with the ratio of loans to equity, then discount window borrowings will not eliminate pressure on interest rates as banks expand loans—only retained earnings accumulated as capital could relieve such pressure. Thus, the conditions under which the money supply curve could be made horizontal are quite strict. Indeed, Moore seems to argue that banks do not care about balance sheet positions and that the discount window is always open to passively supply reserves on demand.

As discussed in previous sections, Minsky's approach to money implies an upward-sloping money supply curve.[18] In his approach, the money supply function is a complex interaction of the behaviors of private borrowers, private lenders, and the central bank. The central bank uses a combination of quantity and price constraints to implement monetary policy. While Minsky agrees that the central bank must operate as a lender-of-last-resort during a crisis, it has a wide range of discretion to utilize quantity constraints during an expansion. This does not necessarily mean that it can control the quantity of loans made, but it does mean that banks must economize on reserves and innovate when the central bank implements quantity controls. As Minsky argues, this action will tend to stretch liquidity and raise interest rates. Eventually, quantity constraints enhance fragility, inducing instability and forcing abandonment of quantity controls. Similarly, the central bank can use a wide range of discretion in setting the price at which it will provide reserves, which then has some influence over market interest rates. Again, if the central bank succeeds in pushing market interest rates "too high," it increases fragility to the extent that it must abandon tight policy to restore stability (Fazzari and Minsky 1984).

Furthermore, banks do not passively supply money on demand in Minsky's model. Some agents will be quantity-constrained because there is no interest rate at which a bank could extend credit to them. That is, the chances of default may be high, so that a high interest rate is warranted. However, the higher the interest rate, the greater is the probability of default. Thus, many agents are always and necessarily credit-constrained. Indeed, one of the primary determinants of the quantity of credit which can be obtained is market share. As Dow and Saville (1988) argue, banks must use quantity rationing because they do not know precisely what interest rate would compensate for risk of default. They can reduce potential losses by placing quantitative limits on each customer with these limits related to collateral, market share, and other factors. Thus, quantity rationing is typical and rational behavior.[19]

Furthermore, as discussed above, banks will not meet all credit demand at a fixed interest rate. As leverage ratios increase, banks will eventually increase interest rates. Innovations and revisions of rules of thumb can postpone this increase, as can central bank accommodation and competition from other financial institutions and from financial markets. Eventually, however, the money supply curve will be upward sloping with respect to interest rates.[20]

Even if the Fed were to supply reserves on demand, banks (and other financial institutions) would stretch liquidity in search of profits when liquidity preference is low. (Since reserves are nonearning assets, profit rates can always be increased by raising the liability-to-reserve ratio—as long as defaults do not occur.) Thus, even when reserves are supplied on demand at a fixed discount rate, banks will increase leverage ratios and will eventually require rising liquidity premia to induce them to continue to expand balance sheets. On the other hand, the money supply would still be endogenously determined even in the absence of central bank provision of reserves. That is, private agents would continue to create money to transfer purchasing power across time. In this case, however, periodic runs to liquidity would generate episodes of debt deflation, during which money could not be created due to high liquidity preference (Wray 1990).

In summary, there are two main strands of the endogenous money approach: the horizontalists, such as Moore (1988) and Kaldor (1982), and those who accept an upward-sloping money supply curve. The key difference between these two strands is over the determination of interest rates: the horizontalists argue that interest rates are exogenously set by the central bank, while the other strand accepts an endogenously determined interest rate. This second approach emphasizes uncertainty, liquidity preference, profit-seeking behavior, and innovations in addition to central bank behavior. The horizontalist strand deemphasizes endogenous factors in favor of central bank determination of interest rates.

Moore (1988) has gone so far as to argue that the major flaw of Keynes' *General Theory* is liquidity preference theory. In the horizontalist model, passive banks and a passive central bank always provide the level of liquidity desired by the public. Unemployment is not caused by any inherent features of capitalism, but by stupid central bank policy that has set the interest rate too high. In contrast, Minsky's version of the endogenous money approach clearly has room for liquidity preference, entrepreneurial bankers, and endogenous instability. Thus, his model retains important Keynesian insights which have been dropped from the horizontalist position.

Policy Implications

Since 1979, central bank policy in the United States has been characterized of tight money, deregulation of the financial system, and frequent lender-of-last-resort intervention. Beginning in 1979, the Fed announced that it would target monetary aggregates. The central bank, however, cannot control the quantity of money because money is privately created during profit-seeking behavior. Attempts by the central bank to constrain the growth of bank reserves tend to reduce liquidity and increase systemic fragility. Thus, the central bank was periodically forced to abandon attempts at quantity constraints to prevent fragility from generating financial collapse. The Monetarist Fed was required to intervene as a lender-of-last-resort more frequently than was any previous Fed.

Inflation and tight money policy combined to raise nominal rates above regulated deposit rates causing disintermediation. As Regulation Q was phased out, deposit rates were permitted to rise to market rates. While this change halted disintermediation, it reduced profitability for those institutions that had financed positions in long-term assets (such as mortgages) on the basis of short-term deposits. This development led to an initial wave of failures, particularly among the thrifts. In partial response to these events, the Fed relaxed restrictions on the types of assets which banks and thrifts were permitted to purchase—in the belief that they could earn higher returns on riskier assets. As is becoming increasingly apparent, banks and thrifts responded by purchasing excessively risky assets so that the numbers of failed and "problem" financial institutions have reached proportions not seen since the Great Depression.[21] Many observers have argued that government willingness to intervene encouraged risk-taking: If the monetary authorities (the Fed, the Federal Deposit Insurance Corporation, and other governmental agencies) guarantee that virtually no financial institution will be permitted to default on its liabilities, market discipline is removed.

According to Minsky, the primary goal of the central bank must be to act as a lender-of-last-resort to prevent debt deflation. As this goal conflicts with the goal of hitting quantity targets, the central bank must abandon such targets. If the central bank intervenes to prevent bank failures, however, this will tend to validate risky bank behavior. Thus, Minsky advocates increased central bank supervision of bank balance sheets. This recommendation, of course, runs counter to the current deregulation movement. Minsky does favor some deregulation of banking (e.g., he advocates elimination of the separation of commercial banking from investment banking). Close supervision is necessary, however, to counter endogenously induced instability. Minsky argues: "rather than assuming a hands-off position on the oversight of activities, the Federal Reserve will have to increase its role in guiding financial behavior along lines that contribute to stability" (Minsky 1988a, 28).

Minsky advocates higher capital requirements and central bank use of the discount window rather than open market purchases to provide reserves (Minsky 1986b, 325). In this way, central bank provision of reserves can be made conditional upon bank purchases of less risky assets and upon lower asset-to-equity ratios. The central bank, for example, could encourage hedge finance by accepting for discount the commercial paper of hedge firms held by banks.[22] "Reforms that tilt the credit arrangements of industrial and commercial firms toward hedge rather than speculative or Ponzi finance are desirable" (Minsky 1988a, 28). Minsky also advocates accommodative policy to bring down interest rates, just as Keynes did in his call for the "euthanasia of the rentier" (Keynes 1964, ch. 24).

Minsky advocates tighter fiscal policy and looser monetary policy in the United States today. Fed intervention as a lender-of-last-resort has eliminated debt deflation, but lent an inflationary bias to the economy as discussed above. This bias can be offset by a government budget that generates surpluses during expansions to place a ceiling on profits and limit speculative booms. Looser monetary policy will tend to reduce inflationary pressure by reducing the size of the markup necessary to generate a surplus. Furthermore, lower interest rates might actually reduce the incentive for banks to grow too fast in an attempt to "grow their way to profitability." As discussed above, rising interest rates tend to squeeze bank profits by raising the interest rate on short-term liabilities more quickly than interest rates can be adjusted on assets. This dilemma provides an incentive for banks to grow quickly to increase the profit rate on equity. Banks can grow rapidly by lowering standards and accepting greater risk. In contrast, falling interest rates (or even low and stable interest rates) would remove this incentive.

Minsky also advocates a regulatory environment which would favor small, independent banks. Decentralization of the financial system would enable the central bank to hesitate longer before intervening, because it could allow a few small banks or financial institutions to fail without fear of generating a widespread debt deflation. While the central bank cannot hold back innovation, it could refuse to validate some financial practices in a financial system comprising small banks (Minsky 1988a, 28).

Central bank supervision of bank assets, increased capital requirements, and central bank intervention as a lender-of-last-resort to prevent debt deflation will help to diminish the consequences of the financial instability which is endogenous to capitalist systems. In conjunction with countercyclical big government deficits, such monetary policy can prevent the reoccurrence of debt deflation without fueling inflation. As mentioned above, floors, ceilings, and other institutional constraints give coherence to a system which is endogenously unstable. Profit-seeking agents, however, adjust their behavior to take account of these institutional constraints. Indeed, unchanging constraints might eventually enhance instability as innovations adapt to them. For example, government insurance of deposits helped to stabilize the system by eliminating the possibility of debt deflation, but agents gradually adapted their behavior to take account of this institutional constraint and created a fragile financial system which expects government bailouts. Thus, it is the task of regulators to continually adjust the institutional constraints to ensure they are appropriate to the financial system which actually exists.

Notes

1. With the lone exception of Rousseas (1986), none of the recent post-Keynesian contributions to the endogenous money approach has specifically cited Minsky's early works on money and financial innovation. Lavoie (1985), Rousseas (1985), and Moore (1988) acknowledge the early work of Kaldor and the Radcliffe Committee, but ignore Minsky's seminal 1957 article. Indeed, Lavoie argues that Minsky's financial instability hypothesis "borders on the lack-of-savings thesis and is quite contrary to both post-Keynesian monetary theory and Keynes's view of the trade cycle" (Lavoie 1985, 77). He clearly would not even include Minsky within the endogenous money approach.

2. Minsky says: "A rising inelastic demand will lead to a rise in the observed price unless supply is infinitely elastic at the existing price. . . . For a variety of reasons—the limited equity base of banks, internal and foreign drains of bank reserves, and, in modern times, central bank (Federal Reserve) actions to restrain the money supply—the supply of finance from banks eventually becomes less than infinitely elastic. This means that after favorable conditions for investment are sustained over some time, the cost of financing investment as it is being produced increases" (Minsky 1986b, 195). See also Minsky (1957; 1986b, 196, 214, 227, 239; and 1978, 20).

3. According to Minsky, banks are not intermediaries: "Banking is not money lending; to lend, a money lender must have money. The fundamental banking activity is accepting, that is, guaranteeing that some party is creditworthy . . . The normal functioning of our enterprise system depends upon a large array of commitments to finance, which do not show up as actual funds lent or borrowed, and money markets that provide connections among financial institutions that allow these commitments to be undertaken in good faith and to be honored whenever the need arises" (Minsky 1986b, 229).

See also Minsky (1957; 1975, ch. 6; 1982, chs. 8 and 13; 1986a; and 1986b, ch. 10).

4. In fact, customers may obtain a line of credit, which is exercised wholly at the discretion of the borrower. See Moore (1988, 16, 25, 50). However, as I will discuss below, not all customers receive credit lines.

5. It is beyond the scope of this paper to examine this trend in detail. See Minsky (1988b) and Wojnilower (1985; 1987).

6. Readers who are unfamiliar with Minsky's use of the surplus and markup theories are referred to Minsky (1986b, ch. 7).

7. See Minsky (1988b) and Schumpeter (1951).

8. See Minsky (1957) and Fisher (1933) for discussions of the debt-deflation process.

9. Initially, demand for finance remains inelastic with respect to the interest rate as firms attempt to meet payment commitments through portfolio adjustments. Wojnilower argues that credit demand is almost perfectly inelastic with respect to interest rates (Wojnilower 1985). The development of floating rate loans has increased this inelasticity since the current short-term interest rate becomes irrelevant except as it influences expectations about future short-term rates. Furthermore, when short-term rates are high, financial institutions relax standards or offer discounts to maintain loan demand. In other words, quantity constraints are reduced to compensate for higher interest rates so that the volume of loans is not affected.

10. While a demand for credit can be met as private institutions increase the supply, a demand for liquidity may not be met since banks may also want liquidity. Thus, just as the nonbank public is trying to "unwind" loans or obtain Ponzi finance (see note 17 below), banks are also trying to liquidate assets and borrow reserves. (See Minsky 1986b, 214–217; 1988a, 6–7; 1978, 17.) Marx also recognized that an expansion occurs by stretching liquidity: "It is precisely the enormous development of the credit system during a period of prosperity, hence also the enormous development of the demand for loan capital and the readiness with which the supply meets it in [expansionary] periods, which brings about a shortage of credit during the period of depression" (Marx 1909, 532). Thus, Marx seems to recognize that credit expansion occurs by leveraging balance sheets, and that because of this, balance sheets cannot be liquidated during a downturn. This is similar to Minsky's thesis.

11. See Wojnilower (1985) and Wolfson (1986) for detailed discussions of recent financial crises. See Wojnilower (1987) for a discussion of the expansion of the Fed's responsibility to include virtually all financial instruments issued by virtually all financial institutions.

12. As Wolfson (1986) argues, the Fed intervened explicitly to protect foreign creditors in the case of the Franklin National Bank failure in 1974.

13. Post-Keynesian contributions to the endogenous money approach include Davidson and Weintraub (1973), Kaldor (1982), Lavoie (1985), Moore (1979; 1984; 1985; 1988), Rousseas (1985), and Wray (1988; 1989; 1990). I will use Moore as the primary representative of the "horizontalist approach," and Minsky as the primary representative of the alternative version of the endogenous approach. See note 17 below.

14. Unfortunately, econometric tests of exogeneity—like those of Sims (1983)—almost certainly provide biased results and are unlikely to settle anything (Moore 1988).

Thus, the exogeneity-endogeneity argument must be settled at the theoretical level.

15. Therefore, quantity controls over demand deposits lead to the creation of other checkable deposits, while controls on checkable deposits lead to the creation of large denomination certificates of deposit, and constraints on asset-to-equity ratios lead to off-balance sheet operations. See Wray (1990 ch. 7).

16. For example, Monetarists argue that the Fed can and should make the money supply curve vertical by hitting announced targets, and castigate the monetary authorities for not doing so in the past.

17. The horizontalist position is accepted by Moore (1988; 1989) and by Kaldor (1982). The alternative is accepted by Rousseas (1985; 1986; 1989), Minsky (1957; 1978; 1988a; 1988b), Dow and Dow (1989), and Wray (1988; 1989; 1990). Davidson (1989) and Goodhart (1989) have raised objections to the assumption that money supply always completely accommodates money demand, but they have not explicitly formulated an alternative.

18. Supply curves are normally drawn at a point in time. The money supply curve I have described would be upward-sloping, but would shift out when innovations occur. Thus, it is not strictly correct to say that the money supply curve is an upward-sloping step function.

19. Moore (1988) reports that only half of the typical credit line has been utilized, but he has not shown that credit lines are uniformly distributed. If they were, it is difficult to see why firms would ever fail for lack of capital, or why the homeless would choose to sleep in the streets. Surely additional debt is always preferable to bankruptcy or homelessness.

20. Recently, Moore (1989) has criticized Rousseas for adopting an upward-sloping money supply curve. Moore argued that an upward-sloping money supply curve implies that interest rates should rise secularly. In fact, as Wolfson (1986) has shown, interest rates do rise over the course of the business cycle (and have risen more-or-less secularly over the past quarter of a century). However, Moore's critique is flawed for it ignores the work of Minsky and Rousseas, both of whom have argued that innovations, central bank intervention, and revisions of rules of thumb shift the money supply curve outward. Furthermore, the secular rise of the interest rate is often reversed over the course of a recession as leverage ratios are reduced due to slow growth of credit.

21. Greider (1989) documents the current problems in the financial sector. Perhaps as many as one-fifth of the thrifts will fail (Greider 1989, 11). In 1988, there were more than 1400 "problem banks" or 11 percent of the total (1989, 27). Things will undoubtedly get worse because financial institutions have taken risky positions. Federally insured thrifts hold 8 percent of outstanding junk bonds, with junk bonds comprising up to one-third of the assets of some thrifts (1989, 46). It is estimated that 57 percent of the financing involved in the typical leveraged buy-out comes from commercial banks. Furthermore, it must be remembered that these problems exist in spite of "the longest peacetime expansion" period of the Reagan recovery. If the economy sputters, failures will increase. A recession like that of 1973–75 would cause fully 10 percent of the nation's corporations to go bankrupt, according to the Brookings Institution. As asset values fall during such a recession, the debt/asset ratio would reach unprecedented levels (Bernanke and Campbell 1988).

22. Minsky has defined a speculative unit as one which has financed a position in an asset which is expected to generate a stream of earnings more than sufficient to retire the debt. However, in the near term, the earnings stream is only sufficient to make interest payments: principle cannot be retired until some future date. A Ponzi unit has financed a position in an asset which does not even generate sufficient income to make interest payments in the near term, so that the interest is capitalized. A rise in interest rates can force a speculative unit to become a Ponzi unit. A hedge unit is one whose earnings even in the near term are sufficient to meet cash commitments. Rising interest rates will not affect the position of a hedge unit. See Minsky (1986b, 70).

References

Bernanke, Ben S., and John Y. Campbell. 1988. "Is There a Corporate Debt Crisis?" *Brookings Papers on Economic Activity*, no. 1, pp. 83–139.

Cooley, Thomas F., and Stephen F. LeRoy. 1981. "Identification and Estimation of Money Demand." *American Economic Review* 71: 825–44.

Davidson, Paul. 1989. "On the Endogeneity of Money Once More." *Journal of Post Keynesian Economics* 11: 488–90.

Davidson, Paul and Sidney Weintraub. 1973. "Money as Cause and Effect." *The Economic Journal* 83: 1117–32.

Desai, Meghnad. 1989. "Endogenous and Exogenous Money." In *Money: The New Palgrave*, John Eatwell, Murray Milgate, and Peter Newman, eds. New York: W.W. Norton, pp. 146–50.

Dow, Alexander C., and Sheila C. Dow. 1989. "Endogenous Money Creation and Idle Balances." In *New Directions in Post-Keynesian Economics*, John Pheby, ed. Aldershot: Edward Elgar, pp. 147–64.

Fazzari, Steven, and Hyman Minsky. 1984. "Domestic Monetary Policy: If Not Monetarism, What?" *Journal of Economic Issues* 18: 101–16.

Fisher, Irving. 1933. "The Debt-Deflation Theory of Great Depressions." *Econometrica* 1: 337–57.

Friedman, Milton and Anna J. Schwartz. 1963. *A Monetary History of the United States, 1867–1960*. Princeton: Princeton University Press.

Goodhart, Charles. 1989. "Has Moore Become Too Horizontal?" *Journal of Post Keynesian Economics* 12: 29–34.

Greider, William. 1989. *The Trouble With Money: A Prescription for America's Financial Fever*. New York: Whittle Direct Press.

Kaldor, N. 1982. *The Scourge of Monetarism*. Oxford: Oxford University Press.

Keynes, J. M. 1964. *The General Theory of Employment, Interest, and Money*. New York and London: Harcourt Brace Jovanovich.

Lavoie, Marc. 1985. "Credit and Money: The Dynamic Circuit, Overdraft Economics, and Post Keynesian Economics." In *Money and Macro Policy*, Marc Jarsulic, ed. Boston-Dordrecht-Lancaster: Kluwer-Nijhoff Publishing, pp. 63–84.

Marx, Karl. 1909. *Capital*. Vol. 3. Chicago: Charles H. Kerr and Company.

Minsky, Hyman P. 1957. "Central Banking and Money Market Changes." *Quarterly Journal of Economics* 71: 171–87.

———. 1975. *John Maynard Keynes*. New York: Columbia University Press.

———. 1978. "The Financial Instability Hypothesis: A Restatement." *Thames Papers in Political Economy*. London: Thames Polytechnic.

———. 1982. *Can "It" Happen Again?* Armonk, New York: M.E. Sharpe.

———. 1984. "Banking and Industry Between the Two Wars: the United States." *Journal of European Economic History* 13: 235-72.

———. 1986a. "Evolution of Financial Institutions and the Performance of the Economy." *Journal of Economic Issues, 20: 345–53*.

———. 1986b. *Stabilizing an Unstable Economy*. New Haven and London: Yale University Press.

———. 1986c. "An Introduction to Post-Keynesian Economics." Washington University. Working Paper no. 88 (January).

———. 1987. "Securitization." Mimeo. Washington University, St. Louis, Missouri.

———. 1988a. "Back From the Brink." *Challenge* 31: 22–28.

———. 1988b. "Schumpeter: Finance and Evolution." Presented at a conference on Evolution of Technology and Market Structure in an International Context. Siena, Italy.

————. 1989. "Financial Crises and the Evolution of Capitalism: The Crash of '87—What Does It Mean?'" In *Capitalist Development and Crisis Theory: Accumulation, Regulation and Spatial Restructuring*, Mark Gottdiener and Nicos Komninos, eds. New York: St. Martin's Press, pp. 391–403.

Moore, Basil J. 1979. "The Endogenous Money Stock." *Journal of Post Keynesian Economics* 2: 49–70.

————. 1984. "Contemporaneous Reserve Accounting: Can Reserves Be Quantity-Constrained?" *Journal of Post Keynesian Economics* 7: 103–11.

————. 1985. "Wages, Bank Lending, and the Endogeneity of Credit Money." In *Money and Macro Policy*, Marc Jarsulic, ed. Boston-Dordrecht-Lancaster: Kluwer-Nijhoff Publishing, pp. 1–28.

————. 1988. *Horizontalists and Verticalists: the Macroeconomics of Credit Money.* Cambridge: Cambridge University Press.

————. 1989. "On the Endogeneity of Money Once More." *Journal of Post Keynesian Economics* 11: 479–87.

Rousseas, Stephen. 1985. "Financial Innovation and Control of the Money Supply: The Radcliffe Report Revisited." In *Money and Macro Policy*, Marc Jarsulic, ed. Boston-Dordrecht-Lancaster: Kluwer-Nijhoff Publishing, pp. 47–62.

————. 1986. *Post Keynesian Monetary Theory.* Armonk, New York: M.E. Sharpe.

————. 1989. "On the Endogeneity of Money Once More." *Journal of Post Keynesian Economics* 11: 474–78.

Radcliffe Committee. 1959. Committee on the Working of the Monetary System. London: HMSO.

Schumpeter, J.A. 1951. "The Creative Response in Economic History." In *Essays on Economic Topics of J. A. Schumpeter*, Richard V. Clemence, ed. Port Washington, New York: Kennikat Press, pp. 216–26.

Sims, Christopher. 1983. "Is There a Monetary Business Cycle?" *American Economic Review* 73: 228–33.

Wojnilower, Albert M. 1985. "Private Credit Demand, Supply, and Crunches—How Different are the 1980s?" *American Economic Review* 75: 351–56.

————. 1987. "Financial Change in the United States." In *Changing Money*, Marcello De Cecco, ed. Oxford: Basil Blackwell, pp. 10–27.

Wolfson, Martin H. 1986. *Financial Crises: Understanding the Postwar U.S. Experience.* Armonk, New York: M.E. Sharpe.

Wray, Larry Randall. 1988. "Profit Expectations and the Investment-Saving Relation." *Journal of Post Keynesian Economics* 11: 131–47.

————. 1989. "A Keynesian Theory of Banking: A Comment on Dymski." *Journal of Post Keynesian Economics* 12: 152–56.

————. 1990. *Money and Credit in Capitalist Economies: The Endogenous Money Approach.* Aldershot: Edward Elgar.

FINANCIAL RISK, GOVERNMENT POLICY, AND MACROECONOMIC PERFORMANCE

A Conference in Honor of Hyman P. Minsky
Held April 20 and 21, 1990

List of Participants

Richard Aspinwall	The Chase Manhattan Bank
Richard Bartel	M.E. Sharpe, Inc.
Anatol Balbach	The Federal Reserve Bank of St. Louis
Robert Brazelton	University of Missouri - Kansas City
James Bullard	The Federal Reserve Bank of St. Louis
Claudia Campbell	University of Missouri - St. Louis
John Caskey	Swarthmore College
Victoria Chick	University College London
David Cleeton	Oberlin College
William Danforth	Washington University
Paul Davidson	University of Tennessee
Domenico Delli Gatti	Universita Cattolica, Milan, Italy
Gary Dymski	University of Southern California
Louis Ederington	University of Oklahoma
Ben Eisner	Telrad Telecommunications Inc.
Warren Farb	Council on Competitiveness
Steven Fazzari	Washington University
David Felix	Washington University
J. Peter Ferderer	Clark University
Piero Ferri	Universitario Bergamo, Italy
Benjamin Friedman	Harvard University
Mauro Gallegati	Universita di Urbino, Italy
Jennifer Gamber	L.H. Meyer & Associates
H. Peter Gray	Rensselaer Polytechnic Institute
Edward Greenberg	Washington University
Sydney Hicks	First National Bank of Dallas

Ric Holt	Baldwin-Wallace College
Martin Israel	Washington University
Kazuo Iwata	University of Denver
John Keating	Washington University
Charles P. Kindleberger	Massachusetts Institute of Technology
Jan Kregel	University of Bologna, Italy
Robert E. Kohn	Southern Illinois University
Maw Lin Lee	University of Missouri
S Jay Levy	Levy Economics Institute
Joseph Losos	Wedgewood Partners
Edward Macias	Washington University
Edward MacPhail	New School for Social Research
Perry Mehrling	Barnard College
Laurence Meyer	Washington University
Hyman Minsky	Levy Economics Institute
Tracy Mott	University of Denver
Richard F. Muth	Emory University
Wilhelm Neuefeind	Washington University
Dimitri B. Papadimitriou	Levy Economics Institute
Robert Pollin	University of California - Riverside
Clemente Ruiz-Duran	Universidad Nacional Autonoma de Mexico
Juana Sanchez	University of Missouri - Rolla
Ved Sharma	Mankato State University
Allen Sinai	Boston Company
John Tatom	The Federal Reserve Bank of St. Louis
Dan Thornton	The Federal Reserve Bank of St. Louis
Chris Varvares	L.H. Meyer & Associates
Mark Vaughan	Washington University
Alejandro Villagomez	Washington University
Murray Weidenbaum	Washington University
John Wenninger	Federal Reserve Bank of New York
Rainer Winklemann	Washington University
Albert Wojnilower	First Boston Corporation
Martin Wolfson	University of Notre Dame
L. Randall Wray	University of Denver
Tim Yeager	Washington University

Hyman P. Minsky

Born: September 23, 1919 in Chicago, Illinois

Academic Degrees

Bachelor of Science - University of Chicago, 1941
Master of Public Administration - Harvard University, 1947
Doctor of Philosophy - Harvard University, 1954

Academic Appointments

Instructor - Carnegie Institute of Technology, Summer 1947
Teaching Fellow - Harvard University, 1947–49
Assistant and Associate Professor - Brown University, 1949–58
Visiting Associate Professor - University of California, Berkeley, 1956–57
Associate Professor - University of California, Berkeley, 1958–65
Professor - Washington University, St. Louis, 1965–1990
Visiting Professor - Harvard University, Summer 1966
Visiting Scholar - St. Johns College, Cambridge University, 1969–70
Visiting Professor - University of California, Berkeley, Summer 1974
Faculty - Centro di Studi Economici Avanzati, Trieste, Italy, 1980-
Distinguished Scholar - Jerome Levy Economics Institute, Bard College, 1990-

Principal Publications

Books

1965 *Labor and the War Against Poverty*, Berkeley, CA: Institute of Industrial Regulations, Center for Labor Research and Education.
1975 *John Maynard Keynes*, New York: Columbia University Press. Translated into Italian, Spanish, German, and Japanese.
1982 *Can "It" Happen Again*, Armonk, New York: M. E. Sharpe. Published in Great Britain as *Inflation, Recession and Economic Policy*. Brighton, Sussex: Weatsheat Books, translated into Italian and Japanese.
1986 *Stabilizing and Unstable Economy*, New Haven and London: Yale University Press.

Academic Articles

1957   "Central Banking and Money Market Changes." *Quarterly Journal of Economics* 71 (May): 171–87.

1957a "Monetary Systems and Accelerator Models." *American Economic Review* 47 (December).

1965   "A Linear Model of Cyclical Growth." *Review of Economics and Statistics* 61 (May): 135–45. Reprinted in Gordon and Klein, eds., *AEA Readings in Business Cycles* 10, Homewood, Illinois: R.D. Irwin, 79–99.

1959   "Indicators of the Developmental Status of an Economy." *Economic Development and Cultural Change* 7 (January): 151–72.

1961   "Employment Growth and Price Levels: A Review Article." *Review of Economics and Statistics* 42 (February): 1–12.

1962   "Financial Constraints Upon Decisions, An Aggregate View." *Proceedings of the American Statistical Association*, pp. 256–67.

1963   "Comment on Friedman and Schwartz, Money and Business Cycles." *Review of Economics and Statistics Supplement* (February): 64–72.

1963   "Can 'It' Happen Again?" *Banking and Monetary Studies*, Deane Carson, ed. Homewood, Illinois: R.D. Irwin, pp. 101–11.

1964   "Financial Crisis, Financial Systems, and the Performance of the Economy." *Private Capital Markets*. Commission on Money and Credit Research Study. Englewood Cliffs, New Jersey: Prentice Hall, pp. 173–380.

1964   "Longer Wages in Financial Relations: Financial Factors in the More Severe Depressions." *American Economic Association Papers and Proceedings* 54 (May): 324–32.

1965   "The Integration of Simple Growth and Cycle Models." *Patterns of Market Behavior, Essays in Honor of Philip Taft*, M.J. Brennan, ed. Providence, Rhode Island: Brown University Press, pp. 175–92.

1965   "The Role of Employment Policy." *Poverty in America*, M.S. Gordon, ed. San Francisco: Chandler Publishing Co., pp. 175–200.

1965   "Overview." *California Banking in a Growing Economy*, Hyman P. Minsky, ed. Berkeley, California: Institute of Business and Economic Research, pp. 1–26.

1965   "Commercial Banking and Rapid Economic Growth in California" *California Banking in a Growing Economy*, Hyman P. Minsky, ed. Berkeley, California: Institute of Business and Economic Research, pp. 175–201.

1966   "Tight Full Employment: Let's Heat Up the Economy." *Poverty American Style*, Herman P. Miller, ed. Belmont, California: Wadsworth Publishing Co., pp. 254–300.

1967   "Financial Intermediation in the Money and Capital Markets." *Issues in Banking and Monetary Analysis*, Giulio Pontecorvo, Robert P. Shay, and Albert G. Hart, eds. New York: Holt, Rinehart and Winston, Inc., pp. 33–56.

1967 "Money, Other Financial Variables and Aggregate Demand in the Short Run." *Monetary Process and Policy: A Symposium*, George Horwich, ed. Homewood, Illinois: R.D. Irwin, Inc., 1967, pp. 265–94.

1968 "Effects of Shifts of Aggregate Demand Upon Income Distribution." *American Journal of Agricultural Economics* (May).

1969 "The New Uses of Monetary Powers." *Nebraska Journal of Economics and Business* 8 (Spring).

1969 "Private Sector Asset Management and the Effectiveness of Monetary Policy: Theory and Practice." *Journal of Finance* (May).

1972 "Financial Instability Revisited: The Economics of Disaster." Board of Governors, Federal Reserve System, *Fundamental Reappraisal of the Federal Reserve Discount Mechanism.*

1972 "An Exposition of Keynesian Theory of Investment." *Mathematical Methods in Investment and Finance*. Amsterdam: Elsevier/North Holland.

1972 "An Evaluation of Recent Monetary Policy." *Nebraska Journal of Economics and Business* 11 (Autumn).

1973 "The Strategy of Economic Policy and Income Distribution." *The Annals of the American Academy of Political and Social Science* (September).

1974 "The Modelling of Financial Instability: An Introduction." *Modelling and Simulation* 5 (Proceedings of the Fifth Annual Pittsburgh Conference, Instrument Society of America). 1974.

1975 "Suggestions for a Cash-Flow Oriented Bank Examination." *Proceedings of a Conference on Bank Structure and Competition*. Chicago, Illinois: Federal Reserve Bank of Chicago.

1975 "Financial Resources in a Fragile Financial Environment." *Challenge* 18 (July/August).

1976 "Our Financial Heritage and the Prospects of 1976." *The Economic Outlook for 1976*. University of Michigan Annual Conference on the Economic Outlook, Ann Arbor, Michigan.

1977 "The Roots of Current Economic Problems." *Public Interest Economics* (December).

1977 "A Theory of Systemic Fragility." *Financial Crisis*, E.D. Altman and A.W. Sametz, eds. New York: Wiley Interscience.

1977 "Banking in a Fragile Financial Environment." *Portfolio Managers Journal*, (Summer).

1977 "How 'Standard' is Standard Economics?" *Society* 14 (March/April): 24–29.

1977 "The Financial Instability Hypothesis: An Interpretation of Keynes and an Alternative to 'Standard' Theory." *Nebraska Journal of Economics and Business* 16 (Winter): 5–16. Reprinted in *Challenge*, volume 20 (March/April 1977).

1977 "An 'Economics of Keynes' Perspective on Money." *Modern Economic Thought*, S. Weintraub, ed. University of Pennsylvania Press.
1978 "Carter Economics: A Symposium." *Journal of Post-Keynesian Economics* 1 (Fall): 42–45.
1978 "The Financial Instability Hypothesis: A Restatement." *Thames Papers in Political Economy*. North East London Polytechnic. Reprinted in Philip Aretis and Thanos Skouras, *Post Keynesian Economic Theory*, Armonk, New York: M.E. Sharpe, 1985.
1979 "The Instability and Resilience of American Banking (1949–1978)." *Quaderno* 16, Associazione per lo Sviluppo degli Studi di Banca e Borsa, Universita Cattolica del Sacro Cuore Facolta di Economia e Commercio, Milano (in Italian).
1979 "Financial Interrelations, the Balance of Payments and the Dollar Crisis." *Debt and the Less Developed Countries*, J.D, Aronson, ed. Boulder, Colorado: Westview Press.
1980 "La Coerenze Dell' Economia Capitalistica: I Fondamenti Marshalliani Della Critica Keynesiana Della Teoria Neo-classica." *Giornale Degli Economisti E Annali Di Economia* (March-April).
1980 "The Federal Reserve: Between a Rock and a Hard Place" *Challenge* 23 (May/June): 30–36.
1980 "Capitalist Financial Processes and the Instability of Capitalism." *Journal of Economic Issues* 14 (June): 505–22. Translated as "Los Procesos Financieros Capitalistas Y La Inestabilidad Del Capitalismo," *Investigacion Economica*, 167, enero marzo del, 1984, pp. 199–218.
1980 "Money, Financial Markets and the Coherence of a Market Economy." *Journal of Post-Keynesian Economics* 3 (Fall): 21–31.
1981 "Financial Markets and Economics Instability, 1965–1980." *Nebraska Journal of Economics and Business* 20 (Autumn): 5–16.
1982 "The United States Economy in the 1980s: The Financial Past and Present as a Guide to the Future." *Giornale Degli Economisti E Annali Di Economia Maggio-Guigno.*
1981 "The Breakdown of the 1960's Policy Synthesis." *Telos* 50 (Winter 1981–82): 49–58. Translated into Italian as "Il Fallimento della Combinazione tra Politiche Rooseveltiane e Keynesian negli Stati Uniti," in Ester Fano, Stefano Rodata and Giacimo Markamao, *Trasformazimi e Crisis Del Welfare State*. Torino, Italy: De Donata Regime Piemonte, 1983, pp. 63–70.
1982 "The Financial-Instability Hypothesis: Capitalist Processes and the Behavior of the Economy." *Financial Crises, Theory, History and Policy*, Charles P. Kindleberger and Jean-Pierre Laffargue, eds. Cambridge University Press, pp. 13–38.
1982 "Can 'It' Happen Again? A Reprise." *Challenge* 25 (July/August): 5–13.
1982 "Debt Deflation Processes in Today's Institutional Environment." *Banca Nazionale Del Lavoro Quarterly Review* (December): 375–95. Trans-

lated as I Processi Di Deflazione Creditizia Nell Odierno Contesto, Instituzionale Moneta and Credito Banca Nazionale De Lavoro (December 1982), p. 140.

1983   "Pitfalls Due to Financial Fragility." *Reaganomics in the Stagflation Economy*, Sidney Weintraub and Marvin Goldstein, eds. Philadelphia: University of Pennsylvania Press, 104–19.

1983   "The Legacy of Keynes." *Metroeconomica* 35 (Febbraio-Giugno): 87–103.

1983   "Notes on Effective Demand." *Distribution, Effective Demand and International Economic Relations*, Jan Kregel, ed. London: MacMillan Press Ltd.

1983   "Institutional Roots of American Inflation." *Inflation Through the Ages Economic, Social Psychological and Historical Aspects*, Nathan Schmokler and Edward Marcus, eds. New York: Social Science Monographs - Brooklyn College Press (distributed by Columbia University Press), pp. 265–77.

1984   "Domestic Monetary Policy: If Not Monetarism, What?" *Journal of Economic Issues* 18 (March). Reprinted in Marc Tool, ed., *An Institutional Guide to Economics and Public Policy*, New York: M.E. Sharpe, 1984, pp. 101–16 (with Steven Fazzari).

1984   "Prices, Employment and Profits." *Journal of Post-Keynesian Economics* 6 (Summer): 489–99 (with Piero Ferri).

1984   "Financial Innovations and Financial Instability: Observations and Theory." *Financial Innovations: Their Impact on Monetary Policy and Financial Markets.* The Federal Reserve Bank of St. Louis, Boston: Kluwer Nijhoff Publishing.

1984   "Banking and Industry Between the Two Wars: The United States." *The Journal of European Economics History* 13 (Fall, special issue): 235–72.

1984   "The Potential for Financial Crises." *The Future of the International Monetary System*, Tamir Agmon, Robert G. Hawkins, and Richard M. Levich, eds. Lexington, Massachusetts: Lexington Books, pp. 91–110.

1985   "Money and the Lender of Last Resort." *Challenge* 28 (March/April): 12–19.

1985   "The Legacy of Keynes." *The Journal of Economic Education* 16 (Winter): 5–15.

1985   "La Structure Financierre: Endettement et Credit." *Keynes aujourd'hui: Thoeries and Politiques*, Alain Barrere, ed. Paris, France: Economica, pp. 309–28.

1985   "Beginnings." *Banca Nazionale del Lavoro Quarterly Review* (September): 211–221.

1985   "An Introduction to Post-Keynesian Economics." *Economic Forum* 15 (Winter 1985–86).

1986   "The Evolution of Financial Institutions and the Performance of the Economy." *Journal of Economic Issues* 20 (June).

1986   "Stabilizing and Unstable Economy: The Lessons for Industry, Finance and Government." *Weltwirtschaft and Unterrelmerische Strategien*, Karl Aiginger, ed. Vienna, Austria: Österrichisches Institut für Wirtschaftsforschung, pp. 31–44.

1986   "Money and Crisis in Schumpeter and Keynes." *The Economic Law of Motion of Modern Society: A Marx-Keynes-Schumpeter Centennial*, H.S. Jagener and J.W. Drukker, eds. Cambridge: Cambridge University Press.

1986   "Global Consequences of Financial Deregulation." *The Marcus Wallenberg Papers on International Finance* 2. International Law Institute and School of Foreign Service, Georgetown University.

1986   "Conflict and Interdependence in a Multipolar World." *Studies in Banking and Finance* 4. Amsterdam, The Netherlands: North-Holland Publishing.

1986   "The Crisis of 1983 and the Prospects for Advanced Capitalist Economics." *Marx, Schumpeter and Keynes: A Centenary Celebration of Dissent*, Suzanne W. Helburn and David F. Braunhill, eds. Armonk, New York: M.E. Sharpe.

1988   "In a World of Uncertainty." *Against the Current* (May/June).

1988   ''Sraffa and Keynes: Effective Demand in the Long Run'' Working Paper no. 126 (November). St Louis: Washington University.

Articles in the Financial Press

1966   "The Evolution of American Banking: The Longer View." *The Bankers' Magazine*, Part I, November, 325–29; Part II, December, 397–400.

1968   "The Crunch of 1966—Model for New Financial Crises?" *Trans-action* (March).

1970   "Passage to Pakistan." *Trans-action* (February).

1970   "The U.S. Economy in mid-1970." *London and Cambridge Economic Bulletin.* Cambridge, England: London and Cambridge Economic Society. Reprinted from *The Times of London*, July 15–16, 1970.

1972   "An Evaluation of Recent U.S. Monetary Policy." *The Bankers' Magazine*, Part I, October; Part II, November; and Part III, December.

1974   "Standard Forecast Questioned." *The Journal of Commerce* (April 16).

1974   "Can and Should the Fed 'Go It Alone'?" *The Journal of Commerce* (April 16).

1974   "The Fragile Financial System Risks Crises, Deflation-Debt Reduction Essential." *The Money Manager* (July).

1974   "Monetary and Fiscal Policy." *J.C. Penney Forum* (Winter).

1974   "The State of the Economy and of Economics." *Washington University Magazine* (Summer).

1978   "The Dollar: U.S. Must be Seen as an Ailing Bank." *The Money Manager* (April 24).

189 HYMAN P. MINSKY

1978   "U.S. Efforts to Prevent a Deep Slump Render Policy Helpless." *The Money Manger* (July 10).
1978   "Unless Corrected, Deficit in Trade Could Trigger Bigger Financial Crisis." *The Money Manager* (December 4).
1984   "The International Ponzi Scheme." *The Boston Globe* (July 5, Op. Ed. Page).
1987   "Curb Speculation, Don't Raise Taxes of Cut Spending." *News Day* (October 25).
1987   "Pollyannas of Capitalism," *New York Times* (October 22, Op. Ed. Page).

Reviews

1974   Review of H. G. Johnson and A. R. Nobay: *Issues in Monetary Economics, Economic Journal* (December).
1974   "Money and the Real World: A Review Article." *Quarterly Review of Economics and Business* (Summer).
1981   Review of N. Kaldor: *Essays on Economic Stability and Growth*, Second Edition, *Journal of Economic Literature* 19 (December).
1981   "James Tobin's Asset Accumulation and Economic Activity: A Review Article." *Eastern Economic Journal* 7 (July-October): 199–209.
1982   Review of Axel Leijonhufved: "Information and Coordination." *Economic Journal* (December): 976–77.
1983   Review of Wallace C. Peterson: *Our Overloaded Economy. Journal of Economic Issues* 17 (March 1983): 228–32.
1984   "Frank Hahn's *Money and Inflation*: A Review Article." *Journal of Post-Keynesian Economics* 6 (Spring).
1985   Review of Michael J. Piore and Charles F. Sabel: *The Second Industrial Divide. Challenge* 28 (July/August).
1985   Review of Christian Saint-Etienne: *The Great Depression 1929–1938: Lessons for the 1980's. Journal of Economic Literature* 23 (September): 1226–27.
1986   Review of Lester G. Thurow: *The Zero Sum Solution: Building a World-Class American Economy. Challenge* 29 (July/August): 60–64.
1987   "Bashing Bigness—But With Blinders," a review article of Walter Adams and James W. Birch: *The Bigness Complex. Challenge* 30 (July/August): 29–31.
1987   Review of Forest Capie and Geoffrey Wood, eds.: *Financial Crises and the World Banking System. Journal of Economic Literature* 25 (September): 1341–42.
1987   Review of Susan Strange: *Casino Capitalism. Journal of Economic Literature* 25 (December): 1883–85.
1988   "A Review Article: Secrets of the Temple: How the Federal Reserve Runs the Country," by William Greider, *Challenge* 31 (May/June).

Government Testimony and Publications

1959   "The Effects of Monopolistic and Quasi-Monopolistic Practices on Price
Levels." *Joint Economic Committee—Employment, Growth and Price
Levels, Part 7.* 86th Congress, 1st Session. Washington, DC: U.S. Gov-
ernment Printing Office.

1966   "The Federal Portfolio." *The Federal Reserve Portfolio.* Joint Economic
Committee, 89th Congress, 2nd Session. Washington, DC: U.S. Government Printing Office.

1968   "Adequate Aggregate Demand and the Commitment to End Poverty."
Rural Poverty in the United States. Report by the President's National
Advisory Commission on Rural Poverty. Washington, DC: U.S. Govern-
ment Printing Office.

1975   "Financial Instability, the Current Dilemma, and the Structure of Banking and Finance." *Compendium on Major Issues in Bank Regulation.*
United States Senate, Committee on Banking, Housing, and Urban Affairs, 94th Congress, 1st Session. Washington, DC: U.S. Government
Printing Office, August, pp. 310–53.

1977   "Statement on the Adequacy of Bank Supervision." *Committee on Banking, Housing, and Urban Affairs of the United States Senate*, March 11.

1978   "Managing Money." *Joint Economic Committee Special Study on Economic Change, Part 3.* 95th Congress, 2nd Session. Washington, DC:
U.S. Government Printing Office, pp. 837–55.

1980   "Finance and Profits: The Changing Nature of American Business Cycles." *The Business Cycle and Public Policy 1929–80: A Compendium of
Papers Submitted to the Joint Economic Committee.* Congress of the
United States, 96th Congress, 2nd Session. Washington, DC: U.S. Government Printing Office, 1980, pp. 230–44.

1991   "Banking Reform." Testimony delivered before the Joint Economic Committee, the United States Congress, May 9.

INDEX

DATE DUE

STEVEN F   Stanford
University   hington
University   ne Levy
Economics   f issues
in macroe   nomics,
including th   portance
of finance

DIMITRI F   nics and
Executive   w York.
He is also   e. He is
editor of *   ution of*
Wealth an   ty in the
U.S. in t   olumbia
University   School
for Social